50 STORAGE PROJECTS
FOR · THE · HOME

50 STORAGE PROJECTS FOR · THE · HOME

Text by Kate Armpriester
Projects and Illustrations by Mary Jane Favorite

Popular
Science
BOOKS

Popular Science Books
Danbury, Connecticut

Published by
    Popular Science Books
    Grolier Book Clubs, Inc.
    Sherman Turnpike
    Danbury, CT 06816

Book design by Linda Watts.

Produced by Bookworks, Inc., West Milton, Ohio.
Illustration assistants: Mary Kay Baird, Linda Ball and
Chris Walendzak. Photography: Karen Callahan and
Nick Engler.

Library of Congress Cataloging-in-Publication Data

Armpriester, Kate, 1947-
    50 storage projects for the home/text by Kate
    Armpriester; projects and illustrations by Mary
    Jane Favorite.
        p.   cm.
    ISBN: 1-556-54043-4
    1. Cabinet-work.   2. Storage in the home.
    I. Favorite, Mary Jane, 1942-   . II. Title.
        III. Title: Fifty storage projects for the home.
TT197.A74   1988   88-28707
684.1'6—dc19   CIP

Manufactured in the United States of America

Introduction

One of the curses of living in a consumer society is that we all tend to accumulate many more things than we can comfortably call our own. Indeed, the good life doesn't always consist of what we have—but how well we can handle it! How many times have you wished for a new home—simply because your present one didn't offer adequate storage space? Finding space where there was none doesn't take a Houdini; rather it takes some ingenious designing and careful building.

This book gives you not 20 or 30 storage projects but a full-blown *50* projects that will make your storage dreams come true. (Actually, there are well *over* 50 projects when you count the many variations of individual projects.) These projects can be used in every room of your house —even out into the backyard! Portables and built-ins... finished wood and utilitarian...for open, visible storage and closed, or hidden storage. There are projects for storing everything from tiny pill bottles to large firewood logs—all in this one book.

50 Storage Projects for Your Home will be a welcome sight in your cabinetmaking or home-improvement library. In fact, it serves both purposes very well. Chapter 1 will get you started in sizing up your storage problem. Chapters 2, 3 and 4 provide you with basic woodworking skills; this section of the book alone will serve as a basic reference for years to come. Chapters 5 through 10 detail, thoroughly, each of 50 contemporary storage projects—projects that you'll find useful no matter what kind of house or apartment you inhabit.

Although the book is titled as 50 separate projects, it should, ideally, be read and digested as one comprehensive volume. Many of the projects will overlap; for example, recessed shelves, although they are presented in the chapter on Bathrooms, can be used virtually anywhere throughout your home. All 50 projects were selected because, as a whole, they provide just about every conceivable storage project that can be executed by a beginner. For these reasons, I recommend reading, or at least, scanning, the entire book before you settle on a project.

In closing, may you learn some basic skills, and may your home begin to fill with shelves, carts, bins, racks, cabinets, caddies, and modules. The right places for all the right things in your life!

Nick Engler

Contents

1

Making Use of Available Space

We live in a 'consumer' society, but that doesn't mean that we consume or use up everything that we purchase. On the contrary, we stockpile goods...save them for a rainy day or retirement...until the bulging closet becomes a monster that sends boxes toppling on our heads when opened.

As we accumulate more and more goods, the goods tend to become more and more disorganized—that is, all our similar possessions are not in the same space. To remedy the problem, we need to create special spaces—storage spaces—around our homes for various types of goods. These spaces make order out of chaos, and render it possible for everyone in the home to find what they need when they need it.

But not all goods require the same sort of storage space. Do you have a home computer...a VCR...tons of toys and games...sporting equipment...sewing supplies...record albums...cassette tapes? All of these items need a specific kind of storage space, custom-built for them. With

the right types of spaces, your home will look more orderly; you'll save time and aggravation in looking for a particular item—and your closets won't attack you.

This chapter will help you determine what sorts of spaces you really need, and the rest of the book shows how to build them. You might elect to purchase ready-made shelving or storage units—but if you build them yourself you will experience the satisfaction of making something with your own two hands. You may also save money by doing it yourself. And you will be able to custom-design and custom-build the storage units to make maximum use of the available space.

Before you begin planning and building, here's an important consideration: Building shelving and other storage spaces almost always involves working with power tools. Consequently, there are safety guidelines to be followed. Even if you are an experienced craftsman, don't skip the section on safety. We can all use a reminder now and then.

The First Step... Taking Inventory

The key to determining what kind of storage space you need is to look at your possessions and note

the frequency with which you use them. Do you and your family read frequently and use reference books often, or do you tend to read paperbacks and magazines once and then eventually get rid of them? Do you collect rare or attractive books for display? As you take an inventory of everything you're storing, decide which goods should be accessible and which can be hidden.

If your storage needs are complicated, you should make a list of every item that is now stored, and, additionally, everything that is now out in the open for which you are seeking a storage space. Be as specific as possible without listing every sweater or photo album you own. Making this list will require that you dig deep into closets, bureaus and chests and also scrutinize all of the shelving units in your home. A complete list of all items in your home (depending on your accumulated goods) could be overwhelming, so you might want to concentrate on one area at a time. For example, if the living area is your problem, make a list of the things that should be stored in that space—or a child's room, or the kitchen.

Once you've made your list, chances are that you've discovered several types of items that fall into the following categories:

■ **Items that you use 'almost never'.** These could include hobby and recreational supplies, musical instruments and toys that you or other members of your family have long since lost interest in. Keepsakes and souvenirs, financial records from past years, and outdated or 'vintage' clothing all fall into this group as do old baby furniture, gifts never used, and broken things 'waiting to be fixed'.

■ **Items that you use occasionally.** These might include seasonal equipment such as snow shovels and sleds, swimming pool and lawn toys, winter or summer clothing and bed linens, window air conditioners and holiday decorations. Other items that might be used infrequently are a slide projector and screen, photo albums, old record albums and cooking or serving utensils for special occasions. In this category also are special kinds of tools, sewing equipment, games and toys —all of these depending on what your current hobbies are.

■ **Items that you use often.** These are the staples of everyday living. Such items include basic kitchen utensils and appliances, laundry and clothing-care supplies, frequently needed home- and car-repair tools. Reference books, current financial records and general office supplies essential to keep paperwork flowing smoothly, clothing that is worn often, favorite toys, games, and records or tapes also fall into this category.

After taking inventory, you should put all your items into these three arbitrary groups. The category that is missing, of course, is 'items that I like but never use'. If you have a special collection of small boxes, antique tools, or kitchen utensils that you treasure and have always displayed, then you'll probably want to include these items in the third category for the purposes of your storage plan. However, if your storage crisis is severe, take a hard look at such items. Are they really treasures or just junk? They may belong in the first category. Depending on the severity of your 'storage crisis', they may be worse than junk—'excess baggage' that belongs in a garage sale.

Articles that end up in that first category are always difficult to deal with. A little bit of mental (and emotional) toughness is sometimes needed. Ask the following questions: How much pleasure does it truly give you? Is there someone you know who could make better use of it? How much space will you gain by getting rid of it? If you plan on giving it to someone at a later date, are you sure that they'll want it? Why don't you use it anymore —have you outgrown the clothes...or the hobby? If you took a picture of it, would the memory be adequately saved?

Think positive. You can donate the goods to charity and possibly get a receipt for a tax deduction. If you have the time and energy, hold a garage sale and use the money to purchase wood to build new storage pieces. Don't get rid of anything that will break your heart (or someone else's), but by all means get rid of the junk and the clutter. Only then will you be on your way to getting organized.

The second category represents items that are definitely needed, but not on a day-to-day basis as are items in the third category. But even these items should be scrutinized. Do you have Christmas tree decorations that are outdated? Lawn chairs that have needed repair work for at least ten years? Have the children simply outgrown a lot of their toys? Once you've whittled this list down a bit, you can begin thinking about the appropriate storage space for the items.

The third category contains the most important home storage items, because you need them and use them so often. Consequently, they should be well within reach—to save you footsteps, stooping, or reaching, and to make them easy to put back in their proper place. They should also be well organized. For example, paperwork is more easily found in file folders than stacked in drawers. Special racks for spices, record albums and tapes make locating and choosing these objects much easier than rooting through boxes or bins to find them.

Identifying the Problem

You've made your list and hopefully narrowed it down a bit by disposing of some unnecessary items. Now you need to totally rethink your home's storage potential. Forget about the way in which things are now being stored. Instead, concentrate on new candidates for storage spaces, areas of your home that could serve well for storage. Remember that some items should be readily accessible while others can be tucked neatly away in harder-to-get-to areas.

Next, take a walk around your house with the express purpose of locating potential storage areas. Homes with nooks and crannies have lots of areas that can be used for storage, but even houses with square, closet-less rooms offer storage space, if you use your imagination. If you're stumped, look at decorating magazines for new ideas. Based on your list, identify large or small, accessible or non-accessible storage spaces. You'll probably find that your home is larger than you think. Shelves can stretch from the floor to the ceiling, and goods can be stored in empty space under stairways. That empty area directly beneath your kitchen cupboards could be converted to useful storage space. The creative wheels in your mind will begin to spin as you discover more and more unused space.

Now for some true rethinking. This could be difficult but imagine your rooms with no furniture. Think about traffic patterns. It's most important that people get around easily and feel comfortable in your home; and your furniture can be rearranged in many different ways to make this possible. By changing the placement of furniture, such as making small groupings instead of 'against every wall', you can acquire new space—space that can be utilized for storage. Of course you might have to get rid of a chair or table to add a shelf-type room divider but, as always, there will be a payoff—in this case a less cluttered and more manageable home.

Another important consideration is the use of the room. Do you have a recreation room, living room, TV room, office and playroom all in one space? If so, it's no wonder that you have a storage

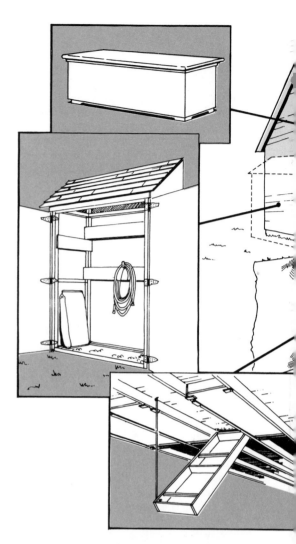

problem in this area! It might be wiser to convert a seldom-used formal dining room or guest room into a TV/music room or office—thus relieving an overstuffed room. This will also give you more practical storage options.

Arriving at the Solution

After you've taken inventory and identified potential storage areas, you're closer to formulating a plan. By exploring the following issues, you'll get an even clearer picture of your storage problems and how to solve them.

Accessibility. This involves the location of the storage area within your home. As mentioned previously, your goods are divided into three types: those used rarely, moderately, and frequently. Using the map that you have made of potential

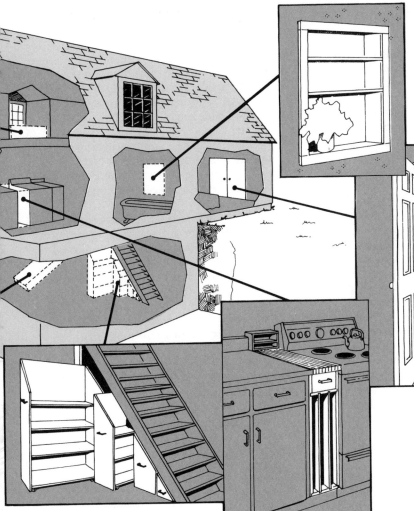

Finding storage space in your home. *This sketch is an example of how to locate available storage space within your home. Once located, you can begin to identify how the space can best be used—how to fill it, who will use it, and what will be stored there.*

storage spaces, match the items with the places so that they will be readily accessible where and when you need them.

If you go fishing or play tennis four times a year, then it's no bother to go to the basement for such equipment. If you do these or other activities once a week, then you should consider putting the equipment in a ground-floor or other handy closet. Keep the most needed things up front, the rarely used things 'in the rear' and carefully plan for the seasonal items. An ice chest might be used only three months of the year but during that time it is used every weekend, so even though it deserves a convenient location for part of the year, maybe it could 'trade places' with the snow shovel and rock salt during the winter months.

Open or Closed Storage. This issue also relates to accessibility. Open storage makes goods more readily available than closed storage. But more than that, it relates to your decorating tastes. For example, if certain dishes are used frequently, open kitchen shelving might be more convenient than traditional cupboards. If the dishes are non-descript, then there is little incentive for removing cupboard doors or building new shelving. But if they accent your kitchen decor, then you might want to display them. By contrast, even though you might use the iron and ironing board often, you probably don't enjoy seeing it day-in and day-out. *Open storage* allows you to display decorative articles and collectibles or any other items that you prefer to keep close at hand. Shelving and counter-tops are common forms of open storage.

Closed storage conceals all the items that we don't want to see. You might open your mail on a daily basis, but you might not want to see the bills after they're opened—until you're ready to make payments. Closed storage, in the form of drawers, cabinets, bins and closets helps us to rid our lives of clutter and 'visual roadblocks'.

Some people work more efficiently in an environment with clean lines and minimal open storage while others thrive in seeming dishevelment—with bric-a-brac and work materials all out in the open, a "wilderness of free association", as one playwright put it. Your decisions between open or closed storage will depend on you and your family's personal needs. They will probably also be influenced by decorating trends.

Updating or Starting Over.   You may discover that a storage space is being used but it isn't being used *correctly*. For example, in your kitchen there is a tall shelf where you keep all of your lids and trays. As you stack and restack them, they invariably slide out and fall onto the floor. Simply adding dividers in this space will help to alleviate the problem, since you can neatly arrange the lids vertically instead of stacking them.

Perhaps you have a very deep closet that, because it's so deep, has wasted space near the back. You can design shelving or carts designed to make better use of this space. These are relatively easy and inexpensive projects that will solve your problem nicely. They're certainly preferable to building a whole new closet!

On the other hand, the time may come when you've utilized storage space to the best of your ability—adding compartments, cubbyholes and mini-shelves to existing cupboards and shelves—and then you simply run out of space. That's the time to start from scratch and plan for new storage areas and/or furniture pieces. When a child grows out of the toddler stage and starts to accumulate larger and larger toys, you may be forced to consider an elaborate shelving unit, or deep toy chest for his bedroom. Or, if you're particular about everything fitting perfectly, you might want to build shelves specially sized for your carousel slide trays, VCR tapes, or paperback books.

The Personal Touch— Who Uses the Space

Once you have determined what you need and where you need it, next address personal factor. You must ask yourself who will be using the storage space and how it can be designed to accommodate their needs. Furniture and cabinetry is sold in standard sizes and these standards are based on average U.S. citizens' body dimensions as determined by government and other surveys. The standard table height is 29 inches; the standard counter height is 36 inches, and counter depth is 24 inches. These are all measurements to use when designing storage spaces or furniture for adults. They allow for moderate comfort and ease when (respectively) sitting at, standing at, or reaching into.

Likewise, there are standard sizes for workbenches, typing tables and other types of furniture, all based on average body sizes. It's recommended that you use these standards when designing your own furniture, especially in a kitchen where major appliances will be of the same height and depth. But, if someone in your family is unusually short or tall in stature, you should consider changing the dimensions slightly to make the pieces more comfortable to use *for the person who's most likely to use them,* especially if that person is going to live in your house for many years. For instance, you don't have to build the standard size 36-inch high countertop. Yours can vary from 32 to 40 inches high, depending on your individual needs. Such adjustments can help to prevent muscle strain, backaches, and other problems.

Designing storage units for children presents other problems since their 'little' bodies grow at an average rate of 2 inches per year between ages five and sixteen. With this in mind, it doesn't seem wise to invest in expensive, undersized cabinetry or shelving for tots. Some practical alternatives are to use inexpensive materials, build units that can accept add-ons, or build units with adjustable shelving. There are other storage problems that are peculiar to kids, and these stem from the fact that kids are pack rats. They collect everything! As you take inventory of children's possessions, you will undoubtedly end up with a group of items that are mostly decorative, seldom used, but absolutely indispensable (according to your kids). These items can be displayed on small shelves or storage units that are up and out of the way.

Planning Ahead...for Permanence or Portability

Closets, cabinets hung on walls and built-in systems are all designed to stay in place when the time comes to sell your home. If you think that you'll be living in the same home for many years and you're quite sure that the designated storage space will always be functional as such, then go ahead and make built-ins. A built-in unit will generally be less expensive because either the back will not be visible or no back will be needed. Built-ins create a small amount of extra space that stand-alone units would take up.

If you're especially fond of your own handiwork or plan on using fine materials, you should build portable storage units—ones that you can take with you. The advantages of knock-down units are obvious. Many designs allow you to reposition and rearrange shelving to meet your changing needs. Boxes or modules can be placed differently according to your decorating whims. Most importantly, if you must move, you can take portable units with you to your new home which might have inadequate storage space.

Determining Dimensions

Another very important variable in planning for storage units is the size of the object being stored. Some standard sizes of commonly stored items are given throughout the book. To be certain of accuracy, however, it's always best to measure the specific item(s). Aside from this you should also consider an economical use of wood and the dimensions of doorways; that is, can you maneuver the newly-assembled storage unit into the room for which it was built without removing a door?

Doing it Yourself— Some Hopes and Cautions

By now, you should know what you need and how to best use the space within your home to take care of your storage problem. The rest of this book is about building those storage units that you need.

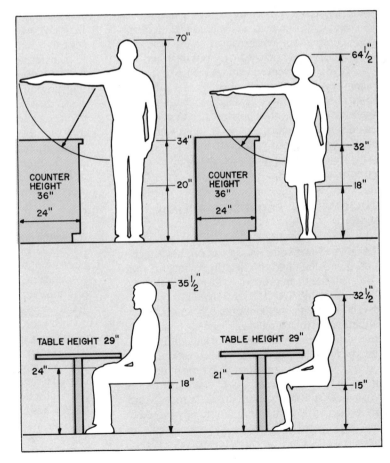

Using adult norms to plan for projects. *Shown are drawings of an average adult woman and adult man whose bodily dimensions have been determined by research statistics. Common furniture, such as cabinets and tables, are manufactured in standard sizes to comply with these norms. Use them as a guide when designing your own projects but vary dimensions when building for taller or shorter adults or for children.*

There are instructions for various methods and techniques, as well as step-by-step instructions for dozens of projects. The benefits of creating such pieces are innumerable: the materials can be your own choice, the size can be for a specific need, the cost will probably be less than purchasing a ready-made piece, and undoubtedly, you'll experience pride in your work.

Realistically, though, there might be storage problems that are better solved by making purchases. If you wish to hang an iron board on the back of a closet door, it only makes sense to buy and mount a rack especially made for this purpose. There is nothing that you could make that would suffice as well or cost less. Organizers such as coated-wire grids, plastic holders or dividers, and baskets are wonderful helpers and, carefully placed, should not detract from your decor.

Larger, factory-built shelving units and cabinets may also suit your needs and your pocket-book just as well—if not better than-making them yourself. Even if you decide to buy such products, you can use this book to understand what it is that you're paying for—what materials were used in construction and how they were put together.

If you've never built things before, it is not recommended that you tackle the larger projects in this book right away. Instead, study and learn the basic skills and then begin with an uncompli-cated, smaller project. Be honest about your own skills, and work your way up. If you've never done it before, merely hanging your own shelves will be an accomplishment.

Safety, The Most Important Issue

Being your own home handyman can be danger-ous, if you don't harbor a healthy respect for your tools and use them properly. Throughout this book, special **WARNINGS** and safety tips are given for specific methods and techniques. In addition, the following is a general list of safety precautions that you should read and adhere to for your own, and your family's protection.

1. When lifting and carrying large or unwieldy items to be stored, seek the help of another person. Also make sure that you are dressed properly and have a firm grip on the item. Your body should be entirely covered and, as an added precaution, you should wear extra-heavy or steel-toed shoes. If you're carrying a storage unit, empty it first. If it has drawers, remove all of them. Lock or tape shut any doors or drawers that cannot be removed. Check the hallway or stairway for obstructions or litter before making the move.

2. When building and assembling, make sure that you have a clear but confined workspace, preferably a workshop. Keep floors clean and free of clutter to avoid accidents. If small children are present in your household, make sure that you keep them away from the tools while you are work-ing. If they are permitted to enter your workspace at all, they should be constantly supervised and you should keep everything harmful far from their reach. Tools, nails, finishes, etc., should be safely locked in cabinets.

3. If you are breaking into walls for built-ins or to hang cabinets or shelves, be cautious. Don't hammer or drill into any areas where you suspect electrical wiring or plumbing might exist.

4. Power tools can be hazardous. If you have small children, keep the tools locked up when not in use. Always buy grounded tools and be sure to read the manufacturer's directions and precau-tions before using them. Keep such brochures handy in case you need the information. Regular non-powered hand tools present dangers also. Keep them within easy reach and make sure that you are gripping them firmly to avoid drops. Most importantly, when you are using any kind of tool —pay attention to what you are doing!

5. When using finishes, glues and solvents, or any kind of substances that give off toxic fumes, work in a well ventilated space. Also, to avoid problems, take breaks often. Smoking is danger-ous. If you must smoke, completely leave your work area and ask any visitors to do the same.

6. Dress for the job. Wear substantial or heavy-weight clothing and sturdy shoes. When working with rough surfaces, put on gloves to minimize nicks, scratches and splinters. Safety glasses or goggles are an absolute must.

7. Stay organized and calm. Have 'a place for everything and everything in its place'. Not only will your environment be safer, but your work will go smoother and faster. Do not work if you're nervous, tired, or angry. These emotional and physical states can be very distracting and cause carelessness. The chances of an accident are slimmer if you're relaxed, rested, and able to fully concentrate on your work.

2

Materials for Storage Projects

The predominant material to be used in this book is wood. Therefore, you should have at least a rudimentary knowledge of this substance and have some guidelines to follow when you first shop for it. Experienced woodworkers know how to spot wood that's green in the blink of an eye, and some even know the species of trees they pass by on their Sunday walks. Never fear, this little primer about lumber and plywood is very brief and organized—telling you only what you *need* to know.

For inspiration, what you should first do is find some finished products—at a woodworker's shop, furniture store, or antique shop—and study the pieces. Find out as much about them as possible...the wood(s), the stain, the finish, the process. Also, scour the library for full-color books on the subject. Once you've seen the beauty of finished wood, go to your local lumberyard and begin your touch-and-feel research on the raw material. Think about your project and where you will place it. You might be tempted to spend a lot of money on fine hardwood, but it's best to go easy if this is your first woodworking experience.

Also covered in this chapter are most 'secondary' materials for storage projects. Fasteners such as screws, nails and glues are described, with charts to help you choose what type you need. Some hardware styles are shown—to spur on your creative thinking. Finally, the subject of finishes is addressed, just to introduce you to some of your choices. Finishing is a huge topic in itself, but it's often a matter of buying the product of your choice and then carefully following the manufacturer's application instructions.

Timber Talk— A Short Lesson on Woods

Wood is divided into two main categories: *softwoods* and *hardwoods*. These terms do not necessarily describe the wood, however. Instead they refer to the trees from which the wood is derived; softwoods come from conifers and hardwoods from deciduous trees. Solid cut pieces of this wood, called *boards, planks,* or *timbers,* all are referred to as *lumber.* Other wood materials are not solid but are plied, glued or compressed together. They include *plywood, particle board,* and *hardboard.*

These materials vary in how they are cut, their strength, how they are sized, graded, and priced. In choosing wood, a good rule of thumb is to use the lowest quality material that will serve its purpose and is acceptable to your tastes. Cabinet backs, drawer bottoms and the backs of facing pieces are all places where you can use wood with defects or of inferior grades—and sheets of plywood do come with one side graded differently than the other side.

When fine appearance is crucial to the finished look, choose unblemished stock, but understand that you will pay dearly for it. Or, where stability is crucial, as for door framing where closet bifold doors will be fitted, select 'clear' wood; knots or warpage could impair smooth operation of the doors. Also, make your selection based on the final finish. For a natural-stained or clear finish, choose better grades of lumber; for a project that is to be painted, choose more economical grades.

All About Lumber

The most commonly used kinds of lumber for storage projects are softwoods—the most popular and widely available of these being pine, fir, cedar, cypress, hemlock, spruce, and redwood. Softwoods are divided into three types for the purpose of grading them. The first two types are boards (wood with a nominal measurement of 1 inch thick) and the third is called *dimension lumber* or *light framing* —lumber with a nominal thickness of 2 inches.

Terminology might vary in different localities but the two types of boards can be graded as either *select (clear)* or *common*. Select or clear boards are more expensive, have fewer blemishes and are rated A through D. Common softwood boards have more knots, are less expensive and are rated No. 1 through No. 5. Dimension lumber, mostly used for framing, but sometimes used for cabinets or smaller projects, is available in four categories: *construction, standard, utility,* and *economy*. Use the chart on this page to determine which grade of softwood to select for your particular use.

Softwood pieces are usually dressed on all four sides at the lumber mill (sometimes desig-

Softwood Lumber Grading

SELECT OR CLEAR (nominal thickness of 1 inch)		COMMON (nominal thickness of 1 inch)		DIMENSION LUMBER LIGHT FRAMING (nominal thickness of 2 inches)	
CATEGORY	DESCRIPTION	CATEGORY	DESCRIPTION	CATEGORY	DESCRIPTION
A	No blemishes. Ideal for natural finishes.	No. 1	Larger tight knots than select grade. Acceptable for painting.	Construction	For use where sturdy framing is needed
B	Tiny blemishes. Fine for natural finishes.	No. 2	More knots; some loose. Can be painted.	Standard	Acceptable for closet framing.
C	Some small blemishes and tight knots. Fine for natural finishes and paint.	No. 3	Splits and holes. Unacceptable for painting.	Utility	Not for closet framing; suitable for cabinets and other small projects.
D	Several small knots. Acceptable for painting.	No. 4	Many splits and holes. Some sections can be salvaged. Do not paint.	Economy	Avoid this grade for storage projects.
		No. 5	Unsuitable for storage projects.		

nated S4S) and the ends will reveal that they are sawn in one of two ways: that resulting in a flat (quarter) sawn grain, and a vertical (plain) sawn grain. There might be a price difference, but choosing the vertical sawn grain will help to ensure against warpage. You should look for standard lumber defects—knots, separations, pitch pockets and warps—and decide how you will treat them before taking your wood home. Most problems can be remedied or, if you're lucky, you can salvage what you need and scrap the sections with the worst defects. Determining whether wood is correctly dried or still 'green' is difficult for an amateur, so to be safe, always order kiln-dried (Kd) wood rather than the less-expensive air dried (Ad) variety.

Sizing is yet another matter and learning this bit of woodworker's language will aid you greatly when the time comes to design and draw your project. Traditionally, in the lumber industry, *nominal sizing* (in name only) refers to the depth and width of wood that has not yet been dried and trimmed to make it smooth. Thus, when you purchase a 2 x 4 you will get a board that was once that size but now measures 1½ inches x 3½ inches. Consult the chart, shown here, for the conversions from nominal to actual sizes and keep it handy when you make project plans. Larger sizes, 4 x 4 through 8 x 8, are not required for most storage projects, so they are not listed.

Nominal sizing does not apply to any pieces of softwood that are smaller than a 1 x 2. Such smaller pieces are considered molding and are sold in exact inch sizes. A board's length, also, will be the actual size in inches that you order. Typically,

Nominal and Actual Sizes of Softwood Lumber (in inches)

NOMINAL	ACTUAL
1 x 2	¾ x 1½
1 x 3	¾ x 2½
1 x 4	¾ x 3½
1 x 6	¾ x 5½
1 x 8	¾ x 7¼
1 x 10	¾ x 9¼
1 x 12	¾ x 11¼
2 x 2	1½ x 1½
2 x 3	1½ x 2½
2 x 4	1½ x 3½
2 x 6	1½ x 5½
2 x 8	1½ x 7¼
2 x 10	1½ x 9¼
2 x 12	1½ x 11¼

softwood comes in even-numbered lengths of 6 to 20 feet.

Hardwoods are distinguished by their beautiful colors and grain patterns, but they're very expensive and they're becoming increasingly scarce. For this reason, woods like oak, maple, birch, and mahogany will be available in random lengths if they are available at all. Generally, hardwoods come in higher grades than softwoods with the number of defects being the determining

Hardwood Lumber Grading

FIRSTS AND SECONDS	SELECT	COMMON	
DESCRIPTION	DESCRIPTION	CATEGORY	DESCRIPTION
No splits or knots on the front or back surface. Fine for natural finishes.	No splits or knots on the front surface; small blemishes on the back. Fine for natural finishes.	No. 1	Some splits and knots on both surfaces. Suitable for painting.
		No. 2	Numerous splits and knots; acceptable for painting.

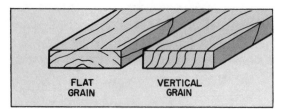

How lumber is milled. *When boards of solid wood are cut from logs at the mill, there are two results: The first,* flat grain (plain sawn) *wood has a grain that runs from side to side, through the width of the board. The second,* vertical (quarter sawn) grain *runs from the top face to the bottom face of the board—either straight up and down or at an angle.*

factor. The accompanying chart lists grades up to No. 2. Though other grades are available, their quality would be unsuitable for storage projects.

Lumber of the hardwood variety is usually sold with smooth surfaces on two or three sides (S2S or S3S). Also, the price might vary according to the grain pattern (flat sawn or vertical sawn). Sizing of hardwoods is actual, not nominal, and standard thicknesses, in inches, are $3/16$, $5/16$, $7/16$, $9/16$, $13/16$, and $11/16$. Widths will vary from board to board and, as mentioned earlier, lengths will be random.

Lumber Pricing. Hardwoods will sometimes be sold by the pound but the most common

Checking for and Working with Lumber Defects

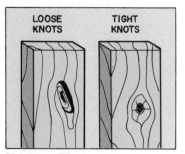

Knots. *The most common defect is knots of which there are two basic types:* loose *and* tight. *Knots themselves are strong but the wood around knots is weakened. Loose knots fall out easily but may be glued back into place. Tight knots may be filled and sanded lightly for painting over. Knots do not always detract from a piece; some woodworkers prefer to leave them visible.*

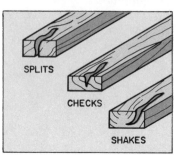

Separations. *Wood separates in three different ways resulting in* splits, checks, *or* shakes. *Splits are cracks that extend all the way through the board; checks are partial cracks. Both of these types occur through growth rings while shakes are cracks that extend between growth rings. If you cannot cut away the defective section of board, you can fill these defects with patching compound.*

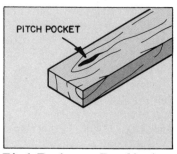

Pitch Pockets. *Found in pine and other evergreen woods, these are openings that ooze resinous pitch. Difficult to fill, the pockets will usually bleed. If you must use a board that contains this defect, first clean away the pitch with turpentine and then apply shellac to the surface before finishing.*

Warpage. *Warpage, caused by improper storage or drying, is not included in the grading of lumber. Therefore, boards should be carefully checked for crooks, bows, twists, and cups. To avoid getting these problems after you take your lumber home, always purchase kiln-dried wood.*

and most current method of pricing, for both soft-woods and hardwoods, is by the running foot. Still, some lumberyards adhere to the traditional method of computing *board feet*. This unit of measurement—actually one square foot of lumber which is 1 inch thick—can be attained in the following way:

For any piece of lumber to be measured, multiply its nominal thickness (in inches) by its nominal width (in inches). Take the resulting total and multiply it by its actual length, in feet. Divide that resulting number by 12.

Plywood and Sheeting Materials

Plywood is lumber that has been manufactured of thin wood layers (called *veneers*) which are plied or glued together. It has many advantages over solid lumber which accounts for its wide popularity. It is resistant to warping, very strong, and comes in large sheets. Moreover, it's considerably less expensive than lumber. Plywood is strong in all directions because the grain of each veneer runs perpendicular to those adjacent to it.

There are two types of plywood, depending on the glue used to hold it together. *Interior grade* is sufficent for indoor use in any area that won't be exposed to moisture or temperature changes. *Exterior grade* should be used outdoors or in other areas where these conditions exist.

Plywoods are divided, like lumber, into softwoods and hardwoods—this designation being based on the condition of the face veneers only. One face may have a different grade than the other. A-C softwood plywood has a good front face and a fair back face.

Examples of *softwood plywood* are Douglas fir, pine, spruce, cedar and redwood, the latter two often serving as house siding. *Hardwood plywoods*, frequently used as alternatives to expensive solid hardwoods, include birch, ash, maple, cherry and oak. Others, domestic or imported, may sometimes be special-ordered. Grading charts are shown here for both softwood and hardwood plywood.

Softwood Plywood Grading★

GRADE	DESCRIPTION
N	No blemishes or knots. Fine for natural finishes.
A	Smooth surface, tiny blemishes that are neatly repaired. Acceptable for natural finishes, ideal for paint.
B	Smooth, firm surface with tight knots and small repair plugs. Suitable for painting; unsuitable for clear finishes.
C	Rough, unrepaired knotholes. Accepts paint poorly. Use only in areas that will not show.
D	Large knots and holes. Use only in areas where strength and appearance are not important.

*Note: Both surfaces of softwood plywood are graded. When ordering, specify the grade desired for the face and the grade for the back; not all combinations are available.

Hardwood Plywood Grading★

GRADE	DESCRIPTION
Premium or A	Well-matched grain and color. No blemishes. Ideal for natural finishes. Very expensive. Not widely available; often specially ordered.
Good or 1	Color and grain are fairly well matched. Ideal for natural finishes. Expensive but worth it for favored projects.
Sound or 2	Smooth, solid surface with some small, tight knots. Suitable for painting or natural finishes.
Utility or 3	Rough surface with knotholes as large as 1 inch and small splits. Not suitable for painting.
Backing or 4	Very rough surface, with defects and large holes. Not recommended for storage projects.

*Note: Both surfaces of hardwood plywood are graded. When ordering, specify the grade desired for the face and the grade for the back; not all combinations are available.

Plywood Core Materials. As mentioned earlier, plywood is composed of a series of veneers all pressed together. While this is true for softwood plywood, it is only partly true with the hardwood type. With hardwood plywood, you will actually have a choice among several types of center or core materials.

Each kind of material offers different advantages. To begin with, *veneer-core plywood* is versatile and inexpensive but its edges leave a lot to be desired in terms of beauty. Sometimes, there are even voids in the edges—especially distracting if they are to be exposed. A few tricks when using it are to cover the edges with molding or with veneer tape once the project is assembled.

Options, when purchasing hardwood plywood, are to purchase *lumber-core* or *particleboard-core* wood. Edges with such solid cores will not only look better, but they will also accept fasteners better. Particleboard cores are basically a slab of wood chips glued together under pressure.

Generally, lumber-core wood is preferable; but refer to the chart shown on this page if you are in doubt about which kind to use.

Plywood Sizes. An advantage of using plywood is that it comes in sheets—the standard size measuring 4 feet x 8 feet. At some lumberyards, half or quarter sizes are available. As for thicknesses, sizing varies according to whether the wood has a softwood or hardwood outer veneer. Softwood plywoods are typically available in ¼-, ⅜-, ½-, ⅝- and ¾-inch sizes. Thicker sheets are available but difficult to find. Hardwood plywoods come in the following standard thicknesses: ⅛, ³⁄₁₆, ¼, ⅜, ½, ⅝, ¾ and 1 inch.

Particleboard. Particleboard, already mentioned as a core material for plywood, is another sheeting material. Also known as *chipboard*, *pressboard*, or *faceboard*, it too is available in interior and exterior grades. Because it is made of wood chips and sawdust glued together under high pressure, it presents several problems that you should be aware of. It's terribly inadequate at holding fasteners; it's very heavy and consequently difficult to work with; and it's very hard

Core Materials of Hardwood Plywood

CORE TYPE	THICKNESS RANGE (in inches)	DESCRIPTIONS
Veneer	⅛ to ¾	Good screw-holding power. Moderate cost. Exposed edges difficult to stain. Susceptible to warpage if used for doors. Difficult to saw.
Lumber	⅝ to ¾	Easy to saw. Edges are easy to trim and stain. Holds fasteners well. Most expensive.
Particleboard	⅝ to 1	Least expensive. Very stable; panels are heavy. Edges are difficult to stain. Poor edge-holding power.

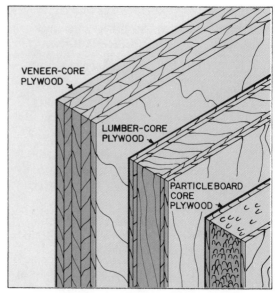

Identifying plywood cores. *When shopping for softwood plywood, you will find only one type available: veneer-core. When selecting hardwood plywood, you will often have a choice of core materials. Besides veneer-core sheets, lumber-core and particleboard-core might also be available.*

on sawing tools—dulling them in a much shorter time-span than other materials.

The benefit, of course, is cost, and particleboard is an acceptable material for cabinet backing, drawer bottoms, small sliding doors and utilitarian projects. Joints and seams may be reinforced with wood blocks. For secure fastening, nails, screws, or bolts should be used in combination with glue. If you wish to paint it, do not use water-base paint which causes the base material to swell. Particleboard is available in thicknesses from ¼ to ¾ inch.

Hardboard. Yet another sheeting material, hardboard is similar to particleboard but has a smooth instead of speckled appearance. Both faces of the board may be smooth or it may have a mesh-like texture on its back. One common type of hardboard has perforations in it. Called *pegboard*, it is very useful for utilitarian storage areas. Also an inexpensive material, hardboard has the same drawbacks as particleboard, so you should use the same guidelines when choosing and using it. It is usually available in ⅛- and ¼-inch sheets.

Moldings, Doweling and Rounds

Moldings can be useful for storage projects in many ways. They can conceal unsightly plywood edges and add interest to an otherwise plain cabinet or other piece of furniture. 'Structural type' molding used at floor and ceiling surface edges can complete the look of closets or built-ins. There is a vast array of styles available—everything from elaborately carved or embossed moldings to simple quarter round.

Available in softwoods or hardwoods, moldings may be unfinished or, in some cases, vinyl coated. They are sold in actual sizes if the piece is smaller than a 1 x 2. For larger pieces, however, sometimes a nominal size (page 11) will be available. If your project plan incorporates such molding, it's best to find out the actual size first to avoid coming up short after your purchase or during assembly. As for length, they're usually sold in random lengths from 3 to 20 feet.

Doweling and rounds are cylindrically shaped wood products that have several applications in shelving and storage projects. Dowels are made from hardwoods. Most notably utilized for reinforcing joints and fasteners, they can also be used as support pegs for shelves. Available in

Tips for Buying Wood and Wood Products

■ Save yourself time by checking with lumberyards by phone. If you know exactly what you want, order by phone.

■ Choose a reputable lumberyard that has experienced salespeople. Especially if you're a novice at checking wood and following plans, you'll need some trustworthy advice.

■ Always take your plans with you. You might need to purchase less wood than you think or you might be able to get by with lesser grades of wood. Often, Common grade softwood can be used in place of Clear, as long as you can cut away the sections with defects. By having your plans with you, you will be able to judge more precisely what you need.

■ Look closely at what you're buying so that you're aware of all defects. Most importantly, check boards for warpage. Caused by improper drying or storage, this problem is not included in the grading of lumber. Warpage can be detected by laying a board down flat and also sighting it on its edge. If you're buying plywood, check the back of the panel for an approval stamp. Markings will include the American Plywood Association name plus the grade of wood (interior or exterior), and the 'face ratings'. In this way, you can verify what you're purchasing.

■ Air-dried wood is more likely to be improperly cured. To be safe, always purchase kiln-dried (Kd) wood.

■ Check out the store's cut-up bin or shop bin for plywood scraps, especially if your project is a small one. The former contains cut-up pieces; the latter contains pieces that might be damaged. In either case, the cost will be considerably lower and you need only cut away the unusable portions.

diameters of ⅛ inch to 1 inch, standard lengths usually measure 3 or 4 feet. Rounds (pine or fir dowels) come in diameters up to 1¾ inch with lengths available up to 20 feet.

Choosing Plastic for Durability

No book on storage would be complete without at least a mention of plastic materials. Though fads have come and gone regarding the use of many types and brand-names, *plastic laminate* seems to be a tried and true favorite for kitchen countertops and other areas of the home that receive constant use—or a dose of abuse now and then. Wood, no matter how it is finished, simply isn't as tough.

As for storage projects, you might consider using this material on shelving, desktops, or children's furniture. The choices will be many because it comes in at least a hundred different colors, patterns, and textures. Though somewhat expensive, one advantage of using it is that it can be laid over inexpensive plywood bases. It's also an excellent material for hiding inaccuracies in construction.

Often homeowners shy away from using this material because they believe that only a professional can install it. While laying large countertops is tricky and requires experience, the process is truly not all that difficult. By beginning on smaller projects, you can learn how to handle the laminate and adhesive and then graduate to larger projects. A router and special trimming bit are used on edges, or they may be trimmed with special hand tools. Still, if you prefer the material but are leery of the process you might be able to purchase counters or plywood sheets that are prefinished with plastic laminate.

Hardware for Wood Projects

Furniture for storage needn't be strictly functional. In fact, unless it will be placed out of the way in a garage, basement or similar utilitarian area, it should be designed to complement your decor. Whether your style is traditional, contemporary or Oriental, you can make your new piece blend in by incorporating decorative hardware. Knobs and pulls for doors and drawers always come to mind but don't forget that you can add additional embellishment in the form of corner trims, side trims and latch plates. Materials vary widely; everything from wood to porcelain, brass-plate, aluminum, steel, or plastic is available. Assortments can be found in home centers or may be ordered from catalogs.

There are rules for adding knobs and pulls (page 71) so be sure that you're choosing the correct kind of hardware as you plan a design. Functioning types of hardware—hinges and catches—will directly affect the design, as shown on pages 65 and 66, respectively. Finally, two

Choosing hardware for storage projects. *Hardware should firstly be functional and then decorative. Use* knobs *and* pulls *on drawers and doors,* tension devices *to secure a bookshelf to a ceiling, and* casters *for movable pieces. Strictly decorative,* corner trim, side trim *and* latch plate *hardware can highlight a plain piece of furniture. Other hardware such as bolts for installation and functional hardware such as hinges, catches, and tracks for sliding doors, are shown elsewhere in this text, along with the processes for mounting them.*

other types of hardware that might be useful for storage projects are tension devices, such as those used to wedge a shelving unit between ceiling and floor, and casters, for movable pieces.

Materials for Fastening Wood

To complete a shopping list for a storage project, you should add the fasteners to it—the screws, nails and glues that will hold the piece together. Don't assume that you will have the correct materials available in your workshop, unless you have a great stock on hand.

Selecting Screws.   If holding power is crucial in your project, choose screws over nails. Another reason for this choice is that if you ever need to disassemble the parts, you may do so with screws. A general rule for determining the size of both screws and nails is that two-thirds of the fastener's shank should penetrate into the second of two pieces of wood being joined.

Screws are available in diameters, or *gauges*, ranging from 0 to 24. Those most often used in woodworking are No. 5 (⅛ inch in diameter) through No. 14 (¼ inch). The thicker the gauge, the stronger the screw's holding power. The flat heads of screws can be countersunk and concealed.

Selecting Nails.   Nails used with glue can create strong holding power and they are quite acceptable for storage projects with light and medium loads. There are many types of nails available but those needed for storage construction fall

Wood Screw Gauges and Lengths

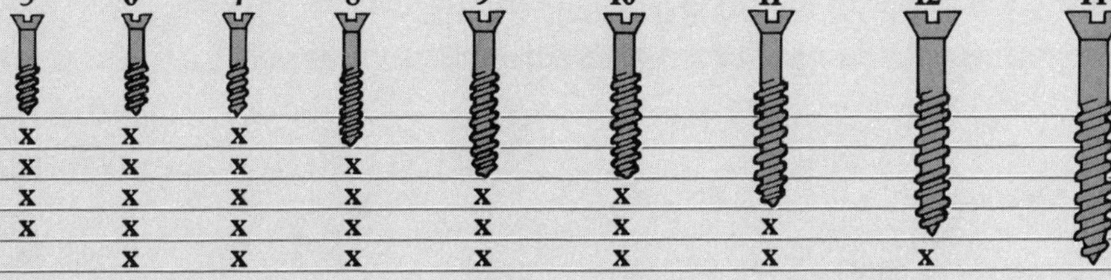

	5	6	7	8	9	10	11	12	14
3/8"									
1/2"	x	x	x						
5/8"	x	x	x	x					
3/4"	x	x	x	x	x	x			
7/8"	x	x	x	x	x	x	x		
1"		x	x	x	x	x	x	x	
1¼"		x	x	x	x	x	x	x	x
1½"		x	x	x	x	x	x	x	x
1¾"				x	x	x	x	x	x
2				x	x	x	x	x	x
2¼"					x	x	x	x	x
2½"								x	x
2¾"									x

*Shown in this chart are typical size (gauge) woodworking screws, beginning from No. 5 (⅛ inch) to No. 14 (¼ inch). Screw lengths are indicated at the left and for every **X** shown under a screw, that particular gauge is available in the given length. For example, a No. 7 gauge screw is available in lengths of ⅜, ½, ⅝, ¾, ⅞, 1, 1¼, and 1½ inches, as is a No. 6 gauge screw. When selecting the length, consider what you're fastening together and measure so that two-thirds of the screw's shaft will penetrate into the adjoined piece of wood. Though only flathead screws are shown here, other types, such as roundhead, ovalhead, and Phillips head, are available.*

into two categories: *common nails* and *finishing nails*. Common nails have greater holding power because they have large heads, but they should be used only where they won't be seen. The heads of finishing nails are very small and permit them to be countersunk and concealed, thus creating a finished appearance.

Nails are sold in lengths from 2 *penny* (or 2d) which measures 1 inch, to 16 penny (16d) which measures 3½ inch. Choose nail lengths using the same guide as for screws.

Selecting the Right Glue. Not all glues are alike and as this substance can literally make or break your project, you should have an understanding of how they differ. Factors involved in making your selection are the load (the amount of strength desired) and the location of the finished project.

In using glues, the proper environment must be maintained since the temperature is often critical in the bonding process. No matter what type of glue is applied, you should always clamp the wood pieces securely (page 30) and wipe away the excess. The latter step is important because in most cases the wood pores will be filled and the affected area will not take a stain.

Although other types are available, these four glues are most often used in woodworking; choose the kind you need for each particular project:

■ **White Glue.** This traditional household and all-purpose glue is fine for light construction but it is not recommended for projects that will be exposed to high temperatures, moisture or great stress. Wood joined with white glue should be clamped until the glue is completely dry—usually about 30 minutes. Do not use it in an excessively warm area, as it will soften.

■ **Aliphatic Resin Glue.** A type of resin-based glue, this has a stronger and more moisture-resistant bond than white glue plus it is a little easier to sand. Even so, it is not waterproof. While

Types and Sizes of Woodworking Nails

Though many types of nails are available, only two will be used for the projects in this book: common nails *and* finishing nails. *Shown are the smallest size (1 inch) and the largest size (3½ inches) of each type. All sizes in between, in ¼-inch increments, are available.*

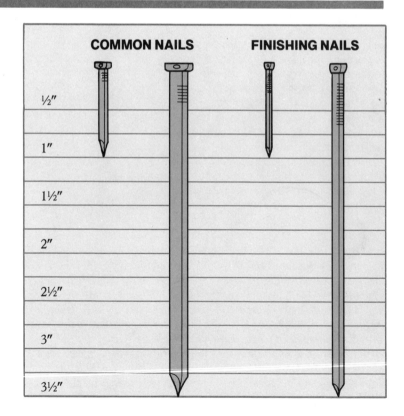

working with aliphatic resin, make sure that the temperature does not go below 50° F. Bonding time is approximately 30 minutes.

■ **Plastic Resin Glue.** Of the common woodworking glues, this type is the strongest. Though not completely waterproof, it is extremely moisture resistant. Available as a powder, it requires the addition of water and an environment of at least 70 degrees F. Once mixed, the glue is only good for four hours, so you should measure for only what you will need immediately. Slower to set than the other types, it requires clamping for four to six hours.

■ **Contact Cement.** Used primarily for laying plastic laminates or bonding wood veneers, contact cement is somewhat tricky to work with because it dries so quickly. It bonds almost on contact so it requires forethought, great care, and correct measuring. Because of its strong bond, clamping is not necessary. If you use the older variety which is highly flammable and noxious, make sure that your area is very well ventilated. A preferred option is to use the new water-base type.

Materials for Finishing Wood

In truth, this subject, if covered thoroughly, requires a book of its own. Instead, here you will learn enough to understand the steps involved in finishing and the basic kinds of products available. There are actually two main steps involved in the process—preparing for the finish and applying the finish—and materials for these steps will be discussed separately.

Fillers, Sealers and Abrasives. Holes, cracks and hammer marks all need to be filled to attain a surface that is level and attractive. The most popular substance for this is called *wood putty* or *wood dough*. Available as a powder, it is mixed with water to the desired consistency. Such a water-based product can be sanded and it responds to stain and paint like real wood. As opposed to plastic-based types, it will not shrink or loosen with time.

Depending on what you intend to finish your project with, you will need to choose other products. If the piece is to be painted, wood putty will be fine but if you are using a clear finish, you might also need to purchase a *putty stick* for coloring the putty to match the wood. Also, wood putty works well for oil-type finishes, but if the

piece will receive a built-up finish such as varnish or polyurethane, you should instead use a *paste wood filler*. To be sure of results, especially if you are applying a stain, first test a scrap piece of wood with the combination.

Sealers are substances for sealing in the stain and filling spots to help prepare the project for final finishing. A common product for this step is shellac although 'sanding sealers' are also available. An alternative is to choose a stain that stains and seals at the same time, allowing you to skip the sealing step.

Another use for sealers is to apply them before the stain so that the stain is soaked into the wood evenly. Plywood of Douglas fir is susceptible to such 'color unevenness' and a special penetrating sealer can be purchased to avoid this problem.

Abrasives include sandpaper of various kinds and occasionally, steel wool or pumice stone. It's also important to use a tack cloth for completely removing all dust and residue. For rough sanding, use Medium Coarse (80#) sandpaper; for general smoothing, use Medium grade (120#) and for the final stage, use Very Fine (220#). Sandpapers are available made of several different types of materials: durable aluminum oxide and less expensive but not as long-lasting garnet and flint. Pumice stone and steel wool are used infrequently—with special finishes.

Stains and Finishes. Stains are most often used to color wood and hide blemishes before the finish is applied. There are several types available: *water stains, pigmented oil stains,* and *penetrating oil stains.* The latter will usually yield the most pleasing results but pigmented oil stains will suffice for most storage projects.

Finishes are clear; they allow the natural color of the wood to be seen. These include varnish, shellac, polyurethane, lacquer, penetrating resin and finishing oils such as tung, Danish or lemon oil. Enamel finishes include oil-base, acrylic-base and polyurethane types.

There is much to decide on when choosing finishes. The only way to know exactly what you're getting is to do a little research on your own. Ask friends who are woodworkers what they used on their storage projects. Look for displays in hardware and paint stores. Within the boundaries of what your taste will permit, you should choose a product that offers ease of use, especially if you're a beginner.

3

Methods of Construction

To build your own storage projects, you need to be familiar with woodworking tools and techniques. In this chapter, we'll briefly review everything from simple, traditional hand tools to elaborate stationary power tools. We'll show some basic techniques and tips for handling most of these. If you're a beginner, this is important information. If you're experienced with tools, you may just want to read those methods that are new to you.

When purchasing tools, we recommend a 'middle-of-the-road' approach. Using just hand tools can be quite laborious, whereas investing in a whole workshop full of state-of-the-art power tools is overkill for the sorts of projects we show in this book. If you don't yet have many tools, start out with a selection of time-saving hand power tools. A power drill, sabre saw, circular saw, orbital sander, and router are all excellent investments if you intend to make more than one storage project. You won't have to spend much time learning to use the tools and you'll be encouraged by relatively quick results.

In order to make the shelves, cabinets, and other projects in this text, you must first learn the basic ways of joining wood. There are six basic joining methods. We'll show you these methods, step-by-step, and tell you the benefits and drawbacks of each. This part of the book is vital; indeed, joining wood is central to building any project. If you have time you should try your hand at making all six types of joints. In addition, you will want to know how to reinforce joints. We'll show you several options for doing this.

Before you begin any project, you always need a project plan or, at least, working drawings and a cutting list. You can't simply go to the lumberyard and pick up what you need, unless your project is very simple. To save yourself money, time, and headaches, learn how to make drawings and figure up a 'bill of materials'. They're truly indispensable. What tools to use, how to handle those tools, joining, drawing, and making a cutting list—that's all you need to know and you're on your way to making storage projects!

Home Workshop Tools and How to Use Them

Whether you plan to make a few storage projects or intend to make building things a lifelong hobby, you will need to invest in some tools. Just how much money you invest is your decision but in the beginning it's recommended that you avoid the large stationary tools. These are not only expensive but they require considerable practice to operate skillfully and safely. Even so, the tools shown here run the gamut from the very basic to the most sophisticated. We show many basic hands-on techniques, but you should also carefully follow the manufacturer's directions, especially when using power tools. Even better, consider taking a shop course.

Sawing and Sawing Tools. At the lumberyard, choose wood that is as close to the sizes you need as possible. You may even want to have some wood sawn right there, especially large sheets of plywood. However, you still need to know how to cut smaller pieces for assembly. Though there are many saws introduced here, they are broken into two categories—those that make straight cuts and those that make curved cuts. Handsaws are inexpensive and can be used for most storage projects but if you prefer the time-saving convenience of power tools, use the circular saw for straight cuts and the sabre saw for curved cuts.

Regardless of what saws you choose for your workshop, there are some basic principles that apply to all kinds of sawing tools—the teeth of the saw, and the handling of materials while sawing.

Along a saw blade, there are a given number of teeth per inch. Saws with fewer teeth per inch make rougher cuts than those with more (and smaller) teeth. For most of the projects in this book, you should use smooth-cutting blades. For example, a handsaw should have from eight to twelve teeth.

If you understand how saws work, you will easily understand the logic involved in sawing techniques. Wherever saw teeth *exit* the wood being cut, there is a chance of getting splinters or 'tear out'. Some saw blades have teeth that point downward while others have teeth that point upward. Make sure that the splinters will appear only on the bad side of the wood you are cutting. Examine both the saw and the wood to figure out which way the teeth face, and what side of the wood they should exit. Follow this general guide: When using a handsaw, table saw or radial-arm saw, cut wood with the good side up. When using a portable circular saw or sabre saw, cut wood good-side down.

Sawing is a skill that requires time and patience to perfect. Each type of saw requires a slightly different technique, so you should practice with several kinds of saws on several types of wood. It's important to always support both halves of the piece you're cutting. If you don't, the saw will

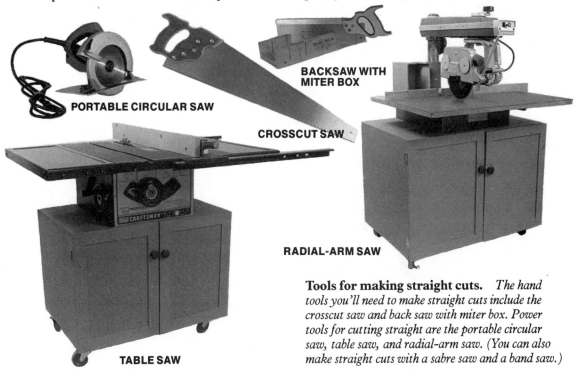

PORTABLE CIRCULAR SAW

BACKSAW WITH MITER BOX

CROSSCUT SAW

RADIAL-ARM SAW

TABLE SAW

Tools for making straight cuts. *The hand tools you'll need to make straight cuts include the crosscut saw and back saw with miter box. Power tools for cutting straight are the portable circular saw, table saw, and radial-arm saw. (You can also make straight cuts with a sabre saw and a band saw.)*

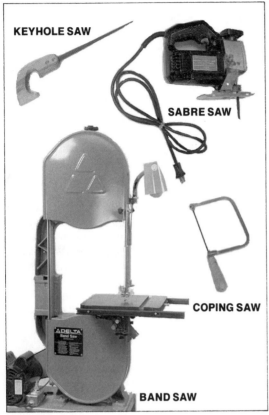

Tools for cutting curves. *The hand tools needed to make curved cuts include the keyhole saw and coping saw. Power tools are the sabre saw and the band saw.*

Using a backsaw and miter box. *The backsaw, unlike the crosscut saw, is held with its blade parallel to the cutting surface. This inexpensive miter box holds small-dimension lumber for making 45° and 90° cuts.*

bind. Also, the unsupported piece will break off as you near the end of the cut. A good way to stop a saw from binding is to wedge a screwdriver in the end of the cut to spread it open a bit.

Using a Crosscut Saw. There are two traditional kinds of handsaws. The *crosscut* saw cuts across the grain of wood while the other type of handsaw, the *ripsaw*, is designed to cut only along the grain. Of the two, the crosscut type is the most useful.

Crosscut saws can be purchased in variable sizes with the blade ranging from 20 to 26 inches. In order to keep a handsaw or any cutting tool in good condition, you should have it sharpened regularly.

When you begin to saw into a piece of wood, you must first make a small notch by sawing upward a few times. As you saw, the groove that the saw creates is called a *kerf*. Once 'set into motion', crosscut saws do about 10 percent of their cutting on the upstroke and 90 percent on the downstroke. Practice sawing techniques on scrap wood to become proficient at using this tool.

Using a Backsaw. The backsaw, so named for its thick 'backbone' on top of the blade, is used mostly for precise cutting and finish work. This feature, along with its short, rectangular design, prevents the blade from bowing. Most commonly, the backsaw is used in conjunction with a miter box to create precise angles across molding or small-dimension lumber. Though they are available in sizes ranging from 12 to 28 inches, a smaller (no larger than 14-inch) one should suffice for the projects in this book.

Typically, backsaws are available with twelve teeth per inch; this is acceptable unless you are doing very fine work. If you are doing fine work, purchase a *dovetail* backsaw, a type with more teeth per inch and a thinner, shorter blade. Likewise, an inexpensive wooden miter box should suffice for your beginning projects, but as you progress you will want to acquire a more precise one.

Generally, working with a backsaw is not as difficult as working with a crosscut saw since the miter box aids you in aligning the saw and the blade is held parallel to the cutting surface instead of at an angle. Note the sawing techniques shown here.

Using a Portable Power Circular Saw. Power saws are great time-savers but they must be used with extreme caution; so plan on doing some practicing before you become proficient in using

METHODS OF CONSTRUCTION

Crosscut Saw Techniques

Prepare the Wood. *To avoid getting splinters where the saw teeth exit, score the backside of plywood with a sharp knife or apply masking tape. For even better results, back the cut with a piece of scrap wood and cut through both pieces.*

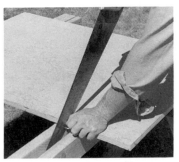

Handling the Saw. *Create a notch by pulling the saw upward several times. Start the cut with short strokes (use the portion of the blade near the handle), and then progress to long smooth strokes, using the entire blade of the saw. Plywood and other sheet materials should be cut with the saw at a 30° angle to the stock; lumber at a 45° angle.*

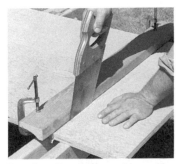

Cutting Straight. *As an aid to help you guide the saw in a straight line, and to help keep the blade square in the stock, clamp a board over the piece to be cut.*

Portable Power Circular Saw Techniques

Using a Guide. *Because these saws are heavy and difficult to maneuver at first, you might want to invest in a long, metal straightedge like the one shown here for making long straight cuts. Clamp the straightedge to the stock and use it as a guide.*

Cutting Large Sheets. *To support and make large pieces easier to manage, cut them on a flat surface such as a floor. Lay scrap pieces of fiberboard or 'builder's board' under the sheet material. Adjust the foot (or platform) of the saw so the blade will cut through your wood, but only partially through the scraps.*

one. Circular saws are sized by their diameters; 6- to 10-inch sizes are available. They also accept a wide range of blade types. Generally, a medium-sized tool (7 to 7½ inches in diameter) and a combination blade (for crosscutting *and* ripping) will be all that you need for basic projects.

When you use this tool, the teeth of a circular saw blade should just barely protrude through the surface of the wood that you are cutting. As mentioned before, you should cut the wood with the good side down. There are also important techniques that you can use to support the wood and also to guide the saw more easily. Study the methods shown here, and practice with your saw—but most importantly, if you're a beginner, use caution and follow the manufacturer's directions and suggestions.

Using a Table Saw. A table saw is basically a power circular saw that is permanently mounted in a worktable. Wood is moved into the blade of the saw rather than the saw being moved over the wood. Additional accessories, like miter

gauges (sliding guides for the wood) and locking rip fences (guide bars that clamp across the table), make this saw your most accurate choice for crosscutting short wooden pieces or for ripping. As with the portable circular saw, a combination blade will suffice for these projects, but other blades are available.

Obviously, this is an expensive and potentially dangerous tool. Unless you plan on doing a lot of woodworking, don't invest in one. If you are using one, gain a lot of practice using it and always observe safety precautions.

Using a Radial-Arm Saw. This saw is also like a power circular saw but it differs in the way that it is mounted. The saw motor and blade are positioned on a movable arm that is suspended above the table. Wood can be positioned on the table and the saw drawn across to make the cuts. (Because of this, the radial-arm saw is most useful for crosscutting long pieces.) Not only can the saw be raised and lowered, but it can also be tilted or swiveled for miter or rip cuts. This tool takes the

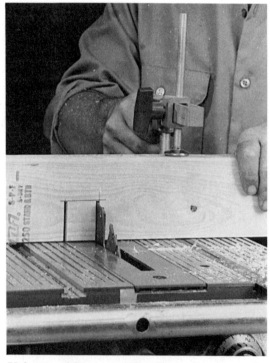

Using a table saw. *The table saw is permanently mounted, allowing you the use of both hands for feeding wood into it.*

CAUTION:

When using power tools, be sure to protect your eyes by wearing goggles.

Using a radial-arm saw. *Ideal for cross-cutting large pieces, this versatile saw is mounted on an arm. It can be raised, lowered, and tilted in several directions. Because of its design, it must be pulled toward the user.*

same blades as a table saw. As with any power tool, you should be extremely careful when using it, don't make any cuts until you're sure of what you're doing, and always follow safety precautions.

Making Curved or Irregular Cuts in Wood. All the saws mentioned previously will make straight cuts only. To make curved cuts in wood, you must use a saw with a thin, narrow blade that is moved in a reciprocating (back and forth) or linear motion. Four kinds of saws will serve this purpose: the keyhole, coping, sabre, and band saw. Of these, the sabre saw and the band saw can also be used for making straight cuts.

Using a Keyhole Saw. Also called a *compass saw,* this tool is ideal for starting cuts in the center of a panel or board from a drilled hole, as well as cutting irregular and curved patterns. The blade measures less than an inch wide at the base or 'head' and is pointed at the tip or 'toe'; lengths vary from 10 to 14 inches.

This small, inexpensive handsaw often comes in kit form—with four interchangeable blades. Some blades are better for cutting long slightly curved patterns; others are good for tight and close patterns. If the kit has a metal-cutting blade, the tool can also substitute for a hacksaw in many operations.

Using a Coping Saw. Another inexpensive handsaw for cutting curves is the coping saw. Distinguished by its strong rectangular frame, it contains a thin, almost wire-like blade. This saw is fine for cutting out intricate patterns. But because the frame isn't very deep, it is restricted to 'edge' work—you can't saw very deep into a panel.

Like the keyhole saw, it will accept blades for cutting metal. Also, depending on how you are supporting the wood to be cut, you can mount the blade to cut on either a pull stroke or a push stroke.

Using a Sabre Saw. The sabre saw, actually a *power jigsaw,* is a good investment since it cuts wood well both on curved and straight lines. Because it is small and relatively lightweight, it also offers easy handling. Many types of blades are available for this saw; it will cut not only wood, but sheet metal, plastic, rubber and other materials.

Because of the way it's designed, you can cut into the center of a board without first drilling a hole (although you shouldn't attempt this if you're a beginner). Also, some models have a feature that allows you to turn the saw blade without turning the body and motor of the saw, making it even more versatile. As mentioned earlier, you should always cut with the good side of the material down since the blades cut upward.

Making a piercing cut with a keyhole saw. *The keyhole saw will cut out a large hole or opening, with no need to cut through the stock from the outside edge. This is called a 'piercing cut'. First drill a small hole in the waste, insert the saw; saw through the waste to your cutline; follow the cutline. Cut with the blade perpendicular to the surface.*

Cutting with a coping saw. *You can make intricate cuts along the edge of a board with this saw, even make piercing cuts if they aren't too far inside the stock. If wood is clamped horizontally, as shown here, point the blade teeth away from the handle and cut on the push stroke. If wood is supported vertically, the blade may be reversed for cutting on a pull stroke. To begin a piercing cut, remove the blade, thread it through a hole drilled in the waste, and reattach it to the saw frame.*

Using a Band Saw. This stationary saw is very powerful because it has a continuous-band blade that rolls between two or more wheels—at least one of which is located above and one below the table. You feed the wood into it, making straight or curved cuts on boards up to 6 inches thick. This tool is indispensable for making all sorts of decorative cuts or intricate joinery, but it's expensive and belongs only in the workshop of a serious woodworker.

Drilling and Drilling Tools. Drilling, the process of boring holes into wood, can be accomplished with either hand or power tools. For building storage projects, using the power tool is recommended. There are several types of hand drills available but of them the most practical and easiest to use is the 'eggbeater' type. Awls, punches and twist tools, though not actually drills, are used to make small holes for starting screws, keeping nails from splitting wood, and so on.

No matter what kind of drill you use, there are several things that you can do to make your operation flow smoothly. Typically, there are three problems encountered when drilling holes: (1) centering the drill bit on your mark, (2) drilling the hole straight into the wood, and (3) preventing the

Using a band saw. *Wood is pushed into the band saw—a powerful tool used for making both decorative cuts and joinery.*

Using a Sabre Saw

Cutting Straight Lines.
Make a guide for straight cutting by clamping a straightedge to the workpiece. You can use the same metal straightedge you purchased for the circular saw.

Cutting Curved Patterns.
Always work with the material's good side down as the teeth of a sabre saw point upward. Because this saw has an adjustable blade that works independently of the saw body, it is especially easy to maneuver.

Making a Piercing Cut or 'Cut-Out'. *Tilt the sabre saw forward on its foot plate, start the motor and slowly lower the tool so that the blade bites into the waste. You can also drill a hole and insert the blade in the hole.*

METHODS OF CONSTRUCTION

backside of the wood from splintering. For the first problem, it helps to use an awl, punch, nailset or even a large nail to create a 'pilot' hole for the drill bit. To keep the bit straight in the wood, use a drill guide.

In order to prevent the wood from splintering, you can either use a scrap wood piece firmly clamped to the backside (then drill into these scraps) or you can drill holes from both sides so that they meet in the middle of the stock. All three of these methods are demonstrated here, as well as

tips for controlling how far the drill bit penetrates the stock. Most importantly, when using an electric drill, always wear safety goggles and follow the safety rules specified by the manufacturer.

CAUTION:

When using power tools, be sure to protect your eyes by wearing goggles.

Drilling Techniques

Keeping the Bit Centered.

To make sure that the drill bit stays on its mark, first punch a small hole with a nailset or large nail. Place the tip of the drill bit in this hole.

Keeping the Hole Straight.

A. *Use a specially-made drill guide for accurate drilling.*

B. *Make your own drill guide by simply predrilling a hardwood block.*

Judging the Drilling Depth.

A. *Use a depth gauge, as shown here, to know how far the bit has penetrated into your workpiece.*

B. *Fasten a stop collar to the bit, so that the bit will only penetrate as far as the collar.*

C. *Place tape around the drill bit, and use the bottom edge of the tape to mark how far you want the bit to penetrate.*

Using an Eggbeater Hand Drill. This drill will suffice if you need to drill only small holes or if you don't want to spend the money on an electric drill. Operated by simply cranking the handle clockwise, it will drill holes up to ¼ inch in diameter with the proper bit.

Using an Electric Drill. This is a highly recommended investment for your toolbox. Power drills come in three sizes, determined by the maximum diameter of the drill bit that can be mounted in the drill's chuck: ¼ inch, ⅜ inch, and ½ inch. The bigger the chuck size, the more power the drill is likely to have—usually. The large-size ½-inch drill will operate slower than the smaller ¼-inch drill, but will be capable of boring through tougher materials, such as hardwoods, metal and concrete. The ⅜-inch size is recommended for general woodworking as the most versatile type for the money spent.

Tools for drilling wood. *For boring holes into wood, use a double-insulated power drill and/or an 'eggbeater' hand drill. Punches and awls can be used to make small 'starter' holes for screws.*

When purchasing a power drill, there are several other considerations. Always get a double-insulated model when buying this or any other power tool. The high-impact, nonconductive material is your extra insurance against electrical shock. Also, consider the drill's operating features. The simplest drill has a trigger that turns the drill either on or off. The next best model has a 2-speed trigger, and an even better model has a trigger that causes the motor to run slower or faster depending on how hard you squeeze it. These 'variable-speed' drills have settings that will freeze the power output at a given level. This is a desirable feature if you plan to drive screws, work on unusual materials or use large attachments. Finally, many drills have a switch to reverse the motor, so that you can remove screws or back a bit out of hard material.

No matter which kind you buy, look for (at least) ⅕ horsepower, a suitable (minimum 90-day) warranty and the Underwriters' Laboratory mark. It's best to shop for a reputable brand. There are drill bits and accessories designed to do everything from sanding wood to trimming hedges, so you will find the tool extremely versatile. For making storage projects, however, you only need a few kinds of bits, which we show here.

Using Chisels. Wood chisels are necessary for cutting grooves and mortises. Even if you have a router, you might have a special problem that calls for these hand tools. Though they often come in sets of four different sizes (¼ inch, ½ inch, ¾ inch, and 1 inch), you might want to purchase individual ones as you need them. Make sure that you don't buy carving chisels; instead, look for chisels that you can hit with a mallet. Typically, these chisels have heavy plastic or wood handles with metal caps. Use a wood, rawhide, or plastic mallet to tap the tops of the chisels. Chiseling techniques, closely associated with making joints, are shown later in this chapter.

Using a Block Plane. Planes are hand tools used to trim away unwanted portions of wood. Though several types are available, the block plane will be adequate for your storage projects. For specialized cabinetmaking purposes like routing, grooving and chamfering, special planes are available. Follow the techniques outlined later in this chapter when using a block plane.

Using an Electric Router. This power tool is a truly marvelous invention. It's an electric chisel, woodcarving knife, and plane—all in one.

Drilling Pilot Holes

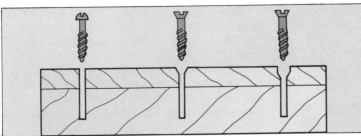

Not all woods need pilot holes for screws; hard, dense woods and other hard materials should have pilot holes; for softer woods and materials they are not required. The best way to be sure is to drive a screw without a pilot hole. If you meet resistance, then you need a pilot hole. The hole's diameter should be slightly smaller than the shank of the screw.

Three kinds of screw holes are shown here: a simple pilot hole, a countersunk hole, and a hole that is countersunk and counterbored. The head of the screw will be visible on the surface of a pilot hole. The top of the countersunk flathead screw will be flush with the surface of the wood. The counterbored screw will be recessed below the depth of the surface, so that you can cover it with wood putty or a wood plug.

The easiest ways to countersink and counterbore screw holes are to use special bits available at most hardware stores. These bits will drill the pilot holes, countersink, and counterbore in one step.

Selecting Drill Bits

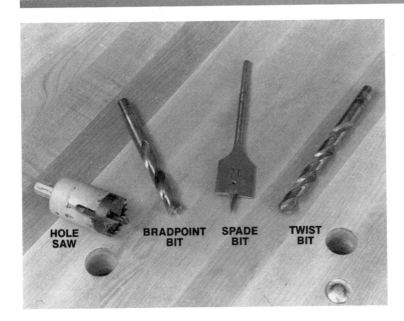

HOLE SAW **BRADPOINT BIT** **SPADE BIT** **TWIST BIT**

Drill bits come in sets or may be purchased individually. Here are some that can be used for storage projects as well as other woodworking functions. Fractional bits or 'twist' bits are used to drill wood, plastic, and metal; they're available in a wide range of sizes. Spade bits, available from ¼ inch up to 2 inches in diameter (in ¹/₁₆-inch increments), are used for drilling rough holes in wood. Bradpoint bits are for drilling smooth holes; they're available in sizes up to 1 inch. Because of the bradpoint, they are easy to center on the work. Hole saws aren't drill bits in the true sense, but they attach to your drill and can make large holes up to 4 inches in diameter.

It cuts grooves of all kinds and also rounds or bevels the edges of boards. With it you can create hinge mortises in minutes. Routers are even used to finish the edges of plastic laminates.

Like any power tool, safety precautions must be followed precisely—and because this one has such high power and speed, you should get plenty of practice handling it *before* you use it on your good wood. Routers are used for several types of joining.

Planing wood. *Begin by checking the sharp edge of the blade; it should protrude very slightly through the slot in the bottom of the plane. Hold it in one hand and apply downward pressure. Cut face grain using long strokes; cut end grain using short strokes. To prevent the end grain from splitting, clamp a piece of scrap wood next to the workpiece and plane both pieces.*

Using Abrasive Tools. Sandpaper is the chief material for abrading and smoothing wood. If you need to do extensive sanding, your best bet is to buy a power sander. There are several types of power sanders, but the orbital sander (shown here) is the most appropriate beginner's tool. It can be used for rough shaping and sanding. However, finish sanding should always be done by hand with a wood block and sandpaper.

Occasionally, there is a need for other 'abrasive' tools to smooth wood or metal surfaces. Files and rasps make easy work of such jobs and they are especially useful for adjustments in small places where routers and planes cannot fit. Available in different sizes and shapes, files and rasps have finer and closer rows of teeth for smooth filing, and larger, coarser teeth for rough abrading. Purchase them only as you need them; examples of each are shown here.

Using Clamps. Clamps have two basic uses: (1) to hold together wooden pieces while they are being joined by glue, and (2) to secure a piece that you are working on so that both of your hands may be freed. (A woodworking vise is merely a large clamp used for this second purpose.) There are many types of clamps available but for these storage projects the only ones that you should need are bar clamps, miter clamps, and C clamps. Each of their uses is discussed here.

Using a Hammer. The standard woodworker's hammer, a *curved-claw hammer*, is needed

An electric router. *A time-saving tool and a must for modern cabinetmaking is the router. It functions as many different tools: a chisel, wood-carving knife, a plane, and a shaper just to name a few. With special accessories, it can do even more.*

An orbital sander. *One of several types of power sanders, the orbital sander is the easiest to handle. It can be used for both rough and finish sanding.*

A file and a rasp. *For general woodworking, touch up trouble spots and rough edges with a wood file; the one shown here is a coarse double-cut, half-round file. The rasp has a rougher surface for even faster abrading.*

METHODS OF CONSTRUCTION

primarily for nailing. Select a comfortable weight and one made of high-tempered steel. Along with the hammer, purchase nail sets which are available in several sizes ($1/32$ and $2/32$ should suffice for your needs). Techniques for nailing and removing nails are shown on page 32.

Using Screwdrivers. You'll need an assortment of screwdrivers. You may wish to begin with the basic four and purchase others as you need them. Equip your toolbox with a large blade, small blade, #1 Phillips, and #2 Phillips screwdriver. Different sizes are needed because if a screwdriver is too small for the head of a screw, it won't work properly but if it is too large, it will gouge the surrounding wood. An advantage of using Phillips screws and screwdrivers is that they won't slip out of the screw heads as easily as a regular screwdriver slips out of the normal slotted ones. If you own a variable-speed drill, you can purchase screwdriver bits to make it easy to drive (and remove) screws.

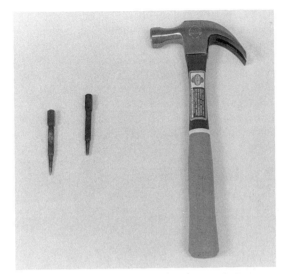

Tools for nailing. *You'll need a curved-claw hammer and two nailsets (size $1/32$ and $2/32$) for storage projects.*

Woodworking Clamps and Their Uses

Long bar clamps *are used for clamping face frames and for clamping across broad materials.* Miter clamps *are used to secure corners, and* C clamps *for clamping materials together or clamping them to a workbench. The woodworker's* vise *is bolted to a workbench or sawhorse; its primary purpose is to hold the stock while you work.*

Generally, you should drill pilot holes before driving screws into wood—the only exception to this being when you are installing small screws into soft wood. In this case, simply begin the hole with a punch or awl. Different types of screws are available, but for the projects in this book, flathead screws will be used most often. Screw sizes are shown in the previous chapter, and instructions for setting them are shown in this one.

Using Pliers and Wrenches. For fastening hardware, you should have an adjustable wrench and a pair of locking-grip pliers. It's also wise to be equipped with a set of inexpensive hex wrenches. The adjustable wrench is most often used in conjunction with a screwdriver to install bolts. Pliers can be used to pull out nails or screws whose heads have twisted off.

Nailing Techniques

Blunting the Nail End. *To avoid splitting woods that split easily, lightly tap the pointed end of the nail with the hammer to blunt it.*

Placing Nails. *Avoid placing nails along the same grain lines since this could cause splitting. Instead, stagger them as shown.*

Using Nail Sets. *Instead of crushing wood with the last few hammer blows, maintain a smooth surface by using a nail set to drive the nail all the way into the wood. Set the nail heads about 1/16 inch below the surface.*

Toenailing. *In some cases, when you can't nail straight through a board into another, you may have to 'toenail' the boards together. Drill angled pilot holes and then drive the nails as shown.*

Removing Nails. *If you must remove a nail, wedge the claw around the nail's shank and rock the hammer backward. To protect the wood's surface, place a stick or block under the head of the hammer.*

METHODS OF CONSTRUCTION

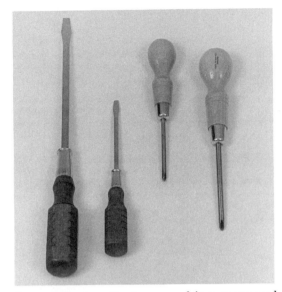

Screwdrivers. *Purchase screwdrivers as you need them, in standard sizes. To begin with, you'll need large blade and small blade screwdrivers, plus #1 and #2 Phillips screwdrivers.*

Pliers and wrenches. *These tools are used for miscellaneous tasks when joining and finishing storage projects.*

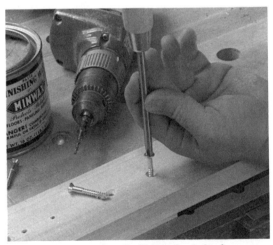

Installing screws. *Drill for pilot holes for screws, countersunk or counterbored as desired. If you meet resistance when installing a screw, remove it and then enlarge the pilot hole slightly. If you're using aluminum or brass screws, it's a good idea to first drive in a steel screw, remove it, and then install the other, softer metal screw. Most importantly, keep the screwdriver squarely seated in the screw head. Screws are easier to drive if their threads have been rubbed with soap or wax.*

Joining—Connecting and Securing Wood Members

Most storage projects are box-like in nature, whether they will become shelving, cabinets, chests, or drawers. *Joining* or *jointing* techniques are used to create the corners and intersections where two members connect to each other. Though there are many types of joints, the time-consuming and complicated ones, like dovetails and mortise-and-tenon joints, are not covered here. With today's strong glues, simpler joints can be just as strong as complex.

Six types of joints are presented here. You should make your choice between them based on several factors: the strength of the joint, its appearance, the tools you'll be using and the degree of skills you possess. Use the chart here to help determine the correct joint for your purposes.

We also show techniques for making butt, rabbet, dado, miter, end-lap and mid-lap joints. Though some are shown using hand tools, you can perform many of the steps more easily by using power tools. Two methods are shown for making dado joints—with a table saw and with a table saw fitted with a dado cutter.

Using Braces to Reinforce Joints.
Normally, a well-made joint does not have to be reinforced. But for storage pieces that will have medium to heavy loads, and especially for pieces that are joined with butt joints, reinforcing with braces is a good idea. Braces can be made of wood or metal; there are several types to choose from depending on the type and size of the joint—and the desired appearance of the finished joint.

The most common types of wood braces are triangular and rectangular wood blocks and *gussets*. Popular kinds of metal braces include those called *flat corner* and *inside corner* braces and *T braces*. These are all shown on page 40.

Choosing the Correct Joint

TYPE		DESCRIPTION	USES AND BENEFITS
Butt		Two or more members joined end to end, end to edge, face to edge, or edge to edge.	The weakest but acceptable for face frame construction when pieces are joined with glue.
Rabbet		A notch cut in the edge of a board. The adjoining board may be similarly notched, or unnotched.	Strong. Often used in carcass construction—for cabinet backs and drawers.
Dado		A groove cuts across the grain of a board. The adjoining board fits in the groove.	Strong; withstands stress from several directions. Often used for drawers and for supporting shelves in cabinets and shelving units.
Miter		Two members are cut at an angle (usually 45°) and joined together.	Medium strength; attractive. Used for molding trimwork on fine furniture cabinets.
End Lap		The ends of two boards are rabbeted to half their depth and joined.	Strong. Requires skill and precision to cut and join but excellent for face frames.
Mid-Lap		A variation of the end-lap joint. The end of one member is rabbeted, the other is dadoed somewhere in the middle of the board.	Strong. Used on frames for large boxes where extra support is needed.

Making a Butt Joint

1. Carefully measure the board before you cut, taking into account the dimensions of any boards that will join to it. For example, if you are making a box which will measure 12 inches on one side, and the side joins an end that is ¾ inch thick, you should cut the side to 11¼ inches long. Lay a tape measure on the piece to be cut and mark this distance by making a small scratch with an awl.

2. Draw a guideline with a combination square. Lay it against the edge of the wood so that the ruler meets the scratch mark made in step 1. With the square held flush against the member's edge, draw a line across it with an awl.

3. If the board is small enough, set it in a miter box and use the 90° guide slot. For larger boards, use a handsaw. Align the saw so that you will be cutting slightly on the waste side of the awl line. Saw with long smooth cuts and, when finished, check it for squareness. If the end is not square or smooth, sand it with medium-grade sandpaper. Cut out the other members using the same procedure. For the butt joint to be secure, as much surface area as possible of one board should contact the other, so be sure to smooth any rough edges.

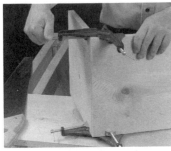

4. Check the fit of the adjoining boards. If you're going to use clamps, 'dry clamp' the pieces together without glue to test the fit—and to see if you have enough clamps. When you're satisfied, remove the wood from the clamps.

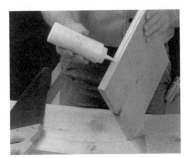

5. Apply glue to members where they will join. If one of the gluing surfaces is end grain, apply extra glue. (End grain soaks up the glue, and an end grain glue joint is never as strong as when you glue face grain or edge grain together.) Assemble the boards and clamp them together while the glue cures.

6. If necessary, secure the joint by nailing or screwing it together. If you use nails, drive the nails at slight angles and vary the angles back and forth as you go. This will help to anchor one board to the other.

Making a Rabbet Joint

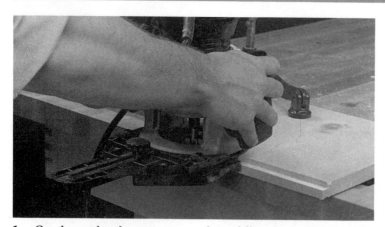

1. *Cut the wood to the proper dimensions, then mark the edge that is to be rabbeted. The technique for making this rabbet depends on the tool you want to use. The two easiest tools are a table saw or a router. If you use a router, mount a straight bit in the chuck and attach a guide to the* base. *Adjust the depth of cut and the position of the guide so that the router will cut a rabbet to the desired dimensions. Turn the router on and draw it slowly along the edge of the board, as shown. If the rabbet is particularly deep or wide, you may want to cut it in several passes.*

2. *To cut a rabbet with a table saw, adjust the height of the blade above the table to cut the depth. Pass the wood over the blade, using the fence as a guide. Be very careful when you do this operation, because you have to remove the saw guard.*

3. *Readjust the blade height to cut the width, and pass the wood over the blade a second time. Once again, use the fence as a guide. Be careful that the waste is not between the fence and the blade. If it is, it will kick back as you finish the cut.*

4. *If the rabbet is particularly wide, you may want to cut just the depth on the table saw, then score the waste several times with the blade, as shown. Remove the waste with a chisel.*

Making a Dado Joint

1. *Like the rabbet, the easiest tools to use when making a dado are the router and the table saw. If you use a router, mount a straight bit in the chuck and clamp a long metal straightedge to the wood to use as a guide. You can use the same straightedge you bought to guide the circular saw. If the dado is particularly deep or wide, you may want to cut it in several passes.*

2. *To make a dado on a table saw, adjust the saw blade to cut the depth of the dado. Cut both edges of the dado. Use the miter gauge to guide the wood, if the board is narrow. Use the fence as a guide if the wood is wide.*

3. *Remove the waste between the two cuts with a chisel. Hold the chisel so that the bevel faces down. This will give you better control. If the bevel faces up, the chisel will want to dig into the wood.*

Option: *You can also use a dado cutter accessory on your table saw to cut a dado (or rabbet). This accessory mounts on the arbor like a normal blade and cuts a very wide kerf. Depending on the type of dado accessory, you can adjust the width of the kerf by either changing the number of blades on the arbor, or adjusting the tilt of the cutter on the arbor.*

Making a Miter Joint

1. You can make miter joints by hand, with a back saw and a miter box, or with a table saw, or with a radial-arm saw. If you make them by hand, place the wood in the miter box and align the mark with the 45° so that you'll be cutting on the waste side of the line. Hold the stock firmly against the back side of the box, and cut with long, slow strokes.

2. To cut a miter joint on a table saw, use the miter gauge as a guide. Check the angle between the face of the gauge and the blade with a 45° triangle to make sure that the gauge is properly adjusted. Clamp the stock in the gauge, and guide it past the blade. Make the cut slowly to avoid splintering.

3. To cut a miter joint on a radial arm saw, rotate the arm so that the blade is 45° to the fence. Check the angle with a triangle. Hold the stock firmly against the fence, and draw the blade across it.

4. When clamping a miter joint, use a special corner clamp to hold the pieces square to one another. Apply plenty of glue to the adjoining surfaces. Miter joints qualify as end grain joints, and end grain soaks up the glue.

5. To reinforce a miter joint, drive nails or screws into both sides of the joint, perpendicular to one another. This will keep the joints from spreading apart.

METHODS OF CONSTRUCTION

Making an End-Lap Joint

1. *End-lap joints are made in much the same way that you make rabbet joints, but the depth of the joint must be equal to half the thickness of the stock. When adjusting the depth of cut on your router or table saw, cut a small lap in the very ends of two scraps and put them together to test the fit. If the top and bottom surfaces of both boards are flush, then the depth of cut is properly adjusted.*

2. *Cut the lap by making repetitive passes with the router or the saw blade. To prevent splintering, score the 'exit' side of the joint (where the blade or cutter exits the stock) with an awl, and make the cut slowly.*

3. *If you wish to make several parts with lap joints, and all the parts will be the same size, you can save time by cutting the laps in the end of a wide board. Then rip the narrower boards you need from the one wide board.*

Making a Mid-Lap Joint

Make a mid-lap joint in roughly the same way that you'd make a dado joint. Cut the full width of the joint by making several passes with the router or the saw blade.

Reinforcing Joints

With Wood Braces. *Attach wood braces by gluing them and/or nailing them into place. Triangular wood blocks (called glue blocks) provide strength and good looks. Gussets, thin wood triangles attached to the edges of corners, are often used to reinforce bottomless or backless boxes. Rectangular wood blocks can be used to strengthen a joint along its entire length. They are also useful for joining two thin pieces of wood.*

With Metal Braces. *Also used for repair work, these three types of metal braces can be used as part of your design to strengthen a joint. The flat corner brace and inside corner brace reinforce corner joints while the T brace is used to strengthen joints where one board joins another midway along its length. Braces are installed with screws, and attached either directly on top of the wood surface or by mortising the wood so the surface of the brace will be flush with the surface of the wood.*

Putting It All Together— Making the Plan

Now that you have determined your storage needs and learned some woodworking basics, you are ready to formulate a plan. You may wish to follow one of the project plans in this book, you may wish to modify a plan to suit your needs, or you may wish to design your own custom-built storage piece. Whichever you decide, you will have to know how to read drawings, or, more likely, how to make your own drawings. If your project is a built-in instead of a freestanding, you must accurately measure the environment where it is to be placed. Once you have made your plan, then you can make up your cutting list.

Paper and Pencil First. Drawings are essential because they are your working plan for every joint used and the dimensions of every piece of wood used. The real value of a drawing is that it forces you to think through your project before building it. The complexity of the drawing is directly related to the complexity of the project.

For simple projects like small shelving units, two drawings will usually suffice—one of the front and one of the side of the unit. For cabinets and desks, or any piece with doors, drawers, and similar details, more views might be necessary—of the top, back, front, side, and bottom. Moreover, each component, such as a drawer, should have an individual set of drawings.

Experienced woodworkers use *isometric* drawings. These provide three different viewpoints—front, side, and top—at one time. Isometrics are not too difficult to read and follow, but they are somewhat difficult for a beginner to execute. Whichever kind and however many drawings you decide to make, the important thing is to show as much as possible. Your drawings will enable you to make up a cutting list for all the needed wood, as well as a shopping list for the hardware.

Make your drawings with graph paper. For most projects, you can let one ¼-inch square of the grid equal 1 inch. (The scale will be 1:4. If that's too big, let one square equal 2 inches, for a 1:8 scale.) When drawing fractions of an inch, as for thicknesses, it is not necessary to draw them perfectly; merely indicate the dimensions in writing on the drawing. When you need to focus on a small section of a component such as a drawer or any section where you need to see specifically how

things are joined, use larger scale 'detail' drawings. For these, you might want to use a different ratio on the graph paper, such as two squares per inch (1:2).

Accurate Measuring for Built-Ins. If you plan to build shelving into a wall or redo a closet, your drawings will include an additional step. You need to first measure all of the surfaces where the piece is to be inserted such as the walls or door openings. These must be measured completely (height, width, and depth) and precisely (using a ¾-inch spring-loaded steel tape). Don't stop there, however. Especially if you live in an older home, your walls might not be perfect. Check for plumbness with a level and for flatness with a straightedge. Often, doorways and other openings are not parallel along their entire length. Measure them at several points to be sure.

Now is the time to completely scrutinize the area for your built-in. If you need to, you can shim out a wall surface to make it even or you can adjust the dimensions of your project to make it fit better. Using the measurements you have recorded, make working drawings.

Making the Cutting List. After you have made your drawings and given some thought to materials, you can compose the cutting list. Determine the type of material you are using for each part and its dimensions. Remember, if you use lumber, to convert the nominal size to actual size. Read your drawings to determine how each part connects to the other parts. What types of joints are used? Answering this question is critical to making an accurate list.

A complete cutting list will include a description of each part, the number of parts that fit that description (if more than one), the material of which the parts are made, and the full dimensions (length, width and thickness) of the parts. Be sure to allow for errors in cutting. Plan for 10-20% waste —10% if you're experienced, 20% if you're not.

With your cutting list made, you are ready to order the wood needed for your project. While you're at it, though, you might as well order everything else needed. Add to your list any other materials—such as fasteners, glue, putty, and sandpaper. Also read over your project plan to make sure that you have all the necessary tools. Try to get everything in one shopping trip to save yourself an aggravating run to the store in the middle of your project.

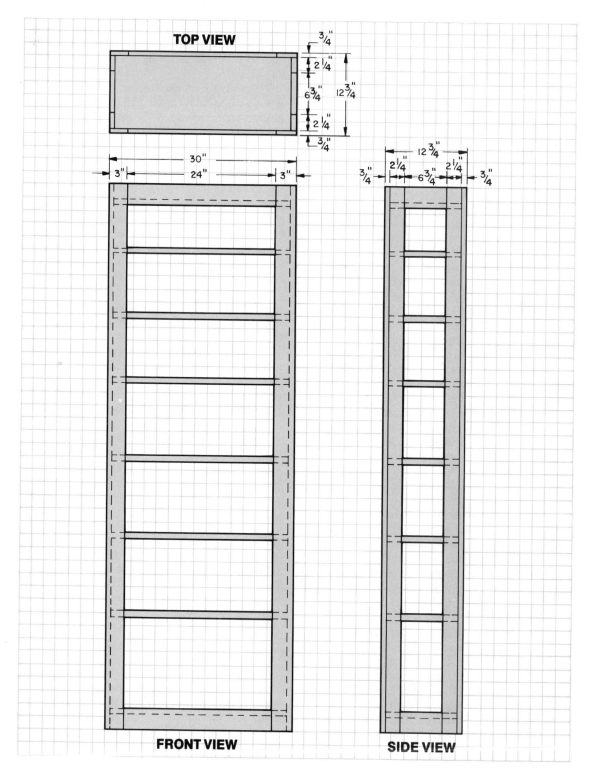

TOP VIEW

$\frac{3}{4}$"

$2\frac{1}{4}$"

$6\frac{3}{4}$"

$12\frac{3}{4}$"

$2\frac{1}{4}$"

$\frac{3}{4}$"

30"

3" 24" 3"

FRONT VIEW

$12\frac{3}{4}$"

$\frac{3}{4}$" $2\frac{1}{4}$ $6\frac{3}{4}$" $2\frac{1}{4}$ $\frac{3}{4}$"

SIDE VIEW

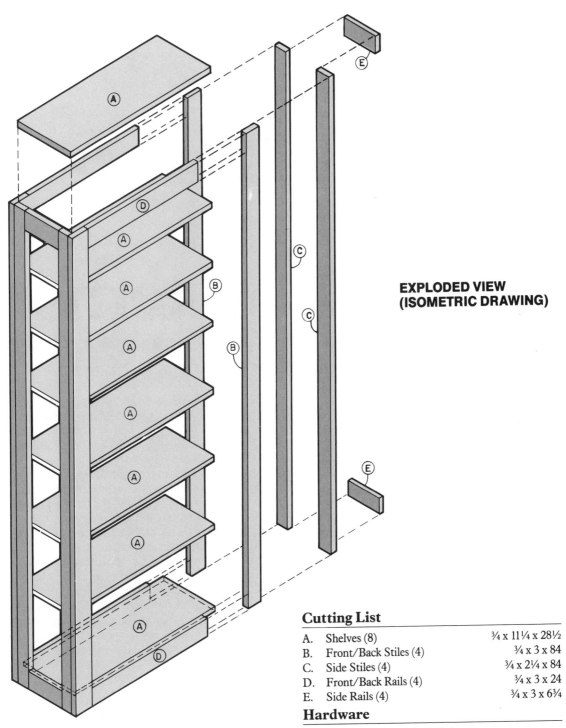

**EXPLODED VIEW
(ISOMETRIC DRAWING)**

Cutting List

A.	Shelves (8)	¾ x 11¼ x 28½
B.	Front/Back Stiles (4)	¾ x 3 x 84
C.	Side Stiles (4)	¾ x 2¼ x 84
D.	Front/Back Rails (4)	¾ x 3 x 24
E.	Side Rails (4)	¾ x 3 x 6¾

Hardware

#6 Finishing or Cut Nails (¼ lb.)
Or #8 x 1¼″ Flathead Wood Screws (6-7 dozen)

4

Storage Basics— Shelves and Cabinet Systems

The two most popular storage projects are shelves and cabinets. They appear different—shelves are open and cabinets are closed—but they share many similar features. In particular, the methods of construction and installation are the same for both projects.

To make shelves and cabinets, you need to understand basic *case construction*. A cabinet is a 'case' (or *carcase*, in some textbooks); it encases whatever is in it. A shelving unit is also a case—that's why they're sometimes referred to as book-*cases*. Case construction is a method (or collection of methods) for building wooden cases. The joinery and fasteners are carefully planned so that the pieces fit together to allow the wood to 'breathe'. Each piece of wood can expand and contract in harmony with the adjoining pieces. If the parts of a case are improperly joined, the joints will

eventually split, the boards may warp or distort, and after a few years, your shelf or cabinet will be useless.

You also need to know how to *install* shelves and cabinets—how to fasten them permanently to your walls, ceilings, or floors. Cabinets and shelving units are installed differently depending on the locations, the load, and the composition of your walls. Furthermore, they must be installed or 'hung' properly so that they remain square *after* the installing. Otherwise, they may not work properly.

A working knowledge of case construction and installation methods comes in handy when building smaller projects, too. The parts of a simple box must be properly joined, if it is to last. While the information in this chapter focuses on shelves and cabinets, it will help you to build all the projects in this book—or even design your own.

The Indispensable Shelf

Shelves are the fastest and easiest of all storage systems to build, although they can sometimes be tricky to design and install. Many factors are

involved—the load, the type of shelves (hanging, freestanding, or stackable), the composition of the wall they are to be hung on, and the available storage space. Let's consider each of these variables, one by one.

Spans and Loads. The span of a shelf and the load of what will sit on it are of primary importance when deciding what type of shelving unit to design and build. The *span* is just another name for the length of the shelf. The technical term for that which the shelf will support is the *load*. An example of a light load is linens; an average load, canned goods; and a heavy load, phonograph records.

Choose your materials in accordance with the load. Solid wood is rigid and unlikely material to bend under loads. Plywood is less rigid and is therefore more apt to bend. Hardboard and particle board are the least rigid. Unless they are properly supported, they may be completely unsuitable as shelving materials. You can test the strength and suitability of a given material by placing the intended shelf board between two chairs. Stack it with its potential load; then check the board to see how it sags.

Generally, the heavier the load, the thicker, wider, and shorter the shelf should be. For example, 1-inch lumber can be used for a heavy load providing that the boards are 8 inches wide and have a span of no more than 30 inches. By contrast, 1-inch lumber only 6 inches wide with a span of 30 inches can be used for a shelf only if it were supporting a medium load. If you want to use ¾-inch plywood as the material for a medium-load shelf, the width of the shelf must be at least 8 inches.

There are several ways to compensate for a heavier load or a longer span by strengthening the material you are using. You can do this by reinforcing the edges of a shelf or by gluing two pieces of wood together for a thicker shelf—or both.

Sizing for Shelf Items. Generally, the load will dictate the minimum size (width and span) of shelves. Of course, so will the size of the objects that the shelf will support. Measure them and adjust the shelf width accordingly. You may also wish to experiment with different ways of stacking or arranging these objects. Also, consider the finished look of the shelves. Do you want the books, albums, or collectibles to be flush with the edge of the shelf or would a slight clearance look more attractive? Experiment with the objects now; decide on the effect that you want to achieve.

Unless you're building adjustable shelves, you must also decide on the distance between shelves. Generally speaking, you should allow for about 1 inch between the tops of objects to the bottom of the shelf above them, or enough space to comfortably remove the object from the shelf. Here is a reference chart for some standard shelf items:

Determining Shelf Spacing

ITEMS	REQUIRED SPACE
Standard paperback books	8 inches
Standard hardback books	11 inches
Oversize hardback books	15 inches
Cassette tapes	5 inches
Record albums	13½ inches
Round slide trays	9¾ inches
Kitchen appliances	7-16 inches
Frying pans	5-8 inches
Pots and pans	6-12 inches
China	9-10 inches
Cleaning supplies	12 inches
Linens	12-14 inches
Hats, small handbags	12 inches

Shelf dimensions may also be affected by the size of the people using them. If you're constructing a freestanding or a hanging shelf for children, make it low to the floor. If your family is tall, treat them to shelves custom-made for their long arms. By making them yourself, you have an opportunity to get exactly what you and your family want.

One final word on designing... be creative! Most people think of shelving as just standard horizontal planks, but remember that you can be innovative—especially if you're building bookshelves. For example, by putting a backstop on your shelves and tilting them backwards, books and objects of the same size will be uniformly seated. You can also make diagonal shelves with partitions, for stacking items on an angle. Still another idea is to slightly tilt the shelves from one end to the other, instead of making them parallel to the floor. This eliminates the need for bookends—gravity will keep the books in place.

Identifying Wall Composition

Drilling a test hole produces:	Wall is composed of:
White dust; drill bit meets little resistance and breaks through quickly.	Drywall, sheetrock, gypsum board, or other thin material.
White dust, then wood shavings. Little resistance at first, then moderate resistance as shavings appear.	Drywall over stud.
White dust, then metal shavings. Little resistance at first, then strong resistance as shavings appear.	Drywall over metal stud.
White and then brown dust. Moderate resistance and breaks through quickly.	Plaster over lath.
White dust, brown dust and then wood shavings. Moderate resistance.	Plaster and lath over stud.
White dust, brown dust and then metal shavings. Moderate resistance, then heavy resistance as shavings appear.	Plaster and lath over metal stud.
Continuous white dust. Continuous moderate resistance.	Thick plaster.
White and then red dust. Moderate resistance, then strong resistance as red dust appears.	Plaster over hollow tile or brick.
White and then gray dust. Moderate resistance, then strong resistance as gray dust appears.	Plaster over concrete block.
Continuous brownish-gray dust. Continuous strong resistance.	Concrete or cinder block.

A Hardware Lesson— Fastening Things to Walls

You can solve a lot of space problems by hanging your shelves on walls, since floor space is sometimes precious. Wall-hung shelves are also easy to construct, as they don't require backs. However, don't assume that you can use any kind of fastener on any kind of wall. You'll need to carefully choose the correct kind of fastener for the wall onto which you are hanging your shelves, especially for shelves with medium to heavy loads.

Consider the Wall. If your shelves will have very light loads you can usually fasten them to a wall with common picture hangers, nails, or wood screws. Of course, it's always preferable that you locate wall studs and attach the fasteners at these points.

There are several methods for locating studs. Experienced carpenters can tell by knocking on the wall where studs are—and where they aren't. Some people have good luck with small gadgets called 'studfinders'. Still, the surest method is to probe into the wall by drilling a tiny hole, angled toward the left or right, and inserting a stiff piece of wire. Keep feeding the wire into the hole until you meet resistance. Then measure the length of the wire that you inserted. Generally speaking, studs will be evenly spaced, usually 16 or 24 inches center-to-center, but this will not always hold true—especially in very old homes where studs are randomly placed.

Often, you may wish to install shelving where studs are not present. In this case you will have to attach fasteners to the wall itself. Although most walls look similar from the outside, they can vary greatly in composition and structure. First, you need to determine whether yours is a solid wall or a hollow one. If it is hollow, you should also find out how thick the wall is. Next, you need to determine the exact material(s) of which the wall is made. Only after you know all this can you then select your wall fasteners.

To gather the above information, drill into your wall. If you suspect that the wall is constructed of dry, flaky plaster, place a piece of clear tape over the spot to be drilled to help prevent crumbling. If you think that the wall might be solid, be sure to use a carbide-tipped drill bit. As you are drilling, observe closely what kind of dust particles or other substances the drill produces and also how much resistance you meet with the drill bit. Then use the chart shown at left to determine the wall's composition.

Using the Appropriate Wall Fastener. Once you've determined the composition of the wall, you can move on to the next step, choosing the kind of fasteners to use. This is dependent on the type of wall, and, additionally, the load of the shelves. The chart on page 48 offers you a choice of fasteners for three different ranges of loads— 0-5 pounds per square feet, 5-10 pounds, and 10 pounds and over. If you aren't sure what the load will be, gather several items that you intend to place on the finished shelves, stack them in what appears to be approximately one square foot, and weigh them on an ordinary bathroom scale.

The chart is conservative and recommends fasteners a bit stronger than might be needed. Nevertheless, it's best to be safe when hanging things on walls, especially heavy loads. The only type of wall not shown in the chart is hollow tile. If you discover that you are working with this kind of wall, regardless of what the load is to be, use a toggle with a ¼-inch diameter bolt. The bolt should be long enough to pass through the thickness of the wall plus the object being hung. Also, the toggle must be able to open within the tile.

Installing Fasteners. As the chart on page 48 indicates, there is a myriad of choices when it comes to selecting wall fasteners. For insertion into studs and other solid walls, some fasteners are inserted into the wall by regular means—hammering, screwing, or bolting—and they adequately provide their own anchor. For hollow walls, however, more elaborate shields or other kinds of expandable features are provided with the fasteners. These work in various ways to grip the wall material or otherwise secure the fastener by actually gripping the wall from behind.

Shown in this chapter are several kinds of fasteners and instructions for how to use them. In order to install these readily-available devices, it is essential that you select the proper size hardware and drill holes of a precise size.

As mentioned earlier, you should determine the composition of the wall by drilling into it. If you find, after drilling, that the wall is hollow, you should also find out the exact thickness of the wall. Do this by inserting a bent piece of wire into the hole, as shown above. Knowing the wall thickness will aid you in selecting the type and size of hardware you need.

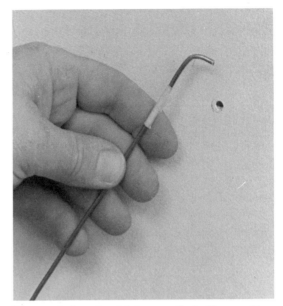

Determining the thickness of a hollow wall.
After drilling a test hole, find the thickness of the wall like so: First, bend the very tip of a thin piece of wire to a 90° angle. Carefully slip this into your test hole. Next, gently pull the wire toward you until the bent tip is stopped by the other side of the wall material. Mark the wire at the point where it exits from the test hole and gently pull the wire out. The distance from the bend in the wire to the mark is the thickness of the wall.

Shelf Supports Mounted to Walls

The fasteners hold either the case or the shelving supports to the wall. Shelving supports are either made from metal or wood, and they are the fixtures upon which the shelves rest. The most popular types of metal supports are *standards* with their adjustable, interlocking *brackets*, and *braces*. Wooden *cleats* may also be used to support shelves, or, as shown later, to support wall-hung cabinets. No matter what kind of supports you use, care must be taken to level them. Use a bubble level or string level to position them correctly on the wall.

Standards and brackets come in many different designs but they all function in the same way. Standards are mounts which are attached to a wall

Choosing the Correct Fastener

Wall Composition	To support 0-5 pounds per square foot	To support 5-10 pounds per square foot	To support over 10 pounds per square foot
Hollow. Drywall, other sheet material, or lath and plaster.	8d to 4d finishing nail. No. 8 to No. 4 self-tapping sheet-metal screws. Picture hangers.	Molly to match wall thickness. Toggle with ¼″ to ³⁄₁₆″ bolt.	Molly to match wall thickness. Toggle with ¼″ bolt, or larger. Caution: Drywall may collapse under heavy loads.
Solid. Drywall or plaster with stud behind it.	4d to 2d finishing nail. Common nail (6d). No. 6 wood screw long enough to be secured at least 1″ into wood.	8d to 4d finishing nail. Common nail (10d). No. 8 to No. 6 wood screw long enough to be secured at least 1″ into wood.	No. 8 wood screw long enough to be secured at least ½″ into wood. Common nail (8d). Hanger bolt or lag of ¼″ diameter, long enough to be secured at least 1½″ into wood.
Solid. Drywall or plaster with metal stud behind it.	Self-tapping sheet-metal screw, No. 4 or larger.	Self-tapping sheet-metal screw, No. 6 or larger.	Self-tapping sheet-metal screw, No. 8 or larger.
Solid. Brick.	No. 6 to No. 4 self-tapping sheet-metal screw with ⅞″ plastic anchor.	Cut nail (6d or larger). No. 8 to No. 6 wood screw with lead anchor. Wood dowel and screw (No. 8 to No. 6). Expansion shield (¼″-diameter bolt).	Expansion shield (¼″-diameter bolt). No. 10 wood screw with lead anchor. Lag anchor with ¼″-diameter lag screw (for heavy loads 2″-3″ long).
Solid. Concrete or cinder block.	Cut nail (6d). No. 6 to No. 4 self-tapping sheet-metal screw with ⅞″ plastic anchor.	Masonry nail (No. 9 to No. 7). Cut nail (8d). No. 8 to No. 6 wood screw with lead anchor. Wood dowel and screw (No. 8 to No. 6).	Expansion shield (¼″ or larger diameter bolt). Lag anchor with ¼″-diameter lag screw (for heavy loads up to 6″ long).
Hollow. Concrete or cinder block.	Cut nail (4d)	No. 8 to No. 6 wood screw with lead anchor. Expansion shield (¼″-diameter bolt). Toggle with bolt long enough to pass through object to be hung plus wall thickness.	No. 8 or larger wood screw with lead anchor. Expansion shield (¼″-diameter or larger bolt). Toggle with bolt long enough to pass through object to be hung plus wall thickness.

Using Wall Fasteners

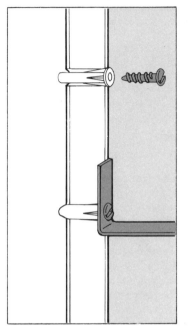

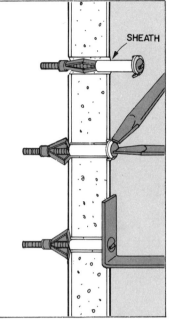

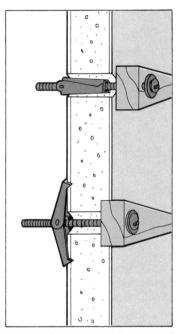

Anchor Fasteners. *These may be used in solid walls or in hollow walls thick enough not to crumble when the fastener is installed. The anchor fastener consists of two parts: a screw and a matching shield that expands when the screw is driven. Although other types are available, the fastener shown here is a plastic anchor which is used with a sheet-metal screw. This type is sufficient for light loads only. To install anchor fasteners, simply drill a hole the exact same size (length and outside diameter) of the anchor. Lightly tap in the anchor; then drive in the screw.*

Mollies. *A Molly™ is always used in a hollow wall; it is sometimes called a hollow-wall anchor. Mollies consist of bolts encased in expanding sheaths and they must be purchased in precise sizes so that the smooth part of their shanks match the thickness of the wall. To install them, drill a hole to match the diameter of the sheath and tap the Molly into the hole. Hold the sheath stationary by inserting the tip of a screwdriver in an open slot in the sheath head. Then, with another screwdriver, tighten the bolt. This will cause the sheath to expand and grip the wall. Be careful not to overtighten. Remove the bolt from the sheath, slip it through whatever you want to hang, and screw the bolt back into place.*

Toggle Bolts. *Toggles are used in hollow walls, and they can support heavier loads than Mollies. They are a machine screw with spring-loaded flanges that open and press against the back of the wall. To install a toggle bolt, drill a hole the diameter of the closed device. With a wire, probe inside the wall to make sure that there is room for the flanges to open. Next, disassemble the toggle bolt and attach the object to be hung. Replace the toggle and push it and the bolt through the wall. The flanges will open and grip the wall as you tighten the bolt.*

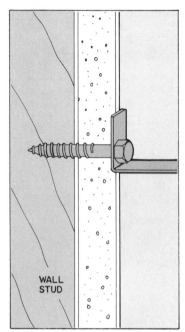

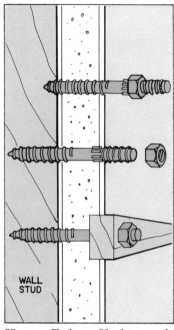

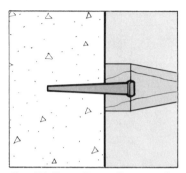

Cut Nails. *Cut nails are used to fasten objects to concrete block, cinder block, or brick. They have blunt ends which can damage soft materials, so they should not be driven into wood without a pilot hole. If you use them to hang a wood object, first drill a hole through the wood slightly smaller than the nail's diameter at its widest point.*

Lag Screws. *Also called* lag bolts, *these fasteners look like wood screws since they are threaded, have a smooth shank and a sharp point. They are not, however, driven with a screwdriver; instead they require a wrench for tightening. Used for hanging heavy loads on walls with wood studs, they may also be used for masonry walls in combination with anchors. Various diameters and lengths are available although screws longer than 1½ inch are difficult to install. To use a lag screw, first drill a hole slightly smaller than the screw's diameter. Next, thread the screw through the object to be hung (usually a metal cleat or brace), and then drive the screw into the pilot hole.*

Hanger Bolts. *Used to attach very heavy objects to walls with wood studs, these bolts are pointed and threaded on one end like wood screws. The other end of the bolts are threaded for nuts. To attach a hanger bolt, first drill a hole slightly smaller than the diameter of the bolt. Turn a nut onto the threaded end. Insert the pointed end into the wall and stud, and tighten it by gripping the nut with a wrench. After the bolt is installed in the wall, remove the nut. Drill a hole through the object that you are hanging. Mount the object over the threaded end of the bolt and fasten it in place with a nut.*

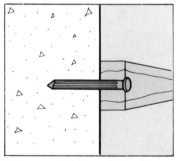

Masonry Nails. *These fasteners, like cut nails, can be used in several types of masonry. Made of hardened steel, they are often finely ridged and are galvanized to prevent rusting. Unlike cut nails, they have a sharp point and require no special precautions when driving them through wood.*

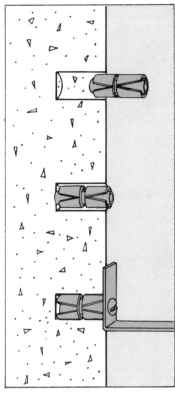

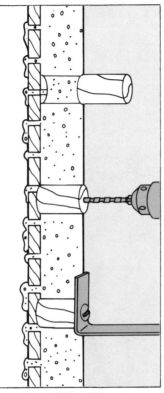

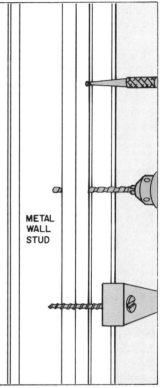

Expansion Shields. *Expansion shields vary in appearance but they all work in the same way—by expanding in the wall as the bolt in the metal shield is tightened. They are used in masonry walls to support heavy loads. The best shields are made of lead. To attach these fasteners, bore a hole in the wall the same diameter as the shield. Tap the shield in the wall. Insert the bolt through the object you want to hang and tighten the bolt in the shield. Make sure that the bolt is long enough to pass through the object you're hanging* plus *the entire length of the expansion shield.*

Dowels and Wood Screws. *Make your own fasteners for masonry walls out of dowels and wood screws; they're especially effective in old or crumbling walls. Begin by cutting a 2- to 3-inch long dowel, ¼ to 1 inch in diameter. Using a carbide-tipped bit, bore a hole in the wall the same length as the dowel but slightly smaller in diameter. Rub the dowel with soap and tap it in with a hammer. Drill a pilot hole in the center of the dowel. Next, insert a wood screw through the object to be hung and drive the screw into the pilot hole.*

Self-Tapping Sheet-Metal Screws. *These fasteners are used exclusively in walls with hollow metal studs. They have slotted or Phillips heads and are threaded along their entire length. To use one, drill a small hole through the wall just to expose the metal of the stud. Make a small starter hole on the metal with a center punch. Using a high-speed steel bit, drill a hole in the stud half the diameter of the screw. Drill a hole in the object to hang it; then drive the screw through the object and into the stud.*

(or other surface) vertically. You then insert adjustable brackets at various heights along the length of the standard. Three popular types of shelf-bracket assemblies are shown here. One benefit of using this hardware is that the heights of the shelves can be changed later.

Standards come in various lengths—for hanging two or more shelves. Shown here is the installation process for mounting a pair of standards vertically side-by-side. However, you may mount more than two if you need to reduce the span of your shelves or support heavier loads. As a rule, mount standards between 20 and 32 inches apart and extend shelves no more than 8 inches on either side of the end brackets. Ideally, secure standards into studs, positioning them 16 to 24 inches apart.

Braces, in contrast, provide 'fixed' shelves, that is, shelves which, once mounted, cannot be adjusted. They are mounted directly to a wall and are not attached to a mounting base like brackets. (In some areas, braces are referred to as brackets, so you might encounter a disagreement over terminology.) Several types are available, and they are generally made of metal in the form of a right angle.

Standards and Brackets—How They Work

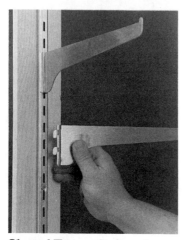  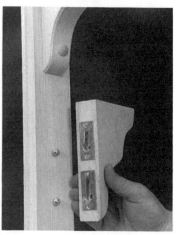

Slotted Type. *Perhaps the most popular type, these devices consist of slotted metal standards and flat metal brackets which hook into them. The standards are three-sided metal strips with vertical slots and screw holes. The holes are usually spaced 6 to 8 inches apart, to attach the standards to the wall. After mounting the standards, the supporting brackets are inserted in the slots; then shelves are laid over the brackets. If you need something more substantial, you can also buy standards with double rows of slots and matching brackets.*

Keyhole Type. *These triangular-shaped brackets are especially strong. Their matching standards have small 'keyholes', so that you can easily insert bolts to anchor them to the wall. To secure a bracket, first slip the head of a bolt into a keyhole in the standard, and push the standard down (or up), so the shank of the bolt rests in the narrow section of the hole. Next, align the bracket and slip it over the standard. Tighten the bracket nut, and simply lay the shelves on top of the brackets. You can also anchor them to the brackets with screws.*

Wooden Corbel Type. *Functional yet decorative, these wooden standards and brackets work in the following way: Mount the standards to a wall; then drive a screw part way into the standard where you want to hang the shelf. The wooden shelf bracket has a metal keyhole-type slot on its back; simply slip this over the projecting screwhead.*

Shown here are several types of braces which are mounted directly to walls for the support of shelves. They are: (1) a stamped metal brace, (2) common angle iron, and (3) a Z-shaped brace or bracket. They are all mounted to the wall in a similar manner; refer to page 54 for complete instructions.

Hanging a Shelf With Standards and Brackets

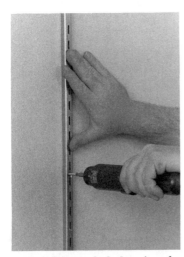

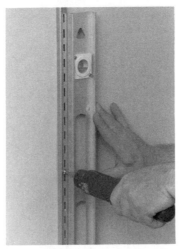

1. *Lightly mark the location of the shelves on the wall. Check the standards you are using to see if they have designated tops and bottoms since some must be installed right side up to work properly. If so, hold the top of one standard against the wall in the location you've designated for an end standard. Mark one fastener hole, preferably a center hole if there are three or more. Drive in a fastener. Do not tighten the fastener; allow enough slack to turn the standard freely.*

2. *Using a spirit level, align the standard with the level, check it for plumb, and mark the exact positions of the other fastener holes. Drill the pilot or anchor hole, if necessary, by first swinging the standard out of the way. When you drill, make sure that the bit is precisely on center. Then install the remainder of the fasteners, mounting the standard to the wall.*

3. *Hook one of the brackets into the mounted standard and fit a bracket into the corresponding slot of the next standard to be mounted. Place the second standard against the wall on the location you've marked for it. Next, have an assistant place a shelf across both brackets. On top of the shelf, place a level. Move the standard up and down until the shelf is level. Mark the wall for the fasteners, and mount the second standard. Repeat this procedure to mount the rest of the standards you need.*

Hanging a Shelf With a Brace

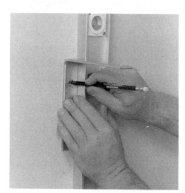

1. *Decide where you want to hang the shelf and determine the composition of the wall. Hold a brace against the wall and place a spirit level next to it. Move the brace until the level shows that it's plumb. Using a pencil or an awl, mark the fastener holes. Drill holes for the appropriate fasteners, being careful to center the drill bit precisely. Then mount the brace to the wall.*

2. *If you are using only two braces to hang a short shelf, decide on the amount of overhang you want at each end. Lightly mark the position of the braces, allowing for the overhang, on the shelf. If you are using more than two braces to hang a longer shelf, mark the position of all the braces, making sure they are as evenly spaced as possible. Depending on the types of fasteners you're using and the*

location of the studs, you may not be able to space the braces all the same.

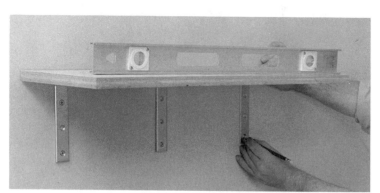

3. *Attach the remainder of the braces to the underside of the shelf at the positions you've marked. Using a combination square, make sure the braces are flush with the back edge of the shelf. Make marks for the screw holes, drill pilot holes, and mount the braces to the shelf with wood screws.*

4. *With the braces attached, rest the shelf on the first brace that you've mounted on the wall. Align the brace with the mark you made for it on the underside of the shelf. Have an assistant place a spirit level on the shelf, and then adjust the position angle of the shelf until it's level. Using a pencil or an awl,*

mark the positions for the fasteners. Set the shelf aside and drill all pilot or anchor holes in the wall. Then have an assistant hold the shelf as you fasten the braces to the wall. Finally, fasten the shelf to the first brace with wood screws.

The most common use for metal braces is in the 'utilitarian' areas of the home. Though usually employed in pairs to support a single shelf, you can also use a row of braces to support longer shelves. Use the same guidelines for mounting them as we gave you for standards, and be sure to check the wall composition and use the correct fasteners. To understand how to mount braces, refer to the instructions for installing stamped metal braces, a widely-used type.

Another popular support for fixed shelves is the wood cleat. Cleats may be mounted to walls or they may be used on the insides of constructed bookcases or cabinets. When used on walls, you need two *opposing* walls, such as the east and west wall of a closet. It won't do to use two walls that form a corner.

Normally, cleats are used to support the ends of shelves. When properly installed, cleated shelves are very sturdy and capable of bridging long spans—especially when reinforced in the middle by another cleat or brace. When using them, select the appropriate fasteners for the wall and the load; also make sure that the cleats are level.

For installing heavier objects such as cabinets, special *mitered cleats* may be used. These are just two strips of wood with beveled edges. The bevels interlock, providing a strong support.

Side Supports for Enclosed Shelves

When you make your own shelving units, the shelves may be a structural part of the case. That is, they may be joined to the supporting uprights with dado or butt joints. Both types of joints offer enough holding power for most loads. However, when shelves are joined to a case with butt joints, the thickness of the lumber should be increased slightly to compensate for the relative weakness of the joint. If the shelf will support a heavy load, you should add cleats under the shelf.

If shelves are not a structural part of the case, then they will have to be supported at their ends by other means. You will need to install supports for the shelves on the uprights inside the case. There are many options available and, as always, make your choice depending on the load to be supported and the look that you are trying to achieve.

Also consider adaptability. You can choose permanent supports or adjustable ones.

You can purchase side supports made of metal or plastic, or, if you prefer the look of all wood, you can use wood *dowels* or cut wood strips to be used as cleats. Of these, the strongest are cleats. In addition to mounting them to the uprights to support the ends of a shelf, you can also install them on the back to support the shelf in the middle.

Other options include *pilasters* with coordinating *clips,* various types of *pins* inserted into drilled holes, and screwed-in *angle irons.* All these are shown in this chapter, along with guidelines for installation. Though the supports are shown in full view, remember that you can always incorporate a face frame on your case to partially hide them.

In-The-Wall Shelving

If you're in need of shallow shelving such as for bathroom toiletries, kitchen spices, or small paperback books, you might consider using a wall's interior space for a shelving unit. This is a fairly easy project, since all you have to do is line the exposed studs with cleats or supports and finish the cut-out section of the wall with a frame.

When selecting a location for your in-the-wall shelving, it's important to check carefully for plumbing and wiring. If you see a nearby plumbing or electrical fixture, then you can make an educated guess about where the pipe or cable is running. But looking at the wall is not enough. Check your basement or crawlspace and also the attic or floor above the location where you're considering putting the shelving unit. To be thorough in your search, also inspect the adjacent room for any signs of plumbing or electrical fixtures. Unless you live in a warm climate, do not consider *outside* walls for in-the-wall shelving. You'll have to remove a large section of insulation, and you'll lose a lot of heat through the uninsulated wall.

Houses vary, but walls are generally between 3½ inches to 6 inches thick. The standard dimension between studs (center to center) is 16 or 24 inches, but this too can vary. Once you've chosen your location, use the 'wire' method shown earlier to find the studs. Then follow the steps we show later in the book to make the shelves.

Cabinets—Most Versatile Storage Spaces

Shelving is wonderful for displaying decorative objects and for keeping items that are relatively attractive within easy reach. But there are certain items which we'd rather not look at, and there are certain areas of the home which we prefer to keep free from clutter. Cabinets of all kinds serve as the traditional storage place for many of the goods that we want to keep concealed.

Hanging a Wall Cabinet. You may think it strange to tell you how to hang a cabinet, even before you've built one. But you may elect to purchase ready-made cabinets, then save money by installing them yourself.

Choosing and Using Side Supports

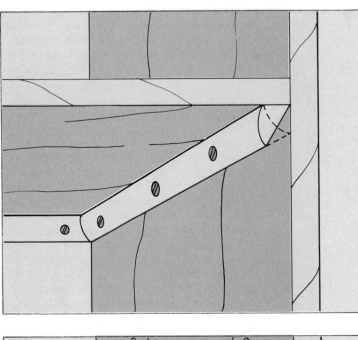

Wood Cleats. *Wood cleats offer you the strongest end support for your shelves. Although they are shown here attached to a shelving unit, you can also attach them to walls with many different fasteners. In addition, you can make them from several different wood materials and moldings. Those that you see here were made from quarter-round molding, and mitered on the front edge to give them a more finished appearance. For heavy loads, attach additional cleats to the back of the case or wall on which you're placing the shelf. If the installation is to be permanent, you may also drive small finishing nails at a slight angle through the shelf and into the cleats.*

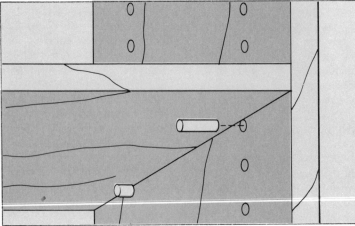

Wood Dowels. *Use wood dowels for an all-wood look in cases. Use small dowels (¼ to ⅜ inch in diameter) for light loads; and larger dowels (½ to ¾ inch) for heavier loads. Use a square and a straightedge to mark the positions of the dowels, then drill holes in the sides of the case the same size as the dowels. Though we show many holes here for adjustable shelves, you may drill fewer holes if you are sure about your shelf spacing.*

To do this, you need to make the mitered cleats we talked about earlier. Cut two strips of *hardwood* (oak or maple is best), each strip as long as the cabinet you want to hang. Bevel one edge of each strip at 45°. Using wood screws, attach one strip to the back of the cabinet with the beveled edge down. Attach the other to the studs in the wall with the beveled edge up. For both strips, the 'points' of the bevel should stand out from the surface, creating two notches. When you hang the cabinet, the point of one bevel will fit into the notch created by the other, so that they interlock.

In order for the cabinet to hang plumb and not tilt forward, you'll also have to shim the bottom edge with another strip of wood, the same thickness as the cleats. Attach this shim to the back

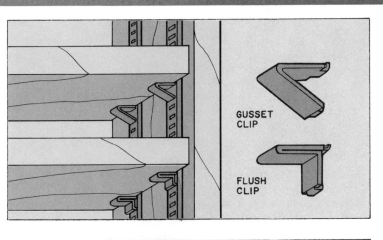

Pilasters and Clips. *Somewhat like miniature standards and brackets, these are slotted metal tracks (pilasters), and metal clips that attach to them. A pair of pilasters is either nailed or screwed to the sides of a case or to a wall. For a neater look, pilasters may be dadoed into the wood. Use pliers for squeezing the clips into place. Shown are two types of clips; the gusset type has more strength than the flush type because of its triangular shape.*

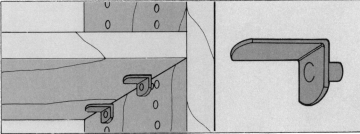

Bracket Pins. *Like dowels, these supports are inserted in small holes drilled to match their diameters. Unlike round dowels, they have a flat surface to hold the shelf. Bracket pins are available made of either metal or plastic. To install them, use the same method as for installing dowels.*

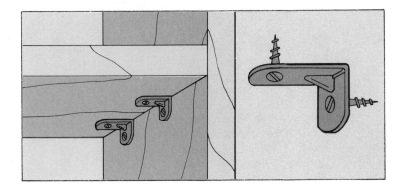

Angle Irons. *Angle irons are relatively strong support devices because they not only support a shelf, but the shelf is secured to them. With their utilitarian looks, they are often used for garage or basement shelving. Although they're shown here attached to a wood case, angle irons may also be wall-mounted. To mount them, use the same method that is used for mounting a brace (page 54).*

Hanging a Cabinet on a Wall

1. Rip a piece of 1 x 4 lumber, slightly shorter than the width of your cabinet, down the middle, with the blade set at a 45° angle.

If you don't have a table saw, you can also use a circular saw or a sabre saw.

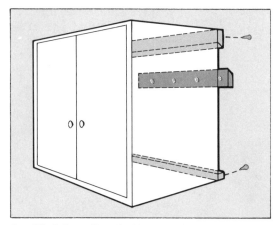

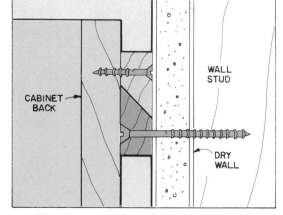

2. Find the wall studs. Fasten one cleat to the wall with the beveled edge up, and the point of the bevel away from the wall. Attach the other cleat to the upper edge of the back of the cabinet. The beveled edge of this cleat must face down, as shown. So that the cabinet hangs straight, cut and attach a strip of ¾-inch molding to the back of it near the lower edge. This molding should be slightly shorter than the cabinet's width.

3. Hang the cabinet by lowering the cabinet cleat onto the wall cleat, so that the two beveled faces of the cleats meet. When you design or construct a cabinet or other storage unit to be hung in this way, make the sides ¾ inch longer than necessary to hide the cleats. Ready-made cabinets are usually constructed in this way.

of the cabinet in the same manner as the cleat. If you wish, you can also screw this shim to the wall studs after you hang the cabinet, to make the installation permanent.

The directions at left are for hanging only one cabinet. Hanging a roomful of cabinets, as in a kitchen, will require precise measuring and constant checks for levelness and plumbness; so plan ahead and proceed carefully.

Cases—Uncomplicated Cabinets.

Now let's discuss how to actually build a cabinet. As we've explained, a cabinet is a case. The simple case is the basic building block for all types of cabinets. No matter what the shape of the finished project, no matter what its size or the materials used to make it, the case will be joined by similar methods. You can make a basic case with just a few pieces (sides, bottom, top, back) and some simple joinery. Once the basic case is built, what remains to be done is simply to install shelves, doors, and drawers where you want them.

Most cases also incorporate a front or *face frame*. This frame has one or more openings for the cabinet doors and drawers. It consists of several vertical pieces, or *stiles* and several horizontal pieces, or *rails*. These rails and stiles can be joined in several different ways. If strength is important, they should be joined with lap joints. If strength is not particularly important, they can be joined by butt joints reinforced with dowels. Attach the face frame to the front edges of the case with glue and screws.

In some projects, the cabinets may also incorporate a *web frame* to support the drawers. Web frames are built exactly like face frames, but they usually have drawer guides attached to the rails and stiles. Join the web frame to the case with cleats, or with dadoes cut into the inside surfaces of the sides.

Simplified Slab Cases.

A very simple case, one without a face frame or a web frame, is sometimes called a box or *slab case*. Slabs of wood or plywood are joined with butt joints or other simple joinery. Open-ended storage cubes are examples of slab cases. Easy to construct, these slab-type cases are not particularly strong. Ideally, their joints should be fastened with screws instead of nails, and reinforced with braces or wood blocks.

When making slab cases with butt joints, there is a very simple guideline for cutting the materials. The finished case will have a height, a width, and a depth. The sides should be cut to the full width and depth. Cut the top and bottom to the full depth and the width minus twice the thickness of the stock. Finally, cut the back to the height minus twice the thickness and the width minus twice the thickness.

If you want your slab cases to have more strength, use something other than butt joints to join the parts. For example, you can use dadoes and rabbets to join the top, bottom, and sides, then set the back in a groove that you've cut in the inside surface of the other four parts. Basically, this is how a drawer is made (although the top and bottom become the front and back, and the back becomes the bottom).

As you can tell, there are many alternatives —different ways to design and build your cases. You can choose between several construction techniques, and many combinations of joints. As always, the factors that should influence your choices are the load you are supporting, the expense involved in choosing materials, and the level of your woodworking skills.

The Addition of Cabinet Doors

Doors are what set a cabinet apart from an open box or a framed shelf. By adding doors, you change not only the looks, but the potential uses of the cabinets. Doors completely enclose what's inside a cabinet, hiding it from view (unless the doors are glass) and keeping it free of dust. Cabinets with doors are great for dishes, glasses, audio and video tapes, and other items that you want to keep clean.

There are two basic types of cabinet doors: hinged and sliding. They each have advantages but, generally speaking, hinged doors are the most common. With a sliding door, you usually can only access half the cabinet at any one time. Hinged doors allow you to open up the entire cabinet.

When designing a cabinet with hinged doors, first consider the clearance. Is there adequate head- or floor-space in your storage area for one very wide cabinet door, or would two narrower doors work better? Consider also the possible use of the inside of the door. Just as your refrigerator door has shelves, your cabinet door has the potential space for narrow pockets, racks, or hooks. Incorporate these ideas early on in the planning stage and choose wood that will accept fasteners for supporting such devices.

Creating a Basic Box or Slab Case With Butt Joints

1. *To join the top, bottom, and sides with butt joints to make a box, first cut all four pieces. With glue and nails (or screws), join the bottom and a side to make an L-shaped assembly, and the top and the other side to make another L. Then join the L's to make a box, and allow the glue to dry.*

2. *True the joint with a block plane (shown here) or with a wood chisel, making the end of the board flush with the surface of the other. Since you're cutting end grain, adjust the depth of cut on your block plane to just barely pare away a paper thin layer of wood. Make sure the plane iron is very sharp. When trued, sand the corner with medium-grade sandpaper to smooth the surfaces.*

3. *Measure and mark a board to make the back (or bottom) of the box. Remember to mark the correct side of the wood so that it will not splinter when cut. If you're using a crosscut saw, mark the surface that will be visible. If you're using a circular saw or sabre saw, mark the surface that will not be seen. Make your cuts just outside the marks.*

4. *Sand and clean the bottom edges of the frame with medium-grade sandpaper; then spread glue on them. Position the back piece on the box. Fasten the bottom with nails, countersinking them at regular intervals. If you wish, fill the countersunk holes and the small ridges between the back and sides with wood putty. Also fill any dents or scratches with the same. Allow the putty to dry; then finish sand the box.*

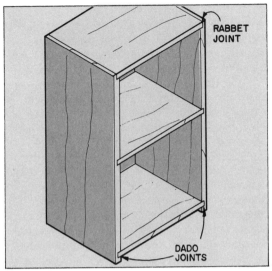

A case made with dado and rabbet joints.
*Most cases are joined so as to hide the edge grains.
Cut rabbets and dadoes in the sides to hold the top,
bottom, and back, as shown. These joints can be
easily cut with a router or dado cutter mounted to
your table saw.*

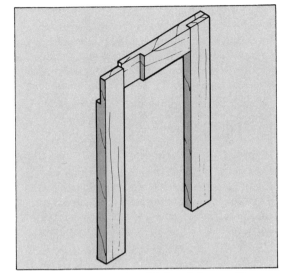

A front frame made with lap joints. *If you
need a stronger front frame, join the frame members
with lap joints. Cut the laps halfway though the
thickness of each board, removing the waste with
a router or dado cutter.*

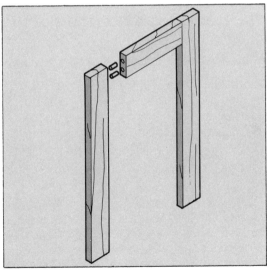

A front frame made with butt joints. *If
you wish to add a front frame to your box or case, the
easiest way to join the boards is with butt joints. Reinforce the butt joints with dowels, as shown. Use a
'doweling jig' to line up the dowel holes.*

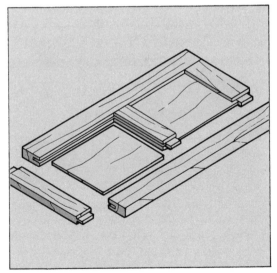

**A web frame made with tongue and groove
joints.** *Web frames are often installed inside large
boxes or cases to support drawers. The web frames
usually rest in dadoes in the sides of the case. The
frame members are assembled with tongue-and-groove
joints. You can make these joints with a router, dado
cutter, or table saw.*

Hinged Doors. Hinged doors can be installed on practically any type of case to create a cabinet. There are three different designs shown in this chapter. Although all these show side-mounted doors, you may also mount doors at the top or bottom edge of a cabinet. And though we depict single doors hinged from the left side, they may, of course, be hinged on the right side. They may also be mounted side-by-side as 'double doors', with or without a center post or stile.

Flush and overlapped doors can be made of solid slabs that are ½ inch to 1 inch in thickness, depending on how large the door will be. Small doors ½ inch thick are usually adequate for most storage cabinets. Large doors on large structures are best made of ¾-inch thick (or thicker) stock, for both strength and appearance; a thin door on a sturdy cabinet looks out of proportion. For proper fit, doors should be made ⅛ inch less in size (all around) than the finished opening.

The most popular material for cabinet doors is plywood. Hardwood plywood with lumber core is best, but others, if selected carefully, will usually serve well. Design your cabinet doors carefully, keeping in mind what the cabinet will be used for. For example, if you will use it for storing large blankets or comforters, then separated double doors will be impractical. The center stile will be in the way when you try to remove the blankets from the cabinet. Also, the stile shouldn't be necessary for support; linens generally aren't very heavy.

Setting Butt Hinges. Hinges come in many forms, so many that they can overwhelm the beginner. But if you start with the simplest kind, the *butt hinge,* and work with it, then you'll see that installing hinges isn't so complicated.

The butt hinge is made of two rectangular leaves which rotate on a central pin. The two basic techniques for mounting it are *surface mounting* and *mortising.* To surface mount a hinge, just attach the hinge to the outside of the cabinet, leaving it exposed. To mount a hinge in a mortise, make a shallow notch between the door and the cabinet so that only part of the hinge, the pin, is visible.

Once you can install a butt hinge in these two ways, you can use the same methods for installing other types of hinges. We've given complete instructions for both procedures—and the variations in surface-mounting for flush and overlapping doors. (Although the hinges shown in the photographs are plain, many decorative styles of butt hinges are available.)

Basic Types of Hinged Cabinet Doors

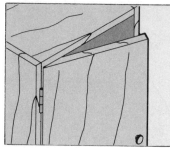

Flush. *The flush door fits inside the cabinet opening or face frame. It must be made from straight, clear lumber so that it will be flush with the surface of the cabinet.*

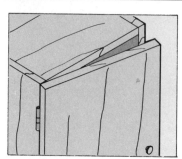

Overlapping. *This is the easiest door to cut and install since it covers the entire cabinet front. Small mistakes in measuring or cutting will not detract from the look of the door. In fact, if you cut the door slightly oversize, you can sand the edges to the size of the cabinet.*

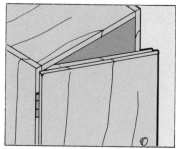

Lipped. *The lipped door has a 'cabinet lip' cut around at least three sides of the door. The lip fits over the cabinet, and the back of the door is partially inset in the cabinet. You can cut this lip with a router or a dado cutter, much the same way you'd make a rabbet joint. This door requires special hinges to allow for the lip.*

Surface-Mounting Butt Hinges

On Cabinets with Flush Doors

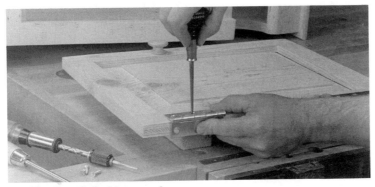

1. First install the hinges on the cabinet door. Place the leaf of a hinge on the front of the door so the pin is perfectly aligned with the side edge. With an awl, mark for screw holes. Remove the hinge, drill pilot holes, and then attach the hinge leaf. Install the remaining hinges in the same way.

2. Set the cabinet upright and wedge the door in place in the cabinet opening; use wood slivers on all sides except the hinge side. With the hinge side flush to the cabinet, mark for screw holes. Drill pilot holes and then attach the hinges.

On Cabinets With Overlapping Doors

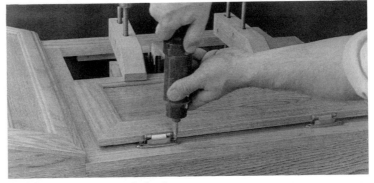

1. First install the hinges on the cabinet door. Place the leaf of a hinge on the side edge of the door so the pin is perfectly aligned with the back surface. With an awl, mark for screw holes. Remove the hinge, drill pilot holes, and then attach the hinge leaf. Install the remaining hinges in the same way.

2. With the cabinet on its back, place the door over the opening. On the side of the cabinet, carefully mark for the screw holes of the unattached hinge leaves. Drill pilot holes and then screw the hinges to the cabinet.

Mortising Butt Hinges

1. *You may wish to mortise a butt hinge into a cabinet; that is, carve out a small recess either to partially hide the hinge or make it flush with the surface of the wood. To do this, first position the hinge on the wood and trace around it with an awl or sharp pencil.*

2. *With a chisel, cut down into the wood, all around the outline of the hinge or hinge leaf. Position the chisel on the outline with its beveled side toward the mortise area (as shown) and tap lightly on the chisel to the desired depth. Do this until you have completely outlined the*

area—to keep the mortise from splitting beyond these marks. Be careful not to cut too deep.

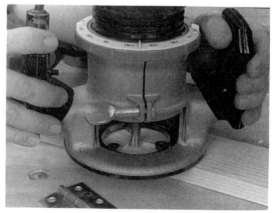

3. *Make a series of shallow cuts within the outlined area, holding the chisel almost vertical. Chip out the waste by holding the chisel almost flat (bevel side up) and tapping it lightly. Shave the mortise smoothly to the exact depth needed. From time to time, lay the hinge or hinge leaf in the mortise to check the depth.*

4. *You can also remove the waste with a router. Use a straight bit and adjust the depth of cut to the thickness of the hinge. As you rout, be careful not to go outside the outline that you have cut with a chisel. After removing as much waste as you can with the router, clean up the corners with a chisel.*

Butt hinges can be used only on overlapping and flush doors. For other types of doors, such as lip doors, specially designed hinges are required. We show several popular types here—and basic instructions for installation. Remember, the information here is just the basics. When you begin to shop at a well-stocked hardware store or from a catalog, you'll find literally hundreds of different hinges in several metals and finishes.

You can determine the number of hinges to use and the amount of spacing between them fairly easily. Unless you're mounting a continuous

Choosing Hinges for Cabinet Doors

Butterfly. *The butterfly hinge is just one of the many decorative types of butt hinges. Made of stamped metal, it is used on flush doors.*

Pivot. *In the past, pivot hinges were used exclusively on overlapping doors. But recently, several companies have developed pivot hinges for flush and lipped doors as well.*

Offset. *These hinges may be used on lipped, overlapping, or flush doors, and they may be surface-mounted or mortised. However, they are most commonly used with lipped doors, mounted to the surface. When using offset hinges on lipped doors, carefully match the dimensions of the offset leaves to the width and depth of the lip.*

Semiconcealed. *Only one leaf of this hinge is visible. Use this type only on lipped or overlapping doors. Mount one leaf to the front of the cabinet and the other to the back of the door. (On a lipped door, the hidden leaf will have a double offset.)*

Continuous. *Also known as a 'piano' hinge, this looks like a long butt hinge that runs the entire length of the door. Continuous hinges are easy to use on flush doors because no mortising is required. Instead, the dimensions of the door are adjusted to allow the closed hinge to fit between it and the cabinet.*

piano hinge, use the following guide: If the length of the door measures more than 2 feet, install three hinges, one in the center and the other two 4 inches from the top and bottom edges. If the door is less than two feet, use two hinges. Divide the length of the door into quarters and place hinges on the top and bottom marks.

Use the following guide to determine what size hinges to use: On doors over 2 feet long, measure the length of the door. The total length of the hinges should be ⅙ the length of the door. For example, if the door length is 36 inches, divide this by ⅙ to get 6. Divide this by the number of hinges, three, and you get 2. You will need three 2-inch long hinges.

Accessory Hardware for Cabinet Doors

Double-Roller Catch. *This popular type of catch consists of an arrow-shaped 'strike' which is mounted inside the door and a spring-loaded double-roller receptacle which is mounted inside the cabinet. Installation requires precise measuring.*

Magnetic Catch. *This catch is made up of a magnet mounted inside the cabinet and a matching metal plate on the inside of the cabinet door. More expensive than the double-roller type, it doesn't require perfect alignment to work properly.*

Bar Latch. *The bar latch, unlike the catch, is mounted on the outside of the cabinet; it is made to be used on flush doors. Often handsomely finished, the bar latch also serves as a handle for opening the cabinet.*

Door Support. *Used in addition to a hinge, this collapsible hardware works to limit the degree to which the door can be opened. Though shown here on a fold-down door, a support may also be used on a side-hinged door. Easy to mount, one part is simply screwed to the inside of the cabinet and the other to the inside of the door.*

Other Options for Doors

Hinges work to hold the door to the cabinet and allow you to open and close it freely. But there are other instances where more than regular hinges are needed. For example, when cabinets are used very frequently, such as in a kitchen, just opening and closing them can be a chore. In such storage areas, consider using *self-closing* hinges. These contain a spring inside to gently but firmly swing the door shut.

Another problem to be reckoned with is how to keep the doors closed. This is a common dilemma with older cabinets, when the doors are slightly warped or misaligned. You may also have a curious toddler in the home, someone that you need to protect from any mischief that they might get into. There are many kinds of hardware available for solving these problems; among the most common are *catches* and *latches*.

Not all doors open from the side. When you have a cabinet door that pulls down, as is frequently the case with a drop-leaf desk, you need to support it. *Stay supports* are the answer for this problem. Once again, the hardware presented here are only the very basic types. If you do a little research, you'll find an abundance of specialty types available. There are low-profile style catches, push-latches that automatically open a door and spring-loaded supports, just to name a very few. Depending on what your cabinet will be used for, you will want to take advantage of these ingenious devices.

Repairing Older Cabinets

As an inexpensive option to building new cabinets, consider recycling older cabinets or even purchasing them at a secondhand store and give them a little first-aid. Often, this involves stripping off the old finish, adding a new finish, or filling cracks and scratches in the wood. If the cabinet has door problems, don't despair. These are sometimes fixed easily. Use the following troubleshooting guide to solve your problems with a faulty door.

Doors That Slide Instead of Swing

When you need to install cabinets in narrow spaces or already-cramped rooms, you should use sliding doors. These are inexpensive and easy to make. The only drawback in using them is that you can access only half of the cabinet at any one time. As always, you should base your cabinet's dimensions on the limitations imposed by the doors. Sliding doors should not be much more than 2 feet high and the cabinet should be at least twice as wide as it is tall.

Troubleshooting Cabinet Doors

TROUBLE	POSSIBLE CAUSE	SOLUTION
Door doesn't stay closed.	Warped door.	Install a bar latch, if possible.
	Loose hinge screws.	Replace all screws with longer or thicker ones.
		Remove original screws and fill holes with wood splinters such as toothpicks.
Door sticks.	Edge of door doesn't clear.	Apply chalk to the door edge; it rubs off at the problem area. Plane and sand this area.
Catch doesn't work.	Misaligned catch.	Remove and reposition the catch strike. Fill old screw holes.

Types of Door Tracks—How to Install Them

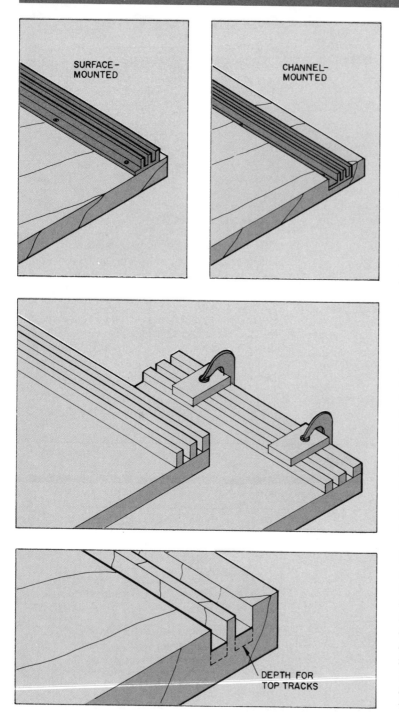

SURFACE-MOUNTED

CHANNEL-MOUNTED

DEPTH FOR TOP TRACKS

Hardware Tracks. *Hardware tracks are available in pairs. Made of metal, plastic, or fiber (for plastic or glass doors), they consist of a deep top track and a shallower bottom one. Although they are available in standard lengths, they can also be trimmed to size with a hacksaw. Surface mounting is easier, but for a better look, mount them in channels that you rout in the cabinet top and bottom. If you rout these channels, the cabinet material must be at least ⅜ inch thicker than the deeper (top) track. Both channels should be positioned at least ½ inch from the front edge of the cabinet.*

Tracks Made of Molding. *Tracks can be constructed of wood molding with three pieces each on the bottom and top of the cabinet. Always make the top track ¼ to ⅜ deeper than the bottom track—this way, you can easily remove and install the doors. Space the molding so the strips are separated from each other by the thickness of the doors plus ¹/₁₆ inch. Glue and nail the strips in place, being careful to clamp them precisely. When completed, apply paste wax to the tracks to help the doors slide more easily.*

Routed Tracks. *These tracks are routed into the cabinet material. This material must be thick enough (at least ¾ inch) to accommodate the routed tracks. The channels should be at least ⁵/₁₆ inch deep in the cabinet's bottom and ¼ inch deeper in the cabinet's top. They should also be ¹/₁₆ inch wider than the door thickness, and about ¼ inch apart.*

These doors must be thin so that they will slide easily, but they should also be thick enough so they won't bend or break. There are many possible materials for these doors: from glass to plastic to high-grade plywood to tempered hardboard.

Tracks made of hardware are the simplest to install. If you prefer the look of wood, you can make your own tracks out of molding or by routing grooves into the cabinet top and bottom. All three processes and their variations are shown in this chapter. No matter which method you choose, you should install or make the tracks before the cabinet is assembled. Remember, too, the other joinery in the cabinet. The tracks must not interfere with the assembly, or in any way weaken the cabinet.

Measuring and cutting the doors requires precise measuring and this must be done after the cabinet is 'dry assembled'—that is, all the cabinet parts are cut and temporarily assembled without glue. Typically, you install recessed pulls in sliding doors; but if you prefer, you can simply drill 'finger holes' in the door panels.

Constructing the Sliding Doors

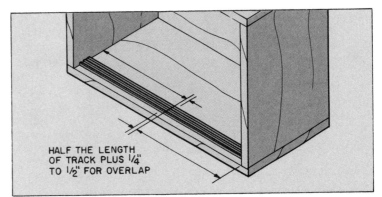

ADD 1/4" FOR DOOR HEIGHT

HALF THE LENGTH OF TRACK PLUS 1/4" TO 1/2" FOR OVERLAP

1. *First, determine the height for both doors by measuring from the bottom of the bottom channel to the lip of the corresponding upper track. To this measurement add 1/4 inch. The doors will rest in the upper channel when they are installed, but you will still be able to remove them by lifting up on them. Next, determine the width for the doors—measure the inside width of the cabinet, and divide by half. Then add 1/4 to 1/2 inch to this so that the doors will overlap slightly.*

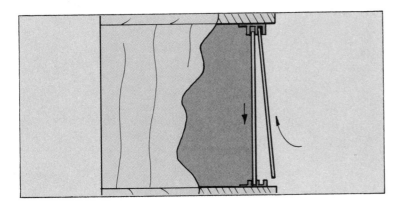

2. *Install recessed pulls in the doors, by drilling or chiseling out an opening in each door to receive the pull. Sand the door edges smooth and apply wax to the bottom edges. To install the doors; simply lift them into their top channels; then let them drop into the bottom ones.*

Drawers—Pull-Out Compartments for Cabinets

Drawers are merely cases that are drawn out of and pushed back into other, larger cases. They must be built with care and precision, however, since drawers take a good deal of abuse, especially if they're used often. The methods and materials that you want to use to make your drawers should all be determined in the planning stages of the cabinet. The following are some guidelines to use when planning for cabinet drawers:

Storage drawers must be strong in order to withstand frequent pulling and pushing. Drawer bottoms have to be sturdy enough not to give way under heavy weights, and firm enough to keep the drawer square. Sides and back have to stay rigid; otherwise the drawer will not slide properly. Yet despite all this, you should make the drawer as lightweight as possible.

Material for drawers should be selected with care. Stock lumber, unless clear and dry, is likely to warp. The best bet, of course, is plywood. If the drawer sides are to be grooved for rails, use ½- to ⅝-inch plywood. Most drawer bottoms can be made of ¼-inch hardboard, a strong material that

won't warp or sag out of shape. If drawers are to be used for storing very heavy things, then bottoms should be of ⅜-inch or even ½-inch plywood. It's rarely necessary to make the drawer bottoms any thicker than this, unless you're storing heavy, hard-edge objects like big woodworking tools.

For small drawers up to 14 inches wide, use ⅜-inch plywood for sides and back, and ½-inch for fronts. Drawers from 14 to 30 inches wide need ½-inch plywood sides and backs, and ¾-inch fronts. If drawers are to be over 30 inches wide, and will be used to hold heavy things, use ¾-inch material for sides, backs, and fronts. Also, for reinforcement, you may want to glue wood blocks or quarter-round molding strips inside the drawers at the corners and along bottom seams.

As a rule, the plywood you select should have the good face veneers turned in on both sides and the back, to assure a snag-free interior. If your budget permits, use plywood with two good sides (or solid wood) for the drawer front. You can, however, use a plywood with only one good side for the front, particularly if the drawer will be lined.

Runners and Glides. There are many ways you can mount drawers in cabinets, but here are two of the more popular methods. The first is

---

Sliding Devices for Cabinet Drawers

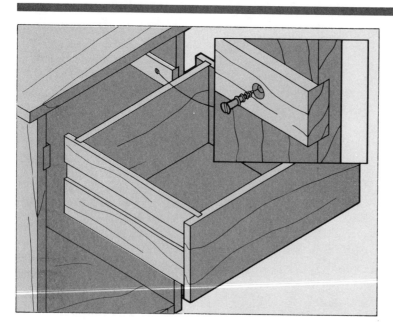

Runners. *The drawer sides are grooved with a router to slide on runners mounted inside the cabinet. Once sanded smooth, they'll give trouble-free service for years. The drawer should be slightly smaller than the cabinet opening—about ¹⁄₁₆ inch smaller all the way around. The drawer runners should be made of hardwood to resist wear. Rout grooves in the cabinet sides and the drawer sides that are half as deep as the runners are thick. Use glue and countersink wood screws to attach the runners to the cabinet.*

to make grooves on the drawer sides and attach wood runners on the inside sides of the cabinet. The second, and perhaps the most trouble-free once installed, is to use drawer-glide assemblies which attach to both the drawer and the inside of the cabinet. Both methods are shown in this chapter, along with basic instructions for installing the drawers.

Constructing the Drawer. As mentioned, drawers are box-like cases that fit into larger cases. Obviously, then, they can be made with the same joints you've used to make cases. But what *combination* of joints should be used to form a drawer? We show three typical drawer plans in this chapter and give instructions for how to assemble one type, the rabbeted and dadoed drawer.

When your cabinet plans call for more than one of the same type of drawers, you should use the 'assembly-line' method for making the parts. Cut all bottoms at the same time, rabbet all sides at the same time, and so forth. You'll save time by not having to reset power tools so often, plus your work and your workshop will be more organized.

If you use glide assemblies to make a drawer, then you will have to add a false front to hide the the hardware. This isn't a bad idea in any case,

since you can make the false front from expensive wood, and use it to hide the drawer's less expensive materials. Installing the false front is an easy process, (page 74), but it calls for careful measuring.

The final step in making a drawer is to add the pull or pulls. (Although the following information covers drawer pulls, you can also use the same basic steps for installing door pulls.) If you're installing a single pull such as a knob, be sure to center it horizontally on the drawer front. To determine the vertical position, remember that you'll get best results if you place the knob on the same plane as the drawer's sliding mechanism. Single pulls are installed by drilling a hole and inserting the mounting bolt for the pull. You should use a drill bit the same size as the bolt and drill entirely through the drawer front. Then insert the bolt (with a washer), and turn the pull onto the bolt.

When a drawer's load will be heavy, use a pair of bar-type pulls, each of which uses two mounting bolts. Locate these bolts approximately 2 to 3 inches from the drawer's sides and align them carefully (page 74). Once the drawer pulls are installed, the cabinet is finished, unless there is more hardware to add. You may want to install

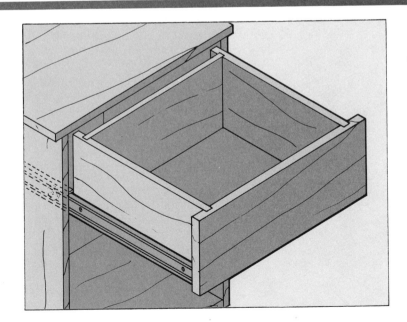

Drawer-Glide Assemblies. *Made of metal, these extension glides are popular because they work smoothly and are available in different lengths and load capacities. The kind shown here allows the drawer to be pulled all the way out without falling. Installing the hardware to the inside of the cabinet and drawer sides requires patience and careful measuring— different brands will require different installation procedures, and these will be provided by the manufacturer. Purchase the glides before making the drawer, so you can be sure to allow enough space between the drawer and the cabinet sides for the hardware.*

Types of Drawers

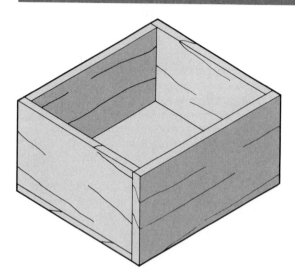

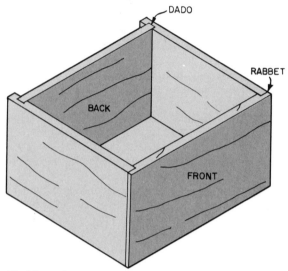

Full Butt-Joined. *This drawer can have a flush or overlapped panel attached to the front, either of which will hide the exposed end grain of the sides. This is the least strong drawer construction since parts depend upon glue, nails, or screws rather than fitted joints to hold them together.*

Rabbeted and Dadoed.
The front is rabbeted, and the sides are attached to it. The sides are dadoed, and the back rests in the dadoes. Usually, the bottom rests in a groove cut on the inside of all four parts. This is adequate for light-to-medium duty drawers.

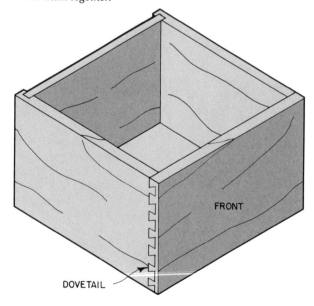

Dovetailed and Dadoed.
This is similar to the 'rabbeted and dadoed' construction, except that half-blind dovetails are substituted for the rabbets. While this looks complex, it's not difficult to make if you have a router and a dovetail template. Of the three types of drawer construction shown this is the strongest.

store-bought legs, casters, or tension rods at this point. Usually very easy to install, they require nothing more than mounting a few fasteners.

Easy Drawer Alternatives. The preceding discussion of drawers has focused on drawers in cabinets, but there is a super-easy option that you can use to make drawer space, even if you aren't constructing a cabinet. Utilizing wall-hung shelves, cabinets, or other structures, you can simply mount glides for drawers on the bottoms of shelves and countertops.

Another simple alternative is to purchase plastic bins that are lipped at the top. Make two L-shaped glides that will hold the lip of the bins; then mount these beneath a shelf or countertop. The glides must be properly spaced so that they will hold the bins, but the bins won't bind when you pull them in or out. These inexpensive makeshift 'drawers' are great for children's rooms and utilitarian areas.

One final word regarding simplicity: If you feel you're not ready to try your hand at drawer-making, then check the home-improvement stores for easy-to-assemble kits. Precut drawers will save you time in building your cabinet, but be sure to purchase the kits first. They come in standard sizes, so you have to plan the dimensions of your cabinet around the size of the drawers.

Assembling a Rabbeted and Dadoed Drawer

1. *Cut all pieces for the drawer, making the bottom ½ inch longer and wider than the drawer's interior. Next, cut the joinery. All the joints on this drawer, including the grooves for the bottom, can be cut using a router, a dado cutter, or a table saw. Dry assemble the parts to check the fit of the joints. Sand the parts where necessary to true the joints.*

2. *Disassemble the drawer and spread glue in the dado and rabbet joints. Do not put glue in the grooves that hold the drawer bottom; the bottom should 'float' free in the grooves so that it can expand and contract with changes in humidity. Put the parts together, and reinforce the dado and rabbet joints with screws or nails. Wipe away any excess glue with a damp cloth, and allow the drawer to dry.*

Installing a bar pull. *To install a bar pull, or any pull with more than one mounting bolt, first carefully measure and mark the drawer front to determine where you want the pull. Rub a little pencil lead on the back of the pull, and press it against the drawer front. This will leave an imprint, showing you where to drill the holes. After you drill the holes, sand the wood to remove the pencil lead. Then install the pull.*

Adding a False Front

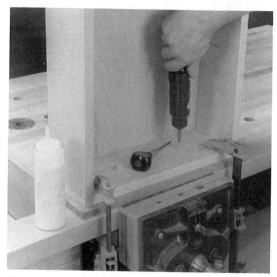

1. *Carefully calculate the dimensions of the false front. If the drawer has a 'flush' front (like a flush door), then the front should be ¹⁄₁₆ inch smaller than the drawer opening, all the way around. If the front overlaps the cabinets, that overlap should be ⅜ to ½ inch, all the way around. Once you've determined the measurements, cut the false front.*

2. *Dry assemble the false front to the drawer with screws. Drive the screws from the inside of the drawer, so that they won't show. Check the fit and the action of the drawer. If you're satisfied with the position of the false front, remove the screws, then reassemble the front to the drawer with glue and screws.*

5

Making the Most of Kitchen Space

The most complex storage area in your home is the *kitchen*. Pots, pans, dishes, appliances, cooking utensils, and canned goods are some of the things in a typical kitchen. Any space with this many items presents storage problems—on a grand scale.

However, there are some easy routes that you can take to update and modernize the storage areas in your kitchen. New products appear on the market every day that are smartly engineered to provide new storage space in the kitchen. Many of them are simply installed in existing cabinets or pantries. If you want to make your own components, there are many ideas to choose from, such as the "Roll-out Bins" or "Cabinet Door Pockets".

Some of the project plans are for special types of cabinets or shelving. For example, the "Wall Pantry" turns an unused wall into a 1-can deep storage cabinet for canned goods. The "Lost Space Storage" cart converts wasted space into usable shelving space, and helps to make small kitchen wares mobile. The "Glass Hanger" stores and displays your glassware simultaneously.

These are just a few ideas for the kitchen. There are others in this chapter, and even more if you take the time to look through other books and magazines. As you plan and design, you'll find new ways to make your kitchen a better organized, more pleasant place to work.

Disheveled Dishes and Other Things

Trends come and go in kitchen design, but there are some important storage needs that remain the same. There is a need to keep major appliances (stove, refrigerator, and sink) in a triangular arrangement, to save the cook as many steps as possible. There is a need to keep foodstuffs covered and stowed away to prevent pests from invading them. But within these boundaries, kitchen design is a matter of personal taste.

We've all seen the sleek modern kitchen where everything except the cook is concealed. On the other end of the spectrum is the little 'pullman kitchen' where baskets, racks, hooks, open shelves and the like expose nearly all of the cook's utensils and even some of the food. One space looks neat as a pin because everything is in closed storage; the other is also very workable because goods and equipment are within sight and easy reach. Both are good storage solutions. With some careful thought, design preferences and storage needs can work together in any type of kitchen.

Perhaps the first thing you need to decide is how much open storage and how much closed storage you need. The available space will be one determining factor, but there are other factors also. Chief among these is the lifestyle of the kitchen's inhabitants. Are they constantly on the go or is there time and energy to reach, bend, and stoop for kitchen work materials? Who does the kitchen chores? Is it one person or is the work shared by many? Are small children part of the household? All these issues will affect how much open and closed storage you should have.

The same considerations will also help you decide what should be stored where. So will this rule of thumb for kitchen design: Always store items near the place where they are *first* used. For example, dishes are most convenient when positioned close to the dining area.

If your kitchen is due for remodeling, you might consider purchasing kitchen cabinetry that is equipped with special pullouts and lazy susans. If, on the other hand, you don't want to remodel extensively, you might want to update your kitchen by modifying the old cabinets. If you're tired of the cabinet fronts or doors, you can change these without pulling the cabinets out. Some companies specialize in custom-building these fronts to fit your existing cabinets. You can save as much as one-half the cost of comparable new cabinets plus avoid much of the mess that a new installation creates.

Another option that will change the look of your kitchen and provide easy access to items is to remove the cabinet doors. This is particularly effective for wall-hung cabinets and is an excellent way to show off fine cookware or stemware. Depending on what kind of hinges the doors have and how the cabinets are finished, you might need to fill screw holes and give your cabinets a new finish. The disadvantage to doing this is that items are liable to get dustier than they would behind doors. But you can prevent the dust with glass or framed-glass cabinet doors.

Solid wood cabinet doors can be very useful, however, and you should think twice about getting rid of them. Small pockets for holding spices or small utensils can be mounted on their backs as can racks and hooks for holding dish towels and potholders.

Take a critical look at your cabinet shelves too. If your cabinets are modern, the shelves will probably be adjustable, supported by standards

and brackets or pins. A very swift remedy for solving storage problems is to simply rearrange the positions of the shelves to accommodate your new equipment.

Shop for Accessories...

There is a good deal of specialty hardware available that transforms a typical kitchen into a wonderfully manageable workspace. There are hinges and pulls that attach to the false fronts of sink cabinets. These pull down to reveal a small tray or pocket for holding scouring pads or other small, necessary, but unsightly kitchen items. We show how to install these in the "Drop-Down Sink Front" project.

Other hardware attaches to the bottoms of wall-hung cabinets. These drop down to reveal cookbook holders, knife racks, message centers, and spice trays, as we show in "Under-the-Cabinet Storage". Yet another great invention is a mixer shelf. This contraption fits inside a standard-size base cabinet where it supports a food mixer. When needed, open the cabinet door and pull out the shelf, complete with mixer. The shelf automatically locks into place at the workable height.

Perhaps the most popular ready-made components are woven wire bins that are mounted on tracks so that they can be pulled out like drawers. These make good lid holders, organizers for containers, and wastebasket holders. They are widely available, and come complete with mounting instructions.

Consider purchasing storage units especially made for your equipment. For example, if you have owned a food processor for five years and realize that you use it more frequently than you had expected, you can buy a wall-mounted holder for the processor blades. Such rearranging will not only put the blades within easy reach but will also free up space elsewhere. If the cost is prohibitive and the design is simple, you probably can make a copy out of wood.

Take advantage of plastic organizers made for standard size products. With the possible exception of the bathroom, plastic works best in your kitchen —because it's so easy to clean. (However, beware of placing any plastic items close to appliances with heating elements.) Colorful plastic bins are ideal for storing fresh produce. Drawer dividers, foil and plastic wrap organizers, and broom and mop holders are just a few more of the low-cost plastic storage products available. Some can be hung on walls or doors; others are simply placed inside drawers.

Let the Ideas Stew

Recipes for 'kitchen storage success' are abundant. Indeed, home magazines, women's magazines, and trade brochures are filled with them. If you can't quickly come up with a plan for your kitchen, then head to the library and do a little research. Here are just a few ideas for kitchen conversions gleaned from such sources:

■ Look up. Note the space above the refrigerator. If there's no cupboard above it, install one.

■ The space above existing cupboards can be used. Fit this area with a 'soffit' cupboard to match your decor.

■ When building pantries, design them to run from the floor to the ceiling to utilize all available space.

You're bound to find scores of usable ideas. Combine these ideas with those shown in this book—or with your own ideas—to plan your own unique projects.

Measure What You Have

Of course, as with any storage project, the way to begin in your kitchen is to first select the items to be stored and rank them according to their importance. Have you been cooking in your microwave oven more, leaving many of your metal pans unused? Does your blender deserve 'front-row treatment' while the waffle iron is used only five times a year? Once these priorities are determined, then you can scrutinize the objects and measure them carefully.

If you're going to build shelving or any kind of built-in components, then you should tailor the space to exactly fit your needs. Every inch of kitchen space is valuable. For example, if you want to fill an empty wall with modules, you could measure every item to be placed on those modules and build them to match.

The most important reason for measuring, though, is to avoid error. Although many kitchen items are relatively small, some are not. If your plan is to build a unit to house a punch bowl or serving tray, you'd be foolish not to measure it

first. Make sure that the cabinet or shelf will provide adequate support, and, if doors are part of the plan, make sure that there will be sufficient clearance.

Shown here is a chart with the dimensions of typical kitchen items. Use this chart for reference in your initial planning stages, but bear in mind that your items will vary. To be safe, always measure.

Standard Sizes of Kitchen Items (in inches)

Cookie Sheet	11 to 12 W x 17 to 19 L x ¾ to 1 D
10 Qt. Stock Pot	13 W (with handle) x 7¾ H x 10¾ dia.
Large Roasting Pan	12½ W x 17½ L x 6 D
Oblong Glass Baking Dish	9¼ W x 14¾ L x 2¼ H
Square Glass Baking Dish	8⅝ W x 10¼ L x 2¼ D
Muffin Tin	10 W x 13 L x 1 D
Spaghetti Cooker	12⅜ W (with handles) x 7½ H x 10 dia.
Soup Can	4 H x 2¾ dia.
No. 2 Can (20 oz.)	4⅜ H x 3⅜ dia.
No. 2½ Can (29 oz.)	4¹¹⁄₁₆ H x 4 dia.
No. 300 Can (14-16 oz.)	4⁷⁄₁₆ H x 3¹⁵⁄₁₆ dia.

PROJECT/Roll-out Bins

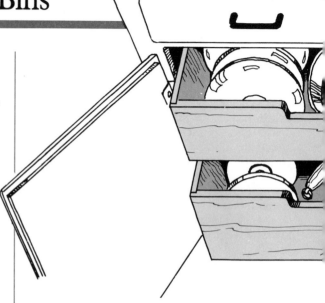

In the kitchen, you can use roll-out bins much the same way you use a file cabinet in an office. Only, in this case, the 'files' are cookware and foodstuffs. The bins are mounted on extension slides, so that they come all the way out of the cabinet, making it easy for you to retrieve whatever you have stored in the bins.

1. Remove the doors from your cabinets, then take out the old, fixed shelves, if necessary. Take care that you don't damage the cabinet case.

2. Measure the height, width and depth of the cabinet, so that you know the space you have to work with. While you're inside the cabinet, take a good look at how it's built and plan where you'll put the supports.

3. Decide how many bins you want to put in the cabinet, and how deep each bin should be. Calculate the dimensions of the bins, allowing ½ inch between each bin. Also allow ½ inch between the bins and the sides of the cabinets, to make room for the extension slides.

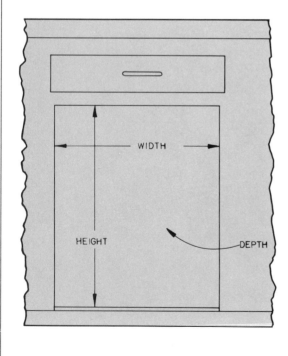

WIDTH

HEIGHT

DEPTH

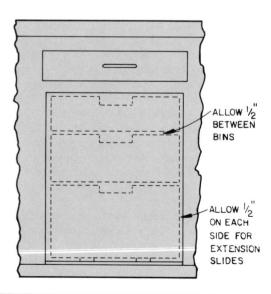

ALLOW ½" BETWEEN BINS

ALLOW ½" ON EACH SIDE FOR EXTENSION SLIDES

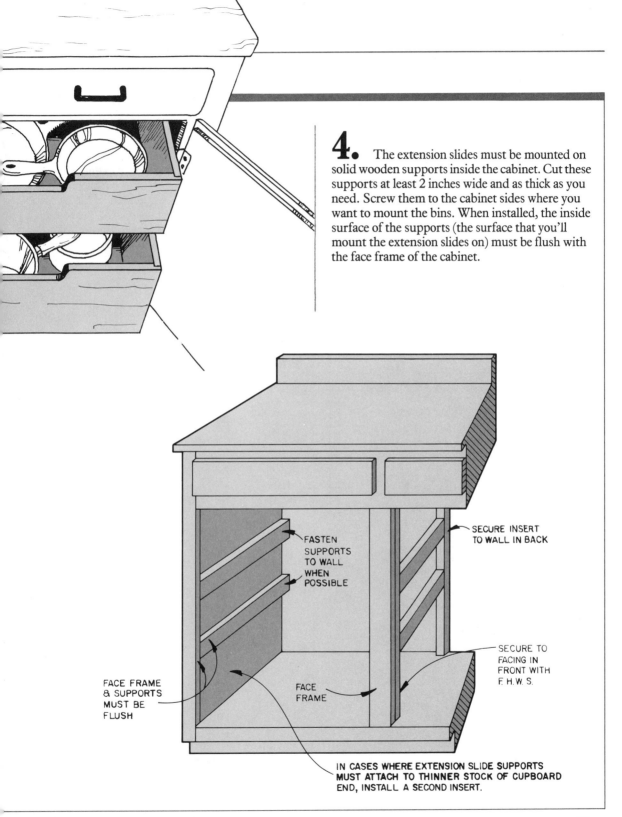

4. The extension slides must be mounted on solid wooden supports inside the cabinet. Cut these supports at least 2 inches wide and as thick as you need. Screw them to the cabinet sides where you want to mount the bins. When installed, the inside surface of the supports (the surface that you'll mount the extension slides on) must be flush with the face frame of the cabinet.

FASTEN
SUPPORTS
TO WALL
WHEN
POSSIBLE

SECURE INSERT
TO WALL IN BACK

FACE FRAME
& SUPPORTS
MUST BE
FLUSH

FACE
FRAME

SECURE TO
FACING IN
FRONT WITH
F. H. W. S.

IN CASES WHERE EXTENSION SLIDE SUPPORTS
MUST ATTACH TO THINNER STOCK OF CUPBOARD
END, INSTALL A SECOND INSERT.

5. If you can't screw the supports to a cabinet side, you'll have to make a simple 'insert'. Nail the support between two 1 x 2's. Then install this assembly in the cabinet, screwing the back 1 x 2 to the cabinet back, and the front 1 x 2 to the face frame. Once again, the supports must be flush with the edge of the face frame.

6. Cut the parts for the bins you need. Cut the front, back, and sides from ¾ inch thick stock, and the bottoms from ¼ inch thick hardboard. Cut a groove near the bottom inside edges of the back, front, and sides to hold the bottom. Cut rabbets in the front to join the sides. With a bandsaw, make a small notch or recess in the top edge to serve as a handle.

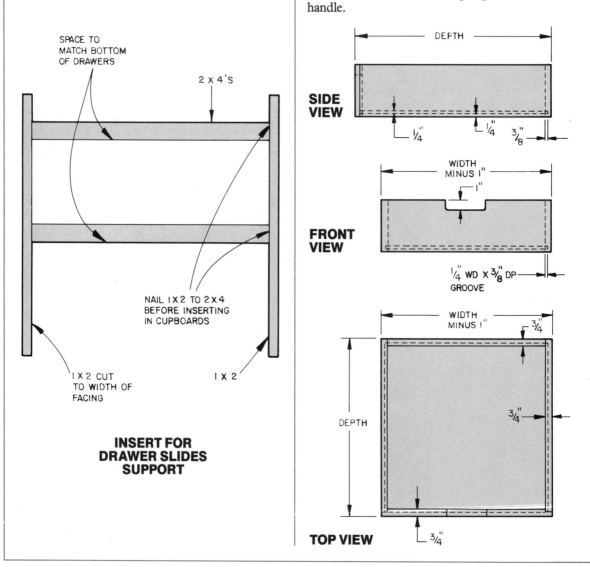

SPACE TO MATCH BOTTOM OF DRAWERS

2 x 4'S

NAIL 1 X 2 TO 2 X 4 BEFORE INSERTING IN CUPBOARDS

1 X 2 CUT TO WIDTH OF FACING

1 X 2

INSERT FOR DRAWER SLIDES SUPPORT

DEPTH

SIDE VIEW

¼"   ¼"   ⅜"

FRONT VIEW

WIDTH MINUS 1"

1"

¼" WD X ⅜" DP GROOVE

TOP VIEW

WIDTH MINUS 1"

¾"

DEPTH

¾"

¾"

7. If you wish, make dividers and special utensil holders to better organize the space inside the bins. Make the dividers from ¼ inch thick hardboard and cut dadoes in the front, back, and sides to hold the dividers.

8. Assemble the bins with glue and screws. *Do not* glue the dividers in place. Let these 'float' in their dadoes so that you can easily remove or rearrange them, should you need to reorganize the bins in the future.

9. Attach the extension slides to the supports. Most extension slides come apart in two pieces—the slides and mounts. Remove the mounts according to the manufacturer's directions and set them aside. Screw the slides to the supports inside the cabinet.

10. Screw the mounts to the bins. Measure carefully where you want to put them—the mounts have to be placed precisely so that the bins will be properly spaced in the cabinet.

11. Install the bins in the cabinets by reassembling the mounts to the slides. Test the sliding action of the bins.

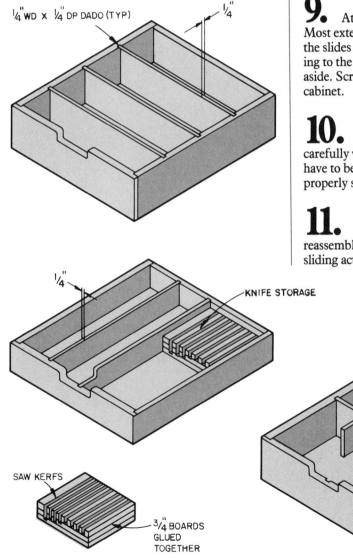

PROJECT/Cabinet Door Pockets

The space behind your cabinet doors can be used for storage if you make some simple 'door pockets'—shelves that attach to the backs of the doors. Be sure to put rails on these pockets, so the items you have stored on them won't fall off every time you open the cabinet doors.

1. Measure the width of your cabinet door openings and the distance you have between the doors and the things that are stored on the shelves. Also measure the size of the items you want to store in the door pockets.

2. If you want to make single pockets, cut out the sides, back, and bottom from ½ inch stock, as shown. Drill holes in the backs so that you can mount them to the doors. Make the rails from ⅜″ dowels. Assemble the pockets with glue and nails.

3. You can also make multiple pockets, if you wish. Cut out the shapes of the sides with a sabre saw or jigsaw.

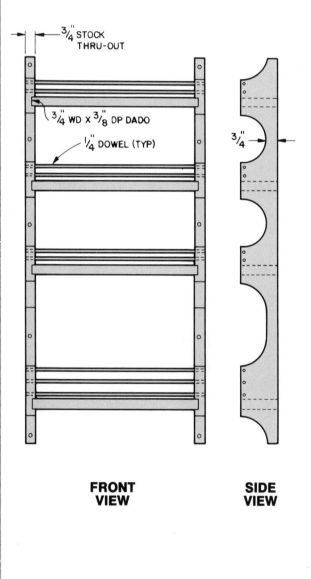

½″ STOCK THRU-OUT   DRILL   ⅜″ DOWEL (TYP)

FRONT VIEW

SIDE VIEW

¾″ STOCK THRU-OUT

¾″ WD X ⅜″ DP DADO

¼″ DOWEL (TYP)

¾″

FRONT VIEW   **SIDE VIEW**

4. Mount the pockets to the backs of the cabinet doors with roundhead wood screws. Be careful that the screws do not go all the way through the doors. Also, be careful to position the door pockets so that they don't hit the cabinet shelves when you close the door.

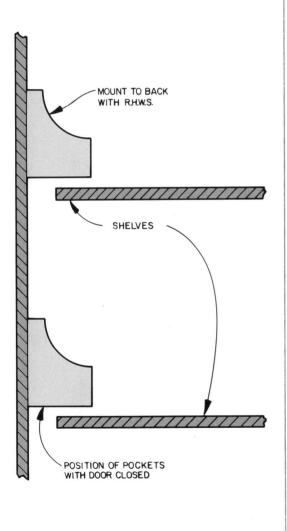

MOUNT TO BACK
WITH R.H.W.S.

SHELVES

POSITION OF POCKETS
WITH DOOR CLOSED

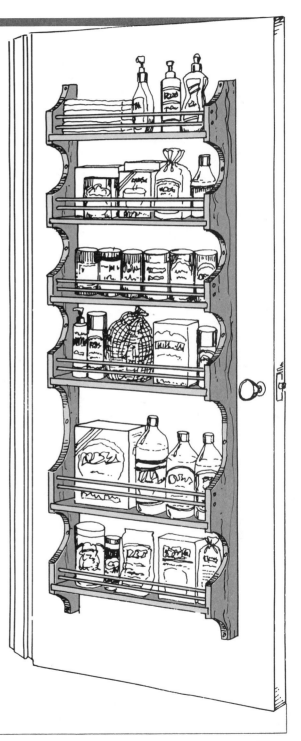

PROJECT/Wall Pantry

Need a place to store canned goods, brooms, and mops? If you have an unused wall, you can make this handy 'wall pantry'. Actually, it's a very shallow shelving unit with doors.

1. Select an unused wall in your kitchen where you can build a cabinet at least 4 inches deep. Ideally, this should be a wall where, for one reason or another, you cannot mount regular 18 inch deep cupboards.

2. Remove the baseboard and any other moldings on this wall.

3. Locate the studs in the wall, and mark them plainly on the plaster or drywall.

4. Measure the distance from the ceiling to the floor. Cut floor-to-ceiling shelf supports from ¾ inch thick stock. These supports should be 4 inches wide or wider. You'll need to put one support every 32 to 36 inches. If you're going to cover the pantry with ready-made doors or shutters, take this into consideration when you plan how to space the supports.

5. Cut 2 x 2 cleats and nail these to the top, middle, and bottom of the supports. Then nail the top and bottom cleats to the floor and ceiling. Take care to get all the supports perfectly straight up and down.

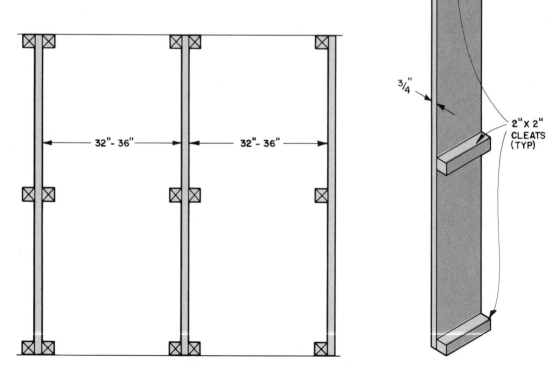

32"- 36" 32"- 36"

¾"

2"x 2"
CLEATS
(TYP)

6. Cut 2 x 2 spacers that fit between the supports, as shown in the drawings. Nail these spacers to the studs in the wall. They should be positioned at the same levels as the cleats.

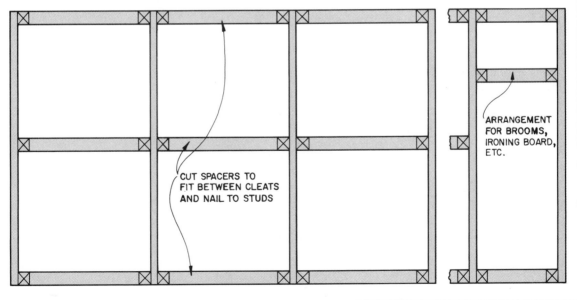

CUT SPACERS TO
FIT BETWEEN CLEATS
AND NAIL TO STUDS

ARRANGEMENT
FOR BROOMS,
IRONING BOARD,
ETC.

PROJECT/Wall Pantry/Cont'd.

7. From ¾ inch thick stock, cut 'permanent' shelves—shelves that will be fixed in the pantry. Nail these shelves to the cleats near the top, middle, and bottom of the supports. These permanent shelves will make the completed pantry more solid.

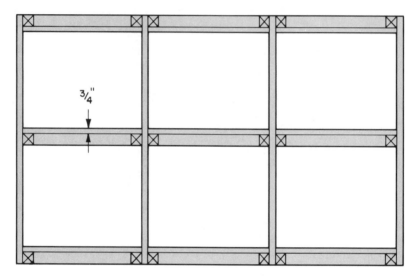

8. Attach shelving standards to the sides of the dividers. Cut 'floating' shelves, and install these on the standards, wherever you want them. As your storage needs change, remember that you can easily adjust the position of these floating shelves.

9. Build a face frame to finish the front of the pantry. Cut the frame rails and stiles from ¾ inch thick stock, and make a lap joint where the frame members will be joined. Assemble the frame with glue.

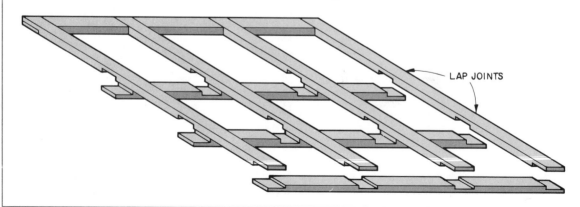

LAP JOINTS

10. Attach the face frame to the pantry with glue and screws. Countersink and counterbore the screws, then cover the heads with wood plugs so you won't see them.

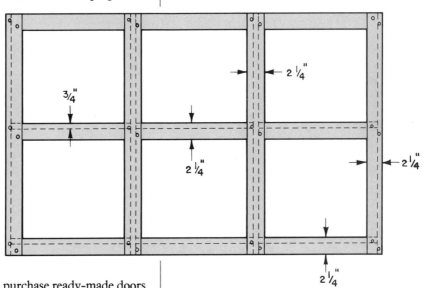

11. If you wish, purchase ready-made doors or shutters to cover the openings in the pantry. These doors should overlap the face frame by ⅜ inch on all sides. Mount the doors to the frame with self-closing hinges, then install pulls on the doors.

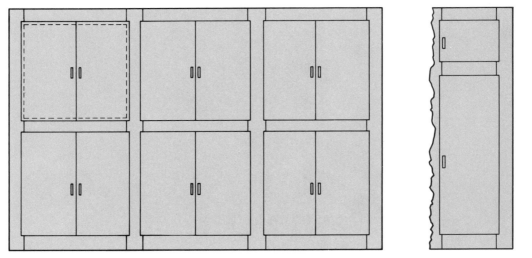

12. You can also make your own doors. The simplest door is just a small sheet of plywood. 'Edge' the plywood so that you don't see the plies, using molding, veneer tape, or plastic or aluminum edging. If you want to get a little fancier, you can also make a paneled door. Each panel door consists of five parts: two rails, two stiles, and a panel. Join the rails and stiles with simple mortise and tenon joints. Let the panels float in a groove cut in the inside edges of the rails and stiles.

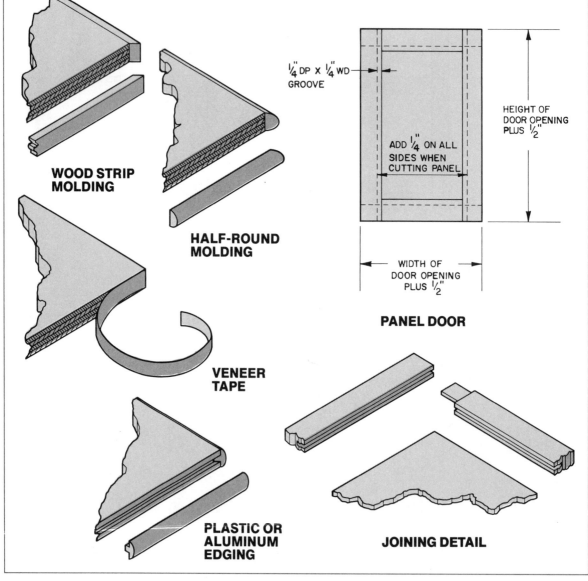

WOOD STRIP MOLDING

HALF-ROUND MOLDING

VENEER TAPE

PLASTIC OR ALUMINUM EDGING

¼" DP X ¼" WD GROOVE

ADD ¼" ON ALL SIDES WHEN CUTTING PANEL

HEIGHT OF DOOR OPENING PLUS ½"

WIDTH OF DOOR OPENING PLUS ½"

PANEL DOOR

JOINING DETAIL

PROJECT/Cabinet Dividers

These inserts divide your cabinet space vertically, making it easy to 'file' certain types of cookware. They are especially useful in organizing baking sheets, shallow pans, and lids.

1. Measure the height and the depth of the available cabinet space. Decide how wide you want to make this insert, and how many dividers you need.

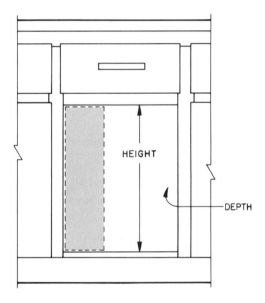

HEIGHT

DEPTH

2. Cut the sides, top, and bottom from ¾ inch thick stock, and the dividers and back from ¼ inch thick hardboard.

3. With a dado cutter, cut grooves in the top and bottom to hold the dividers. Make an indentation on the sides and the dividers with a band saw or sabre saw. This indentation will help you retrieve the cookware from the compartments.

4. Assemble the parts with glue and nails. If you wish, do *not* glue the dividers in place. Let them 'float' in their grooves. That way you can remove them or rearrange them if your storage needs change.

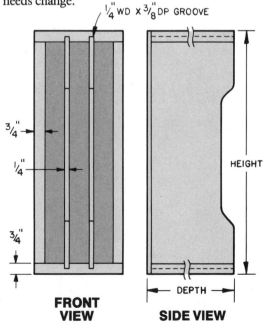

¼" WD x ⅜" DP GROOVE

¾"

¼"

¾"

HEIGHT

DEPTH

FRONT VIEW   **SIDE VIEW**

PROJECT/Slide-out Shelves

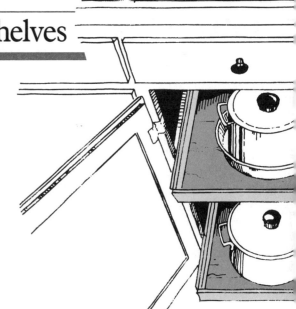

Oftentimes, it's hard to see what you have stored on a fixed shelf. You don't always know what's hiding behind the items in the front row. It's also hard to retrieve things on a fixed shelf. You have to move everything in front of the item you want. A slide-out shelf neatly solves both these problems. You can see what you have on the shelf when you pull it out, and retrieve what you want without having to move anything else.

1. Remove the doors from your cabinets, then take out the old, fixed shelves, if necessary. Take care that you don't damage the cabinet case.

2. Measure the height, width and depth of the cabinet, so that you know the space you have to work with. While you're inside the cabinet, take a good look at how it's built and plan where you'll put the supports.

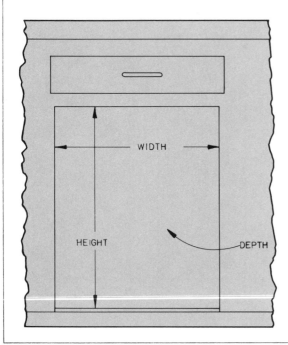

3. Decide how many shelves you want to put in the cabinet, and where to place them. Plan carefully; unlike adjustable shelves, these slide-out shelves cannot be easily rearranged once installed. Calculate the dimensions of the shelves, allowing ½ inch between the shelves and the sides of the cabinets, to make room for the extension slides.

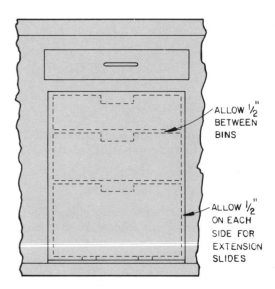

ALLOW ½" BETWEEN BINS

ALLOW ½" ON EACH SIDE FOR EXTENSION SLIDES

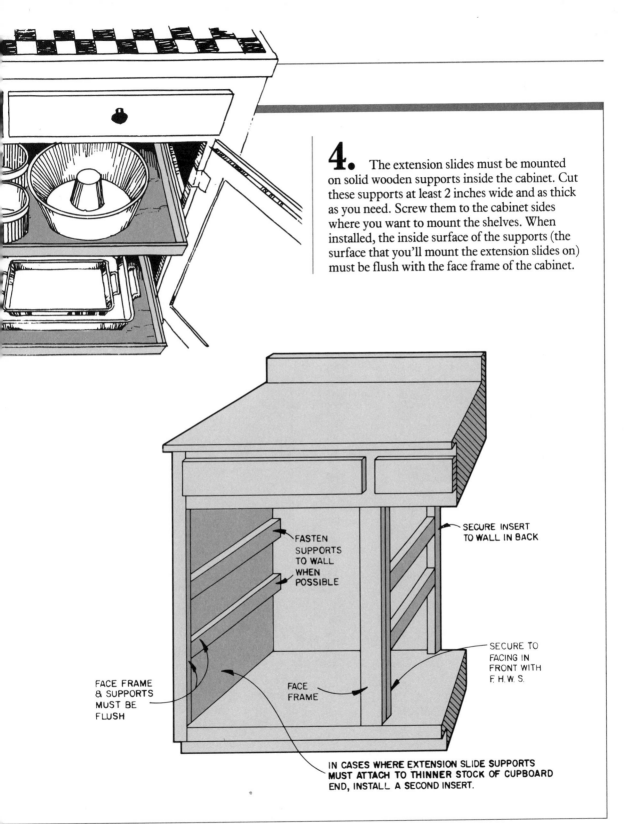

4. The extension slides must be mounted on solid wooden supports inside the cabinet. Cut these supports at least 2 inches wide and as thick as you need. Screw them to the cabinet sides where you want to mount the shelves. When installed, the inside surface of the supports (the surface that you'll mount the extension slides on) must be flush with the face frame of the cabinet.

SECURE INSERT TO WALL IN BACK

FASTEN SUPPORTS TO WALL WHEN POSSIBLE

SECURE TO FACING IN FRONT WITH F. H. W. S.

FACE FRAME & SUPPORTS MUST BE FLUSH

FACE FRAME

IN CASES WHERE EXTENSION SLIDE SUPPORTS MUST ATTACH TO THINNER STOCK OF CUPBOARD END, INSTALL A SECOND INSERT.

PROJECT/Slide-out Shelves/Cont'd.

5. If you can screw the supports to a cabinet side, you'll have to make a simple 'insert'. Nail the support between two 1 x 2's. Then install this assembly in the cabinet, screwing the back 1 x 2 to the cabinet back, and the front 1 x 2 to the face frame. Once again, the supports must be flush with the edge of the face frame.

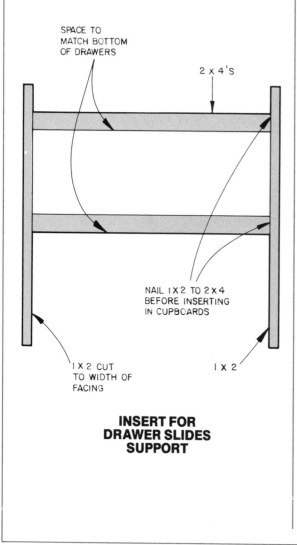

SPACE TO
MATCH BOTTOM
OF DRAWERS

2 x 4'S

NAIL 1 X 2 TO 2 X 4
BEFORE INSERTING
IN CUPBOARDS

1 X 2 CUT
TO WIDTH OF
FACING

1 X 2

**INSERT FOR
DRAWER SLIDES
SUPPORT**

6. Cut the parts for the shelves you need from ¾ inch thick stock. Each shelf should have a lip around it to keep items from falling off when you slide the shelf in or out. This lip should be at least 2 inches wide, so you have enough room to attach the extension slides. Assemble the shelves with glue and screws.

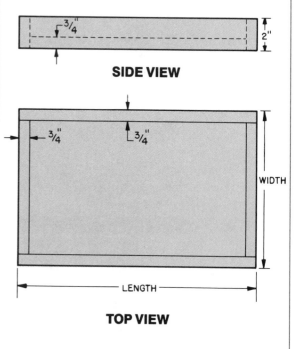

¾"

2"

SIDE VIEW

¾"

¾"

WIDTH

LENGTH

TOP VIEW

7. Attach the extension slides to the supports. Most extension slides come apart in two pieces—the slides and mounts. Disassemble the mounts from the slides according to the manufacturer's directions. Screw the slides to the supports inside the cabinet, then screw the mounts to the shelves.

8. Install the shelves in the cabinets by reassembling the mounts to the slides. Test the sliding action of the shelves.

PROJECT/Sliding Trays for Drawers

To increase the available storage space in a drawer, install sliding trays. These trays will add room at the *top* of the drawer to store small items. However, they slide out of the way and allow you to easily reach what you have stored in the bottom of the drawer.

1. Measure the length (or the width) of the drawer, and cut ½ inch x ½ inch cleats to fit. Attach these cleats to the sides of the drawer, about half-way up. Depending on what you want to store *under* the drawer, you may want to adjust the height of the cleats.

2. Build a simple box from ½ inch thick stock to make a tray. The tray should be as wide as the drawer, but only half the length. The depth must be no more than the distance from the top of the drawer to the cleat. If you wish, cut dadoes in the sides of the tray (*before* you assemble it), and use these dadoes to hold dividers. Assemble the tray with glue and nails, then place it in the drawer so that it rests on the cleats.

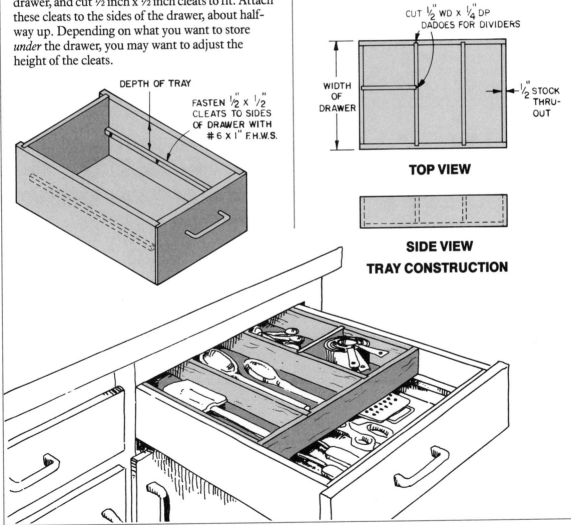

DEPTH OF TRAY

FASTEN ½" X ½" CLEATS TO SIDES OF DRAWER WITH #6 X 1" F.H.W.S.

CUT ½" WD X ¼" DP DADOES FOR DIVIDERS

WIDTH OF DRAWER

½" STOCK THRU-OUT

TOP VIEW

SIDE VIEW
TRAY CONSTRUCTION

PROJECT/Overhead Pots and Pans Rack

To store much-used pots and pans where you can get at them easily, you can mount a rack on a wall or suspend it from the ceiling.

1. Make a simple grid from 1″ dowels. Fasten the dowels together with #8 x 1½ inch flat-head wood screws, countersunk. Drive the screws from the top (or the back) so they won't show when you mount the rack. If you're going to hang this project from the ceiling, install eye screws instead of wood screws at the four outermost corners.

2. Mount the rack. To hang this project from the wall, drive screw hooks into the wall studs, then set the hanger on the hooks. This way, it can be easily removed to clean or paint the wall. Use large S-hooks to hang kitchen utensils from the rack. You may have to bend or 'spread' the S-hooks slightly so that they will slip over the dowels easily.

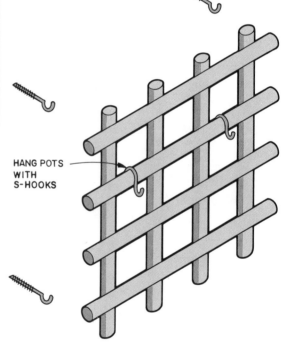

HANG POTS
WITH
S-HOOKS

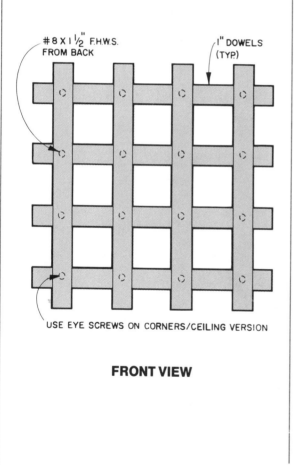

#8 X 1½″ F.H.W.S.
FROM BACK

I″ DOWELS
(TYP.)

USE EYE SCREWS ON CORNERS/CEILING VERSION

FRONT VIEW

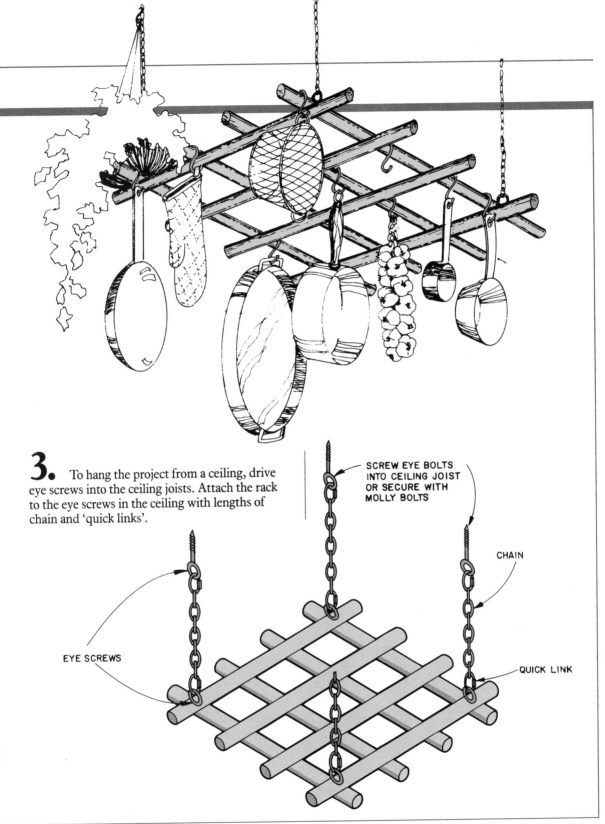

3. To hang the project from a ceiling, drive eye screws into the ceiling joists. Attach the rack to the eye screws in the ceiling with lengths of chain and 'quick links'.

SCREW EYE BOLTS
INTO CEILING JOIST
OR SECURE WITH
MOLLY BOLTS

CHAIN

QUICK LINK

EYE SCREWS

PROJECT/Glass Hanger

Stemware, such as wine glasses, can be easily hung from a simple 'glass hanger'. Not only does this help organize the glasses and make better use of otherwise wasted space, it shows off your fine glass.

1. Decide where you want to hang or mount the glass hanger. It can be hung from the ceiling most anyplace, or mounted underneath a cabinet. Measure the available space, and determine the dimensions of the hanger. Usually, each row of glasses will be 3⅜ inches wide. But this may change depending on the make of the glasses and how you make the hanger molding.

2. Cut the wine glass molding you need on the table saw. The molding requires four separate passes: two passes to cut the top and two to cut the beveled sides. You can also purchase this molding from several mail-order woodworking supply houses. One such source is The Woodworker's Store, 21801 Industrial Blvd., Rogers, MN 55374.

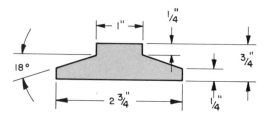

WINE GLASS MOLDING DETAIL

3. Cut the stiles and rails needed to make a frame for the glass hanger. These parts should be ¾ inch thick and 1 inch wide.

4. Assemble the rails, stiles, and moldings with glue and screws. If you're going to hang this project from the ceiling, install eye screws in each corner of the assembled frame.

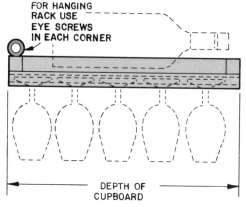

SIDE VIEW

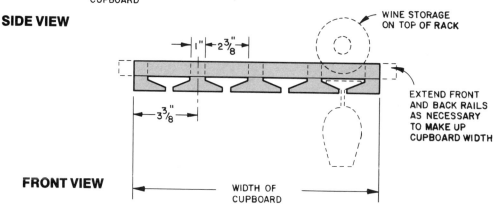

FRONT VIEW

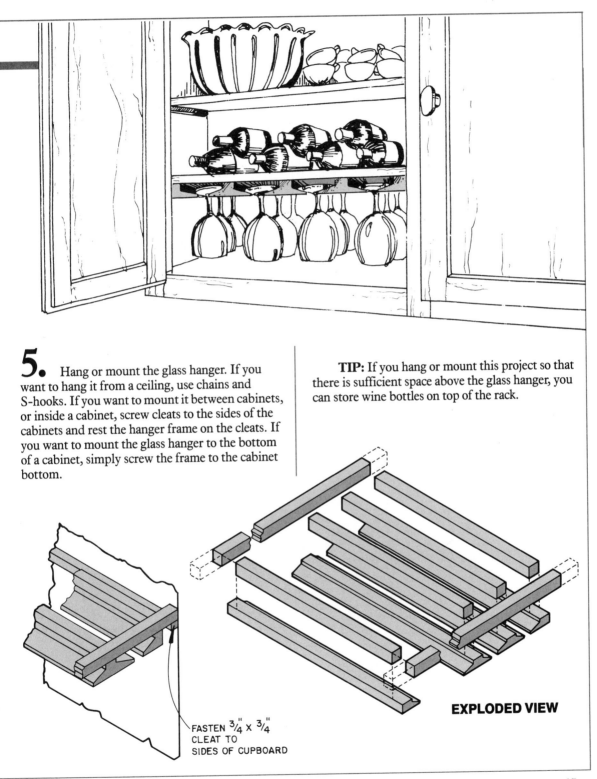

5. Hang or mount the glass hanger. If you want to hang it from a ceiling, use chains and S-hooks. If you want to mount it between cabinets, or inside a cabinet, screw cleats to the sides of the cabinets and rest the hanger frame on the cleats. If you want to mount the glass hanger to the bottom of a cabinet, simply screw the frame to the cabinet bottom.

TIP: If you hang or mount this project so that there is sufficient space above the glass hanger, you can store wine bottles on top of the rack.

FASTEN $\frac{3}{4}$" X $\frac{3}{4}$"
CLEAT TO
SIDES OF CUPBOARD

EXPLODED VIEW

PROJECT/Utensil Racks

These racks mount to the backs of cabinet and pantry doors, in the same manner as 'door pockets'. However, they are much more specialized than door pockets. Most of them are made for specific kitchen utensils.

1. Measure the width of your cabinet door openings and the distance you have between the doors and the things that are stored on the shelves. Also measure the size of the items you want to store in the racks.

2. Decide how you want to construct the racks. We show four variations, all designed to hold common kitchen utensils—a knife rack; a rack for large utensils; a rack for food processor attachments and cookware lids; and a rack for storing long, narrow objects, such as meat thermometers, pizza cutters, skewers, and so forth.

3. To make the *knife rack,* cut a back and a front from ¼ inch thick hardboard. Then cut long, narrow wooden dividers, a little more than half as thick as the knife handles. Glue the parts together, sandwiching the dividers between the front and back.

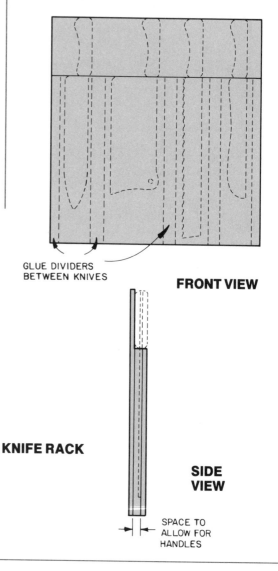

GLUE DIVIDERS
BETWEEN KNIVES

FRONT VIEW

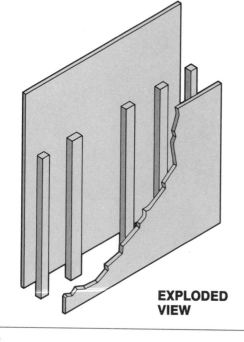

KNIFE RACK

EXPLODED VIEW

SIDE VIEW

SPACE TO ALLOW FOR HANDLES

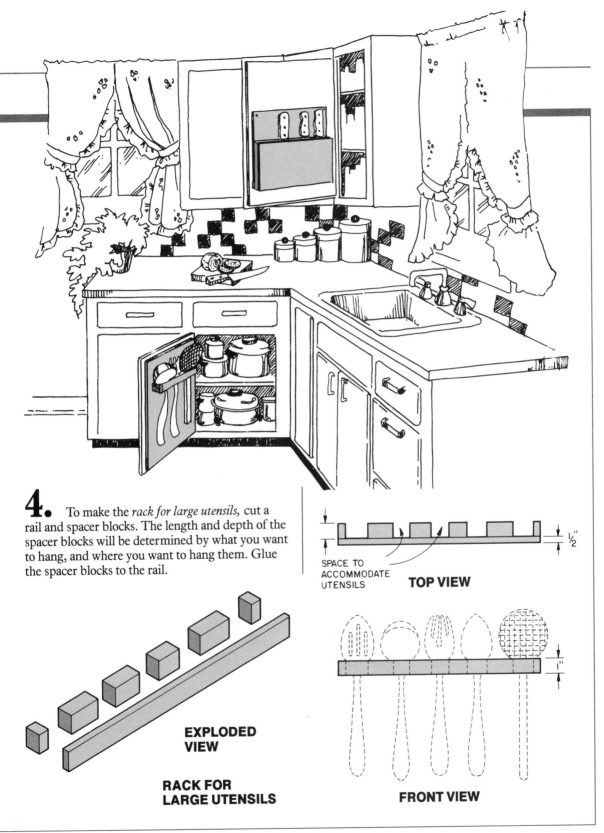

4. To make the *rack for large utensils,* cut a rail and spacer blocks. The length and depth of the spacer blocks will be determined by what you want to hang, and where you want to hang them. Glue the spacer blocks to the rail.

SPACE TO ACCOMMODATE UTENSILS

TOP VIEW

½"

EXPLODED VIEW

RACK FOR LARGE UTENSILS

FRONT VIEW

1"

PROJECT/Utensil Racks/Cont'd.

5. To make the *rack for food processor attachments or cookware lids,* cut a front and a back from ¼ inch thick hardboard. Also cut a wooden bottom and dividers. Notch the front, if needed, to accommodate the attachment's shaft or the lid's handle. Glue the parts together, sandwiching the bottom and dividers between the front and back.

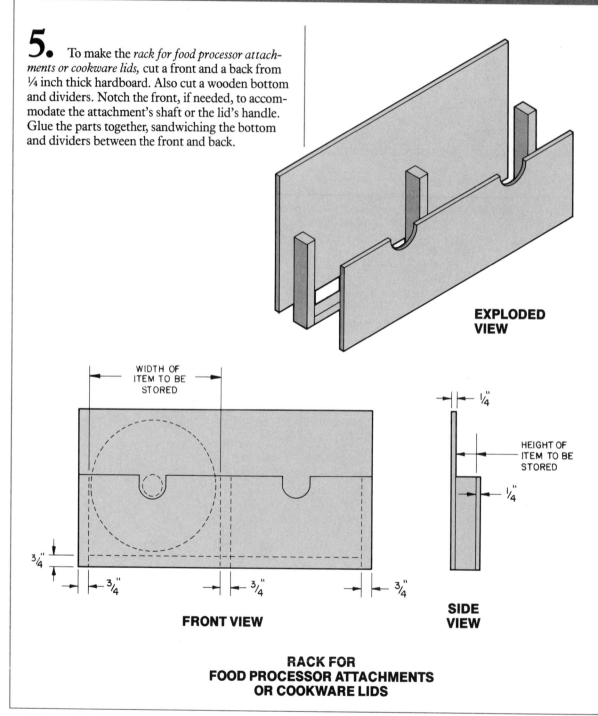

EXPLODED
VIEW

WIDTH OF
ITEM TO BE
STORED

¼"

HEIGHT OF
ITEM TO BE
STORED

¼"

¾"

¾"

¾"

¾"

FRONT VIEW

**SIDE
VIEW**

**RACK FOR
FOOD PROCESSOR ATTACHMENTS
OR COOKWARE LIDS**

6. To make the *rack for long, narrow objects,* cut a back from ¼ inch thick hardboard. Cut a wooden bottom, dividers, and front strips ½ inch wide and ¼ inch thick. Glue the dividers and the bottom to the back, then glue the front strips to the dividers.

7. Position the racks on the doors so that they won't hit the shelves when you close the doors. Then screw them to the doors, being careful that the screws don't come through the fronts of the doors.

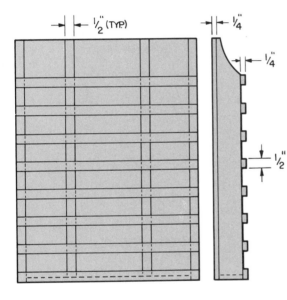

FRONT VIEW   **SIDE VIEW**

RACK FOR LONG, NARROW OBJECTS

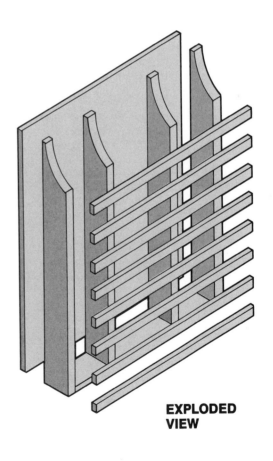

EXPLODED VIEW

PROJECT/Stacking Vegetable Bins

Certain vegetables and fruits—potatoes, onions, apples, and so on—are best stored at room temperature, in the open air. If the air around them gets stagnant and humid, these foodstuffs may rot. These vegetable bins provide good open air storage—the food is ventilated from both above and below. Furthermore, you can stack up as many of them as you need.

1. Cut out the wooden parts for the bins you need from ¾ inch thick stock. To properly ventilate these bins, the bottom is made from woven wire 'hardware cloth'. However, if you want to make the bins with a solid bottom, you can substitute ¼ inch thick plywood. Hint: Consider using Aromatic Cedar for the wooden parts in these bins. Cedar repels insects and helps keep foodstuffs fresh.

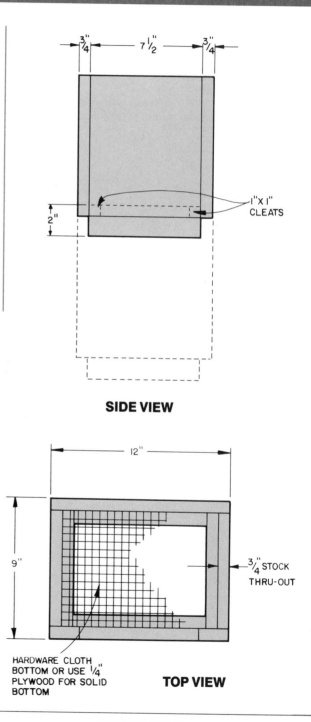

SIDE VIEW

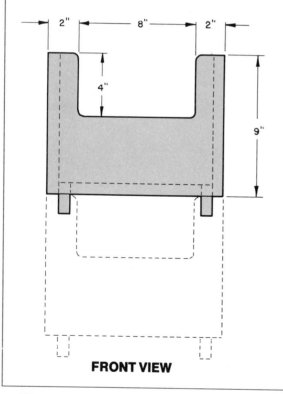

FRONT VIEW

HARDWARE CLOTH BOTTOM OR USE ¼" PLYWOOD FOR SOLID BOTTOM

TOP VIEW

2. With a band saw, cut a recess in the front. This will enable you to reach in the bin without having to unstack them.

3. Assemble the wooden parts of the bins with glue and nails. Note that the two side cleats, which are wider than the back and front cleats, stick out below the bins. When you stack the bins, the side cleats on the bottom of the top bin fit into the opening in the top of the bottom bin. This keeps the bins neatly stacked.

4. Attach hardware cloth to the top surfaces of the cleats with staples.

EXPLODED VIEW

PROJECT/Under-Cabinet Storage

There's a lot of unused storage space immediately beneath your wall cabinets. You can use this space to store small kitchen items by making this swing-down shelving unit.

1. Measure the space you have under your cabinets, and the items you want to store in that space. From these measurements, determine the dimensions of the swing-down shelves.

2. Make the shelves as you would a small box with dividers. Cut the frame and the bottom from ½ inch thick stock, and the shelves from ¼ inch thick stock. Rout dadoes in the sides to hold the shelves. Finally, cut a length of cove molding to use as a handle on the front of the completed shelves. Assemble the parts with glue and nails.

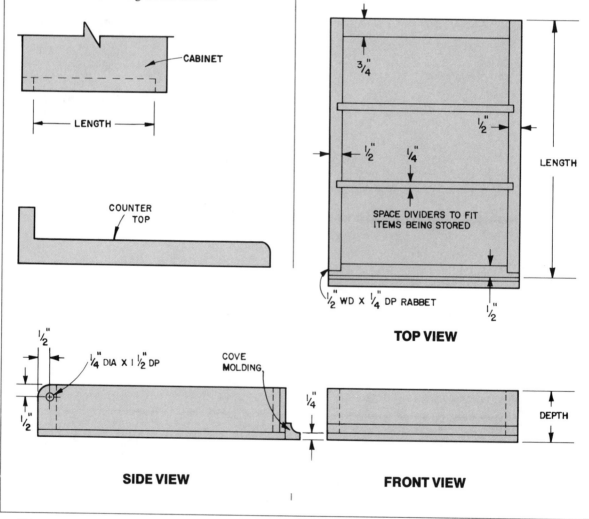

CABINET

LENGTH

COUNTER TOP

3/4"

1/2"

1/2"   1/4"

SPACE DIVIDERS TO FIT ITEMS BEING STORED

LENGTH

1/2" WD X 1/4" DP RABBET

1/2"

TOP VIEW

1/2"

1/4" DIA X 1 1/2" DP

COVE MOLDING

1/4"

1/2"

DEPTH

SIDE VIEW

FRONT VIEW

3. To hang the shelves, cut two boards, ¾ inch thick and as long and as wide as the shelves. Drill pilot holes edgewise through these hangers so that you can screw them to the bottoms of the cabinets. Also, drill holes in the back top corners of the hangers, so that you can mount the shelves to them.

4. Mount the hangers to the bottoms of the cabinets with roundhead screws. Position the hangers so that the shelves will fit between them with approximately ¹⁄₁₆ inch clearance on either side.

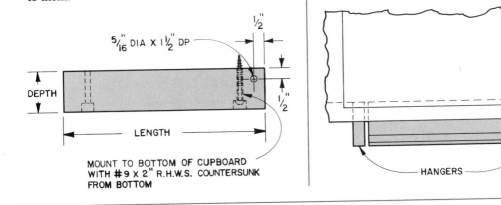

5/16" DIA X 1½" DP

½"

½"

DEPTH

LENGTH

MOUNT TO BOTTOM OF CUPBOARD
WITH #9 X 2" R.H.W.S. COUNTERSUNK
FROM BOTTOM

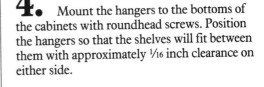

HANGERS

PROJECT/Under-Cabinet Storage/Cont'd.

5. Round the back top corner of the shelves with a block plane and sandpaper. Drill holes for the pivots, then mount the shelves to the hangers, using ¼ inch dowels as pivots.

1/4" x 2 1/4" DOWELS
1/4" WASHER

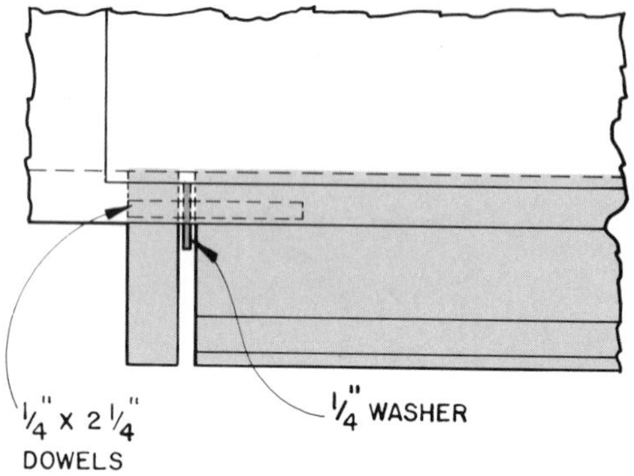

6. To keep the shelves in the 'up' position, install a turnbutton near the front corners of both hangers. Turn the turnbuttons to the inside, and they will hold the shelves up. Turn them toward the outside, and the shelves will pivot down.

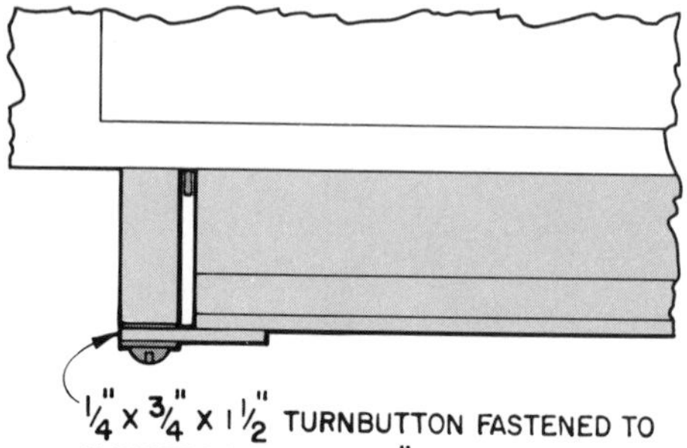

1/4" x 3/4" x 1 1/2" TURNBUTTON FASTENED TO HANGERS WITH # 6 X 1" R.H.W.S. & TWO WASHERS

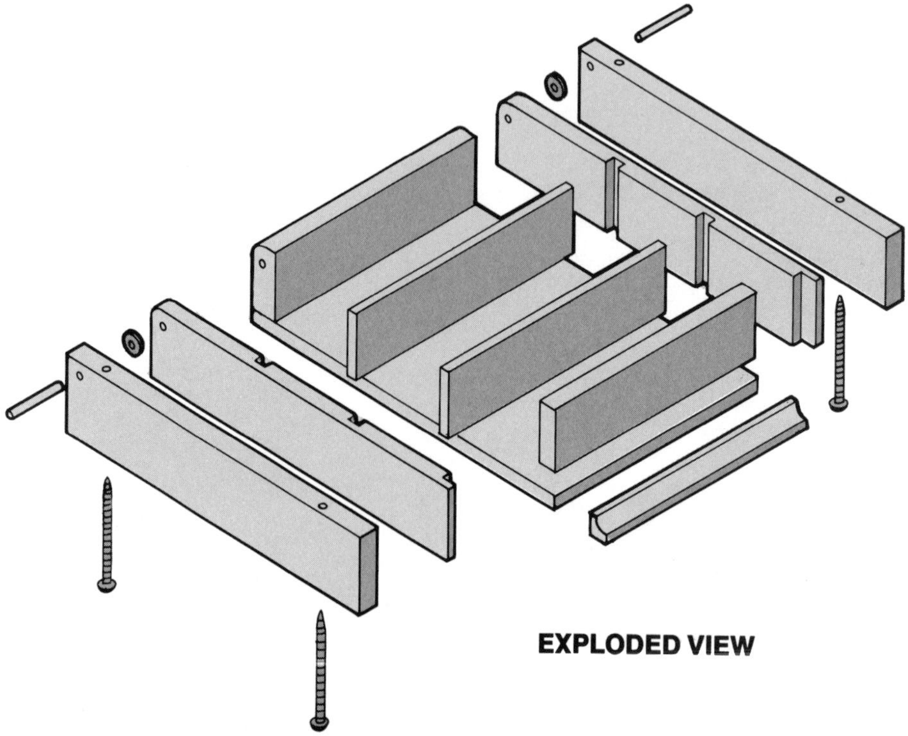

EXPLODED VIEW

PROJECT/Lost Space Storage

There's plenty of 'lost space' in your kitchen that can be reclaimed and used for storage. Possibly the most obvious lost spaces are the gaps between counters, wall, and appliances. Example: Check out the gap between your stove and the kitchen counter, or the gap between the wall and the refrigerator. If the gap is wide enough, you can fill it with a skinny cabinet or cart.

PROJECT/Lost Space Storage/Cont'd.

1. Measure the gaps between walls, counters, and appliances in your kitchen. Consider how you might fill them. You can make either stationary cabinets to put in these gaps, or roll-around carts.

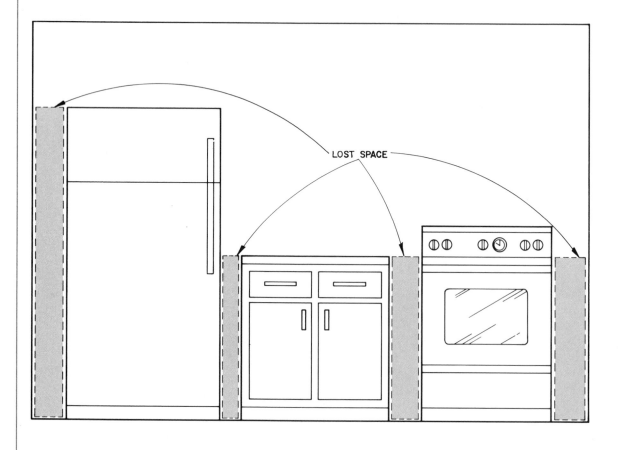

LOST SPACE

2. If you elect to build a *stationary cabinet:* Cut the case parts from ¾ inch thick stock, and any dividers you think might be necessary from ¼ inch thick stock. If your kitchen cabinets are built with a 'toe space', be sure this new cabinet has a matching toe space. Assemble the parts with glue and screws, and finish the project to match your existing cabinets.

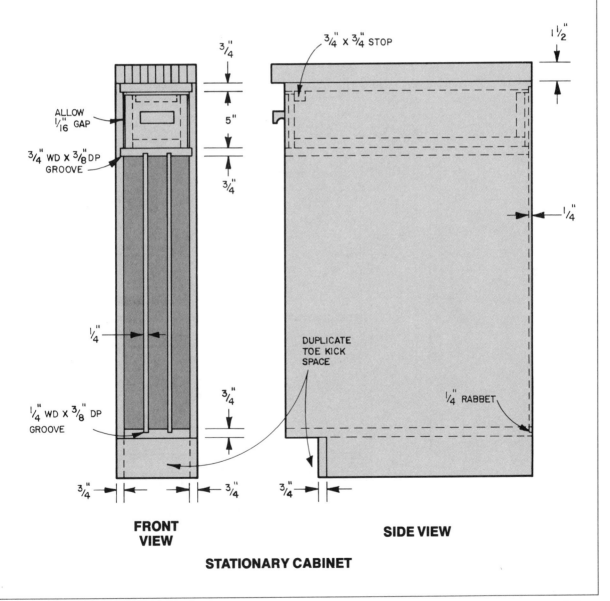

FRONT VIEW

SIDE VIEW

STATIONARY CABINET

PROJECT/Lost Space Storage/Cont'd.

3. If you choose to make a *roll-around cart:* Design the cart without sides. Mount shelves in between a front and a back. You can access these shelves from the sides whenever you roll the cart out of the gap. Mount the finished cart on casters.

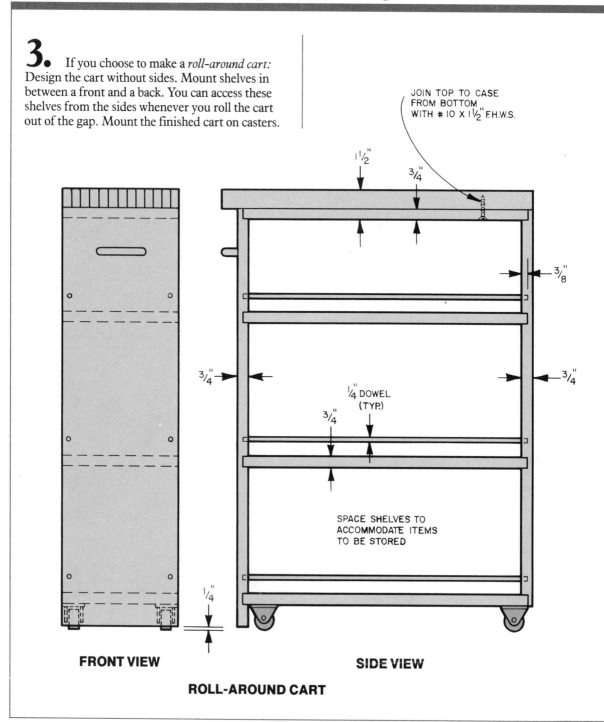

JOIN TOP TO CASE FROM BOTTOM WITH # 10 X 1½" F.H.W.S.

1½"

¾"

¾"

¾"

¾"

¾"

¾"

⅜"

¼ DOWEL (TYP.)

SPACE SHELVES TO ACCOMMODATE ITEMS TO BE STORED

¼"

FRONT VIEW

SIDE VIEW

ROLL-AROUND CART

4. As an option, consider putting a cutting board on top of your new cabinet or cart. Make this cutting board from strips of hardwood, glued together with waterproof resorcinol glue.

5. You may also wish to add a drawer to your cabinet or cart. Shown here is a simpler version of the 'rabbet-and-dado' drawer, described earlier in this book. This version dispenses with the dado. If you make a drawer, carefully plan your clearances. There should be a $1/16$ inch gap on all sides of the drawer, so that it works smoothly.

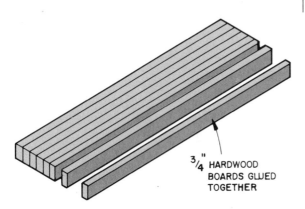

**BUTCHER BLOCK TOP
CUTTING BOARD**

$3/4$ " HARDWOOD BOARDS GLUED TOGETHER

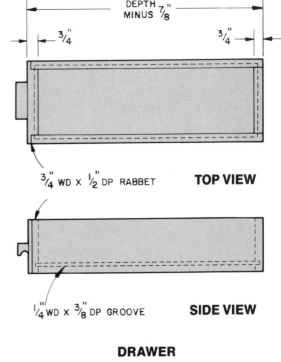

DEPTH MINUS $7/8$"

$3/4$" $3/4$"

$3/4$" WD X $1/2$" DP RABBET   **TOP VIEW**

$1/4$" WD X $3/8$" DP GROOVE   **SIDE VIEW**

DRAWER

PROJECT/Drop-down Sink Front

One of the most perplexing storage problems in the kitchen is where to keep all those unsightly scrub brushes, strainers, and pads of steel wool. Well, there's plenty of space right behind the false front on your sink cabinet!

1. Remove the top front panel or panels from your kitchen sink cabinet. Some cupboards may have a center stile behind a long, single panel. If so, this stile will have to be removed, as well. Saw it off at the top and the bottom.

2. Measure the area that you have uncovered. If necessary, cut a new front panel. The panel should overlap the cabinet face frame on all sides by ⅜ inch.

3. Measure the distance from the face frame to the sink, and determine how much room you have for a bin behind the front panel. Figure the dimensions of the bin front, back, sides, and bottom. Leave at least a ⅛ inch clearance between the front of the sink and the back of the bin, and ⅛ inch clearance on either side, between the bin and the face frame.

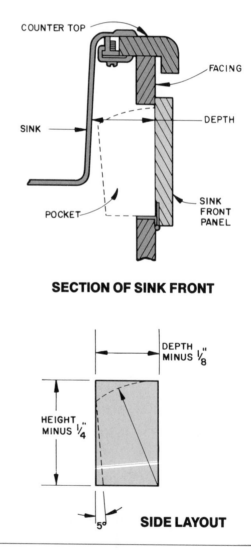

SECTION OF SINK FRONT

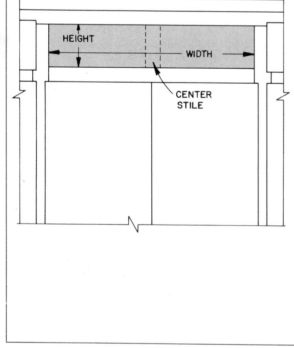

SIDE LAYOUT

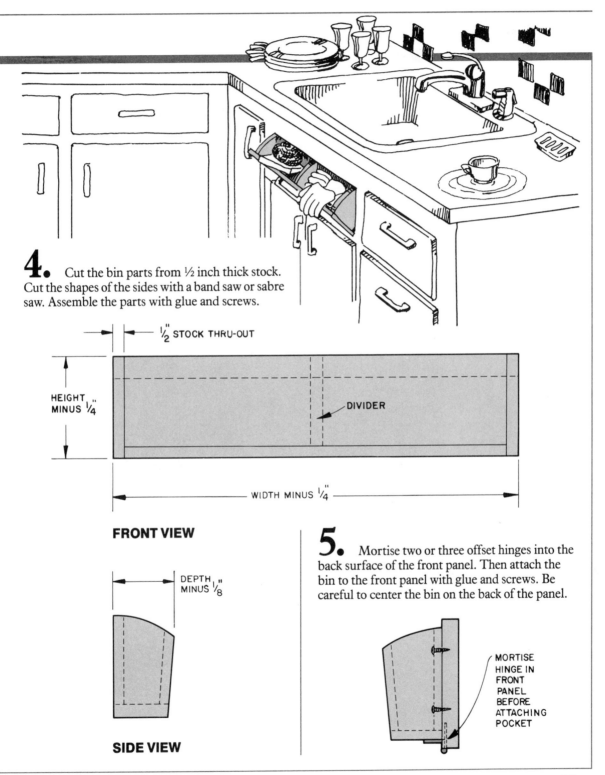

4. Cut the bin parts from ½ inch thick stock. Cut the shapes of the sides with a band saw or sabre saw. Assemble the parts with glue and screws.

½" STOCK THRU-OUT

HEIGHT MINUS ¼"

DIVIDER

WIDTH MINUS ¼"

FRONT VIEW

DEPTH MINUS ⅛"

SIDE VIEW

5. Mortise two or three offset hinges into the back surface of the front panel. Then attach the bin to the front panel with glue and screws. Be careful to center the bin on the back of the panel.

MORTISE HINGE IN FRONT PANEL BEFORE ATTACHING POCKET

6. Mount the bin in the cabinet, screwing the hinges to the edge of the face frame.

7. To keep the front panel from dropping down too far and spilling the contents of the bin, you'll have to make a simple 'stop'. Have a helper swing the panel down part way, exposing the bin so that you have easy access to it. While the helper holds the panel in that position, reach behind the face frame and make a mark on the side of the bin, using the back of the face frame as a straightedge. You can mount a stop anywhere along this mark.

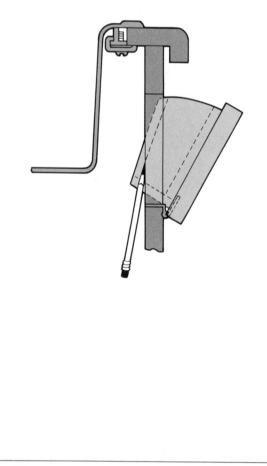

8. Drop the front panel down completely and drill a small pilot hole in the side of the bin at the mark.

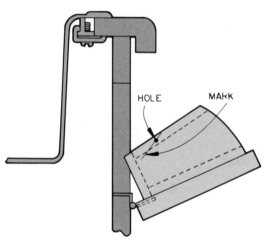

HOLE   MARK

9. Close the front panel, and screw an L-hook into the pilot hole in the side of the bin. Make sure the 'L' faces up or down, parallel to the mark. When you open the front panel and allow the bin to drop down, the L-hook will catch on the face frame and prevent the bin from going too far.

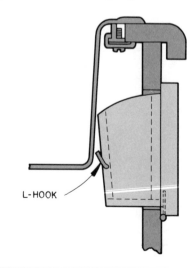

L-HOOK

6

Closets—
Traditional
Catch-Alls

Some architect in antiquity invented the closet; and the words that were immediately spoken were "Close it!".

In every home, there was a need to have a place in which things could be stored. This was so important that it became part of the structure of the house. Now we have guest closets, linen closets, bedroom closets, and cleaning closets—all special little rooms for keeping one kind of, or one person's, belongings.

Closets should be made to work for their user or for the special purpose intended, but often they are woefully inadequate. In older homes these structures are especially notorious for having wasted

space. They are often far too deep and have one humongous shelf at the top.

How can you update your present closets to suit your needs? The key is to be flexible and to do some hard calculating about what your needs are. In this chapter, we present suggestions for reworking a typical adult's closet; but these can be altered to create a linen closet or a child's closet, or whatever you need. There are also projects for storing everything from belts to blankets. Most importantly, remember that your work does not necessarily have to be permanent. By installing modern hardware, you can adjust shelves and rods as your hobbies change or as your children grow.

Creative Thinking About Closets

Closets are small chambers or rooms that offer plenty of closed storage space. They usually have a hinged or sliding door, but just because the doors can be closed does not mean that closets have to be messy, disorganized, or overloaded. On the contrary, a carefully planned set of shelves, poles, and other storage compartments within a closet can

create better organization—and even more storage space.

Some homeowners make the error of thinking of closet space in rigid terms. (The entry closet should be used only for coats and umbrellas; the linen closet only for linens.) A little creativity on your part can yield some interesting results, and exciting possibilities. You can free up storage space throughout your home by utilizing closet space in novel ways. This is particularly true if you have many closets. You can use a 'cool' closet (on an outside wall) to hold a wine rack. Another somewhat eccentric example is to store audio equipment, complete with record albums and tapes in a closet. If you have period decor (country, federal, Victorian, etc.), this will keep the modern-looking knobs, dials, and switches out of sight. It will also keep your expensive equipment beyond the reach of small children—at least initially.

You can combine several functions in one closet as long as they are compatible. As an extreme example, don't store children's play equipment with toxic household cleaners. Most importantly, create accessible storage space for the things that are in current use. A young child's closet can be filled with shelves for toys and games with only a little space left for hanging clothes. As the child grows and the wardrobe changes, more space can be devoted to clothing.

When you're taking inventory and gathering ideas, you should shop at home improvement stores. There are many kinds of hardware and accessories that will aid you in making your design. Bins, racks, hooks, and clamps can all be used, not only on the inside walls of the closet but also on the door.

There are some general principles to keep in mind when you go about filling a closet. The main rule is to make things accessible. If you store items three deep, then you will inevitably raise havoc when the time comes to hunt for them. This problem can be alleviated by the simple use of a marking pen; put labels on boxes, bags, or even shelves if it will help you and your family to remember where everything goes. Install a light in the closet if it's located in a dimly-lit area of your home; or keep a small flashlight inside it.

Shelves and rods are closet basics, but don't feel limited by these structures either. You can add drawers, compartments, or even tabletops if you wish. A drop-down or pull-up leaf is great to add to a linen closet, as a space for folding laundry before it is stored on the closet shelves.

The Basic Closet—Redesigned

The problem with the traditional closet design is that it ignores what people usually keep in them. Certain areas are overcrowded; the space in other areas is mostly wasted. Typically, closets have a single rod running down the middle of them, about 66 inches off the floor, and a single shelf above that. The clothes, no matter what their length, are hung on the rod; the shoes are piled on the floor; and everything else is precariously balanced on the shelf. The result is usually a cluttered shelf and floor, and a lot of dead air in between.

Consider how clothes are designed and how they are hung: Most of the clothes you store—shirts or blouses, pants or skirts, sweaters and jackets—take up less than 36 inches of vertical space when hung on hangers. A few types of clothes require more vertical space. But the rod in your closet has been installed as if all you owned were full-length dresses and overcoats. The result is a lot of wasted space under your clothes. Use this wasted space wisely and you'll increase the shelf space without sacrificing hanger space.

Making the Plan. To begin, make a sketch of your closet as it exists, without any shelves or hangers. Draw a single shelf running the length of the closet, 80 inches above the floor. This is probably 10-12 inches above where your present closet shelves are installed. Next, draw a simple vertical shelving unit with six to seven shelves that measure 18-24 inches wide. This unit should fit under the long shelf, dividing the closet in two parts. It should also be offset from the center, so that you can reach the shelves easily when you open one door.

In the larger of the two sections, put two hanger rods, 38 inches and 76 inches off the floor, respectively. Both these hangers will hold 'short' clothes. In the other section, draw a single hanger rod 63 inches off the floor for 'tall' clothes. If you wish, put another shelf immediately above this rod. What you've sketched will look something like the typical layout shown here.

If you do some measuring and comparing, you'll find that this arrangement will increase the shelf space in your closet by 250% or better, and the hanger space by at least 130%. Clearly, this is a better use of the available space.

Experiment with the design for a bit, rearranging the elements to suit your own needs. Depending on the types of clothes, or other gear, you own, you might want to make one side of the closet longer or narrower. You may need more or less shelf space than is shown here. Perhaps you have a few ideas of your own—for a clothes hamper, a stash for jewelry, or whatever suits you.

Once your design is completed, consult the first project in this chapter for instructions on how to renovate the closet. In this particular project, cedar 'closet liner' was used for mothproofing, although it can, of course, be omitted. Note also that in this project the shelves and closet poles are fixed. If you prefer more flexibility, substitute heavy-duty standards specifically made to hold closet poles and shelves.

If you don't want to completely revise your closets, consider building the projects following the "Redesigned Closet". These projects are suggestions for shoe and pants racks, non-standard pole and shelf arrangements and various kinds of storage bins and modules that will fit inside a closet. Used individually or in combination, they will help you to make better use of the closet space you now have.

Reorganizing a Closet

BEFORE...

AFTER!

PROJECT/Redesigned Closet

There's a lot of wasted storage space in most closets. You can increase *both* the hanging space and the shelving space by simply repositioning the poles and the shelves.

1. Carefully measure the inside of your closet. Draw up a plan to reorganize the storage space. Here are a few suggestions: Raise the top shelf to 80″ above the floor. Beneath this shelf, plan a tall, narrow shelving unit that divides the closet into two areas for hanging clothes. In one area (preferably the largest of the two areas), draw two poles, 38″ and 76″ off the floor, respectively. These poles can be used to hang shorter clothes, such as shirts, skirts, and pants. In the other area, draw a single pole 63″ off the floor. This can be used for longer clothes, such as coats and dresses. If you wish, plan another shelf directly above this pole. In your plan, be sure to include not only the rods and shelves, but also uprights, cleats, and pole hangers that you'll need.

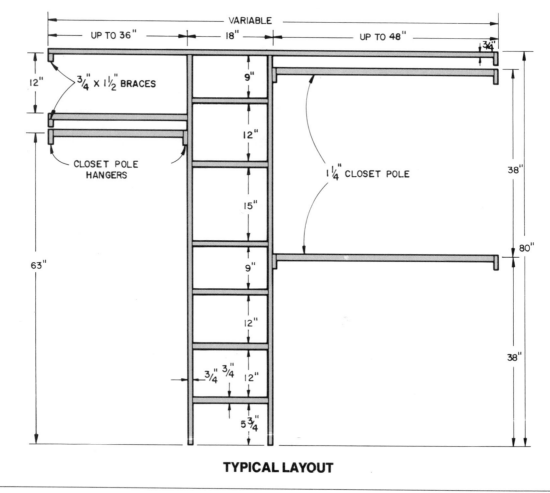

TYPICAL LAYOUT

2. Remove the shelves, poles, and any hardware that are presently in your closet.

3. If you wish, line the inside of your closet with aromatic cedar chipboard. This relatively inexpensive material will protect your clothes against pests and keep them smelling fresh.

4. Cut the shelves, rods, uprights, cleats, and hangers to the size and length that your plan calls for.

5. Build the shelving unit. With a helper, nail or screw the shelves between the uprights. This unit will seem wobbly at first, but when you install it in the closet, it will become quite rigid.

6. Make the pole hangers that you need. With a holesaw, cut 1⅜″-diameter holes in the hanger stock. Then 'open up' the top edge of the hole with a band saw or sabre saw.

7. Install the shelves in the closet. Stand the shelving unit in place and put the long shelf on top of it. It will keep the shelf in place while you install the cleats. Screw these cleats to the side walls where you want them to support the long shelf. Be certain that they are secured to the 2 x 4 studs in the walls. Nail or screw the top shelf to the cleats and to the uprights of the shelving unit. Secure the bottom of the shelving unit to the floor with metal brackets.

8. Install the poles. Attach the pole hangers to the side walls and the uprights with screws or nails. Then rest the poles in place in the hangers.

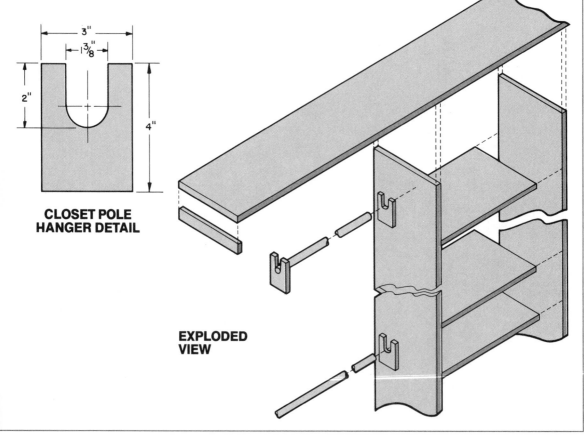

CLOSET POLE HANGER DETAIL

3″

1⅜″

2″

4″

EXPLODED VIEW

PROJECT/Shoe Rack

Nothing clutters closets more than a dozen pairs of shoes, spread out all over the floor. A shoe rack will organize those shoes, and help relieve the clutter. This particular rack is mounted on casters.

This allows you to wheel the rack in and out of the closet, so that you can easily reach the shoes you need, even at the back of the rack.

1. Cut the parts to size. Cut the ends, shelves, rods, and other parts to their proper length and width. You can make the ends of the rack from plywood, or glue two 1 x 10's edge to edge. If you use plywood, you'll need to cover the edges with molding so that you can't see the plies. Cut the molding to size, also, mitering the ends where shown in the *End View.*

2. Drill ¾″ holes through the ends, where shown in the *End View.* These holes will hold the rods.

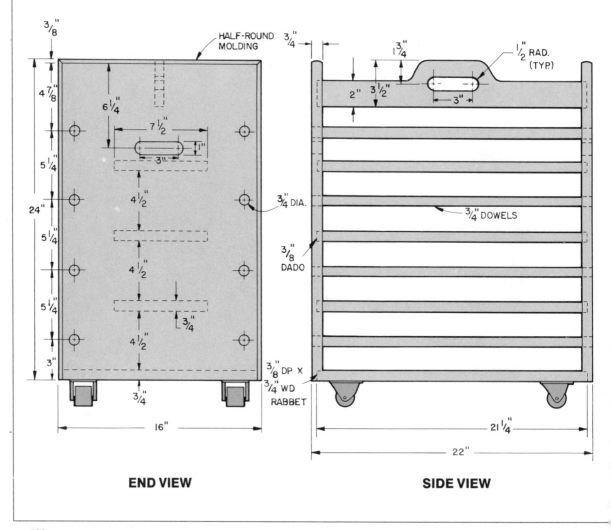

END VIEW

SIDE VIEW

3. Cut the dadoes and rabbets in the ends to hold the bottom, top stretcher, and shelves or 'toe rests'. Mount a ¾″ straight bit in your router to make these joints. To guide the router while you're cutting, clamp a straightedge to the stock. Square the ends of the dadoes with a chisel.

4. Cut the openings for the handles. Drill 1″ holes to make the ends of the handle openings. Then cut out the waste between the holes with a sabre saw.

5. Cut the shape of the top stretcher with a band saw or sabre saw.

6. Assemble the ends, toe rests, top stretcher, and bottom with glue and #10 x 1¼″ flathead wood screws. Counterbore and countersink the screws, then cover the heads with wooden plugs. If you've made the ends from plywood, attach the moldings with glue and brads.

7. Paint or finish the rack.

8. Attach casters to the bottom of the completed rack.

EXPLODED VIEW

PROJECT/Pants Rack

There's nothing worse for pants than hanging them on wire hangers. The slender wires leave creases where the pants fold over them. A special pants rack, attached to the wall of the closet, not only relieves this problem, it also frees up hanging storage space.

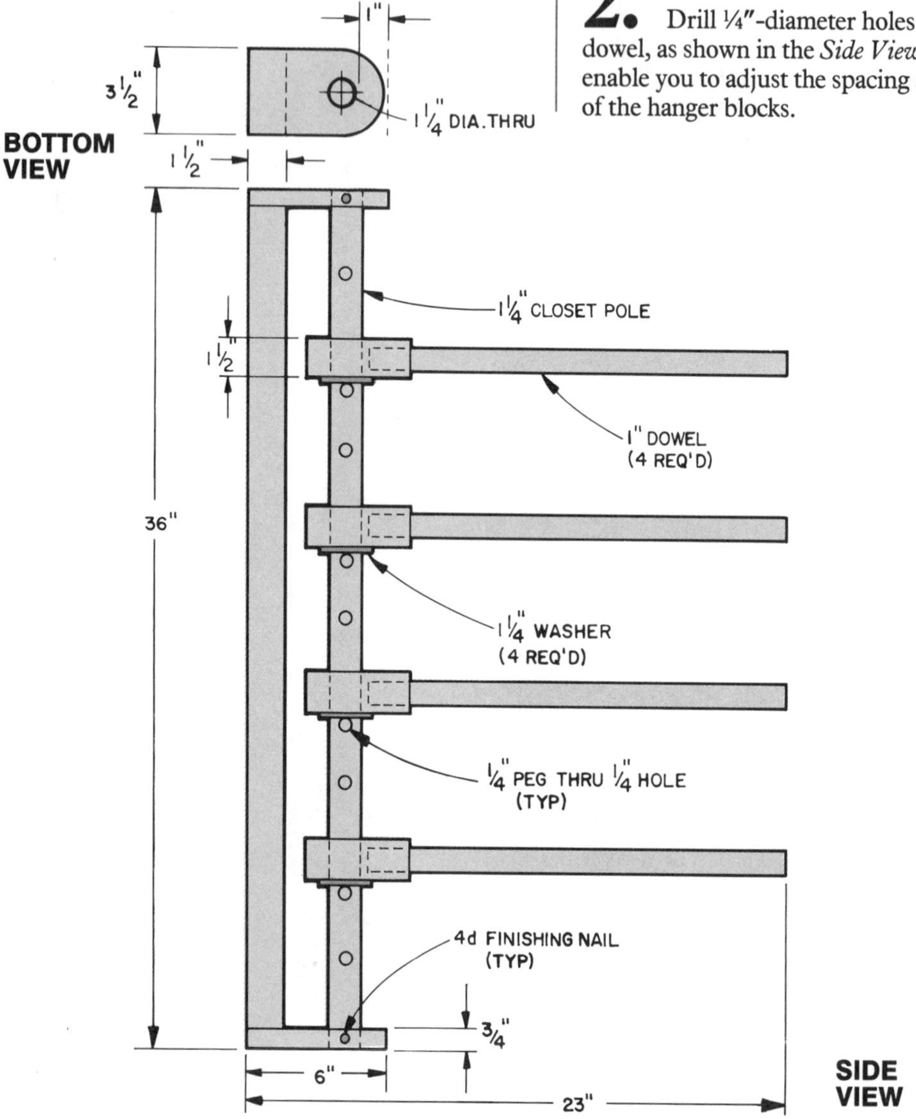

1. Cut the pole, dowels, and other wooden parts you need to make the pants rack. Saw out the shapes of the individual hanger blocks with a sabre saw, then sand off the saw marks.

2. Drill ¼″-diameter holes in the pivot dowel, as shown in the *Side View*. These holes enable you to adjust the spacing and the height of the hanger blocks.

BOTTOM VIEW

3½″

1″

1¼″ DIA.THRU

1½″

SIDE VIEW

36″

1½″

1¼″ CLOSET POLE

1″ DOWEL (4 REQ'D)

1¼″ WASHER (4 REQ'D)

¼″ PEG THRU ¼″ HOLE (TYP)

4d FINISHING NAIL (TYP)

¾″

6″

23″

3. Drill or saw holes in the hanger blocks. Make two holes in each block—a hole 1¼″ in diameter through the wood so that the block will pivot, and a 1″-diameter stopped hole for the hanger dowel, as shown in the *Hanger Detail*. Use a holesaw to make the larger hole, then enlarge it slightly with a rasp. It should turn on the closet pole without binding.

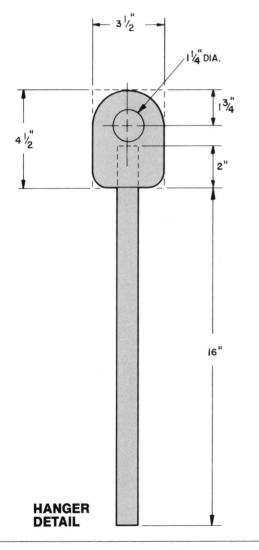

HANGER DETAIL

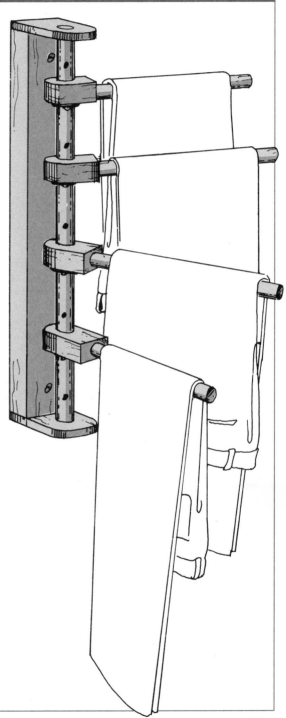

4. Cut 1¼"-diameter holes through the bottom and top of the rack. Once again, use a holesaw to make these holes.

5. Sand the parts of the rack. Be especially careful to smooth the hanger dowels. Make sure they are free of splinters.

6. Assemble the hangers. Glue the hanger dowels in the stopped holes in the hanger blocks.

7. Assemble the rack. When the glue on the hangers cures, place them on the pivot. Put a 1¼" I.D. washer under each hanger, as shown in the drawings. Screw the bottom to the post, and insert the lower end of the pivot into the hole in the bottom. Insert the upper end into the top, and screw the top to the post. Keep the pivot from slipping out of the hole in the bottom or the top by pinning it in place with 4d finishing nails. Drive these nails through the sides of the bottom and top parts.

8. Mount the rack in the closet. Drive wood screws through the post and into a stud in the wall. Adjust the hangers to the vertical height that you want, and keep them in place with ¼"-diameter pegs. Insert these pegs in the holes in the pivot.

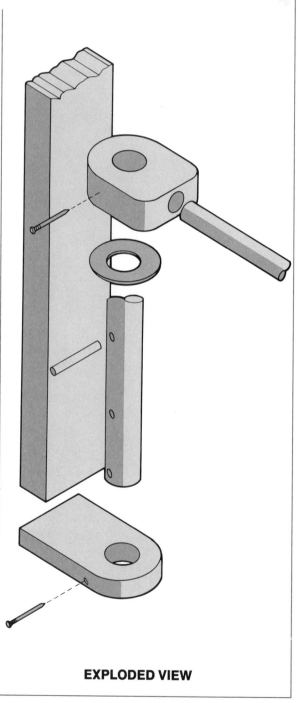

EXPLODED VIEW

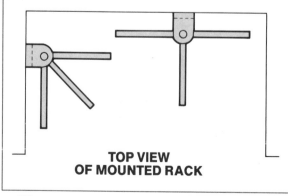

**TOP VIEW
OF MOUNTED RACK**

PROJECT/Closet Bins and Shelves

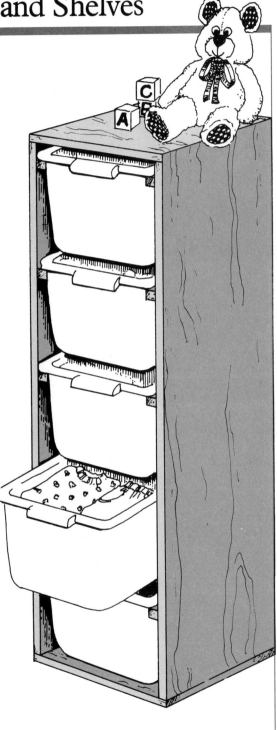

Are you short of drawer or shelf space? Here's a plan for an easy-to-make project that will give you more of both. Purchase plastic tubs to rest on the cleats inside this closet insert, and you've got extra drawer space. Or cut squares of plywood, and you've got extra pull-out shelves.

1. Plan the size of the project. Measure the closet where you want to put this bin/shelving unit, and decide how big you can make it. Then visit your local hardware or variety store and measure the plastic tubs they have available. This will determine the final dimensions of the unit.

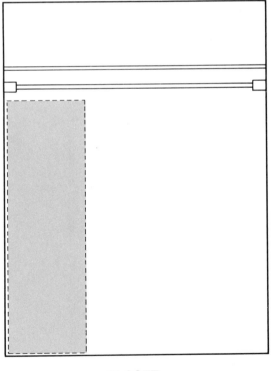

**CLOSET
WITH PROPOSED INSERT**

2. Cut the parts of the unit to size. Make the cleats from ¾"-thick solid wood. The sides, back, top, and bottom can be made from plywood or particleboard. If you use plywood, you may want to cover the plies in the front of the unit with molding so they won't show. If this is the case, cut the molding to size, too.

3. Attach the cleats to the sides. Carefully measure and mark their position, then glue and nail the cleats in place.

4. Assemble the unit. Glue the top and bottom to the sides, and reinforce the joints with nails or screws. Be certain that the unit is square, then nail the back in place. If you've made the unit from plywood, attach the moldings to the front edges with brads.

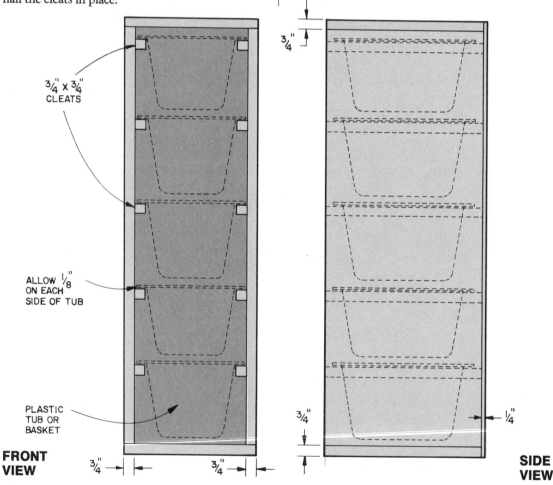

¾" x ¾"
CLEATS

ALLOW ⅛"
ON EACH
SIDE OF TUB

PLASTIC
TUB OR
BASKET

FRONT VIEW

¾"   ¾"

¾"

¾"

¼"

SIDE VIEW

5. To make pull-out shelves, cut them from ¾"-thick plywood. These shelves should be ⅛" narrower than the inside of the unit, so that the shelves will slide in and out easily. Drill two 1"-diameter holes near the front edge of the shelves for finger-holds. If you want to cover the plies, attach molding to the front edge with brads.

6. Paint or finish the unit. Then slide the bins and shelves in place.

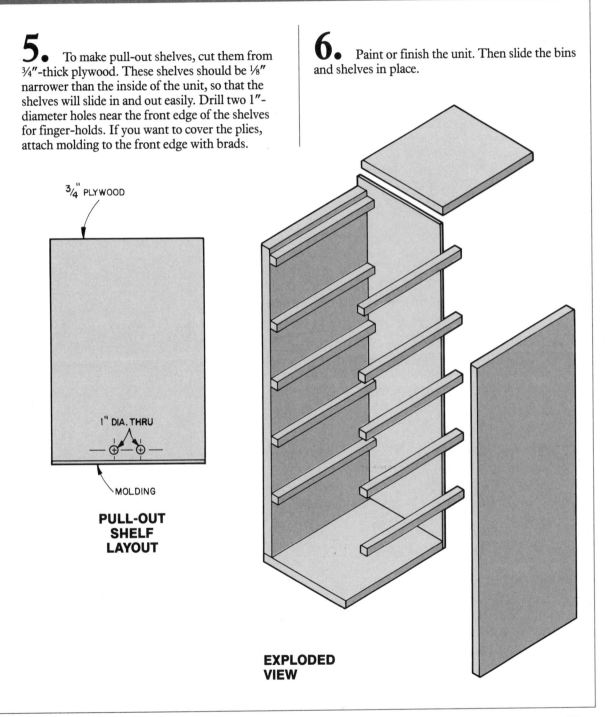

¾" PLYWOOD

1" DIA. THRU

MOLDING

**PULL-OUT
SHELF
LAYOUT**

**EXPLODED
VIEW**

PROJECT/Double Closet Poles

Perhaps the easiest way to add extra hanging storage space in your closet is to add another closet pole. This pole hangs from your existing one, giving you 'double poles' in part of your closet. Hang short clothes (shirts, skirts, and pants) in the spaces under the double poles, and longer clothes (dresses and coats) on the original pole where the poles aren't doubled up.

1. Determine how long you need to make the second or 'double' closet pole. This will be determined by the quantity of 'short' hanging clothes that you have.

2. Cut the pole, dowels, and the hangers to the sizes you need.

3. Drill ¼"-diameter holes through the new closet pole, near each end.

4. Make the hangers. With a holesaw, cut two 1¼"-diameter holes in each of the hangers, one hole near each end. Then use a sabre saw to 'open up' the upper holes from the side, as shown in the *Hanger Layout/Side View*.

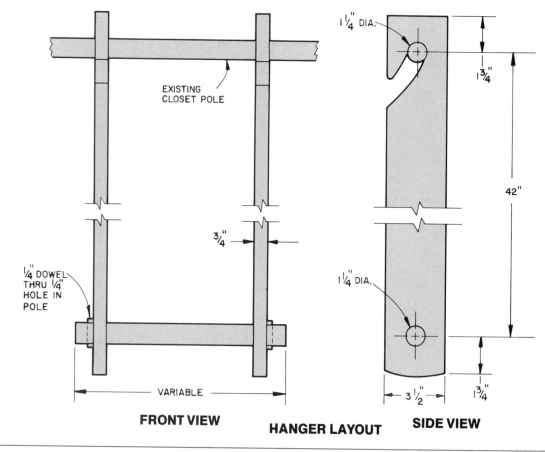

1¼" DIA.

1³⁄₄"

42"

1¼" DIA.

EXISTING
CLOSET POLE

¾"

¼" DOWEL
THRU ¼"
HOLE IN
POLE

VARIABLE

3½"

1³⁄₄"

FRONT VIEW

HANGER LAYOUT

SIDE VIEW

5. Sand the parts of the project smooth. Apply a stain or a finish, if you wish.

6. Assemble the double closet pole. Suspend the hangers from the original pole, then insert the new pole in the holes at the bottom end of the hanger. Keep this new, second pole from slipping out of the holes in the hanger by gluing ¼″- diameter pegs in the holes near the ends of the pole.

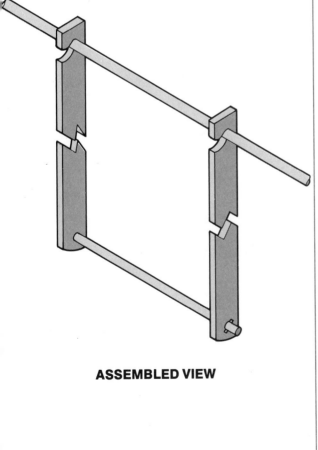

ASSEMBLED VIEW

PROJECT/Blanket Rack

Blankets and bed linens should be stored in the fresh air. If you fold them up and store them away in a closed chest, they may get musty. This wall-mounted rack provides a place to hang blankets where the air will circulate around them.

1. Measure the space where you wish to mount the rack. Also, measure the blankets that you want to hang. This information will help you determine the size of the rack you want to build.

2. Cut the dowels, sides, and stretchers. Consider making the sides from aromatic cedar. This will repel pests and keep the blankets smelling fresh.

3. Drill ¼"-diameter holes through the back stretchers. You'll use these holes later to mount the completed rack inside the closet.

4. Cut the shapes of the sides. Lay out the sides on the stock. Drill 1"-diameter holes to make the bottoms of the notches. Then cut the shape of the sides with a sabre saw. Sand away the saw marks.

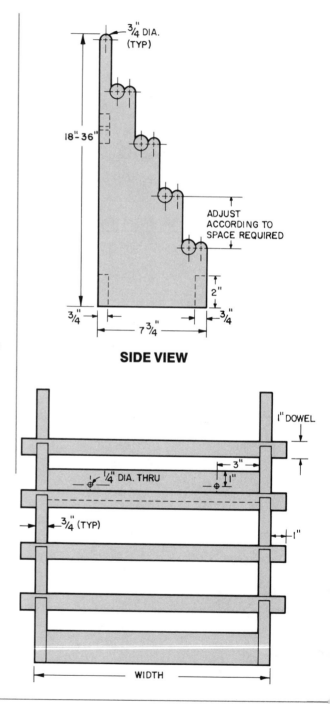

SIDE VIEW

FRONT VIEW

5. Assemble the rack. Sand all the parts smooth, then screw the sides to the stretchers. Paint or finish the rack, if you wish. (*Don't* apply a finish if you've made the sides from cedar. This would seal in the scent of the wood.)

6. Mount the rack to a wall inside your closet. Drive wood screws through the stretchers and into the studs in the wall. If you must mount the rack to the wall at a place where there are no studs, use molly anchors. Put the dowel in place on the rack and drape blankets over them.

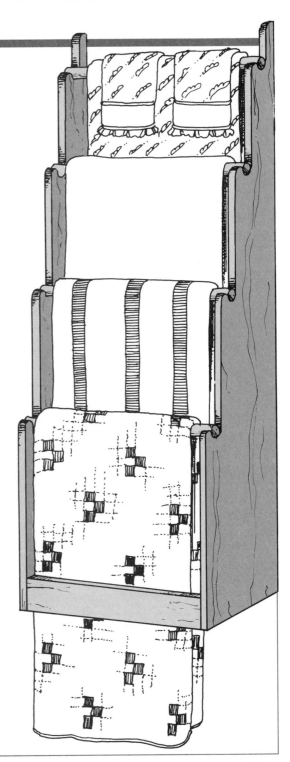

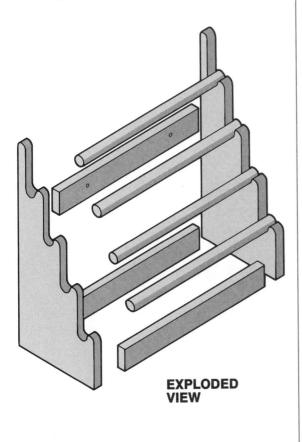

EXPLODED VIEW

PROJECT/Wall Storage Modules

These clever modules make use of the wasted wall space at the back or on the side of your closet. They hang from a ladder-like rack, and can be easily rearranged as your storage needs change.

1. Measure the wall where you intend to attach the rack. Draw up a plan for the rack and determine the size and number of the parts you'll need to make. If possible, plan your rack so that you can attach the uprights to the studs in the wall.

2. Assemble and finish the rack. Cut and rip the slats and the uprights to size, then nail the slats to the uprights. Paint or finish the rack to suit yourself.

3. Attach the completed rack to the wall of the closet. Drive wood screws through the uprights and into the studs in the wall. If you must attach the rack to hollow spaces in the wall, use molly anchors.

4. Decide what storage modules you want to hang on the racks, and what sizes these modules should be. There are several to choose from: a hanging 'pocket', a shelf, belt or tie rack, a divided tray, a bat or racket holder, and a boot hanger. You may also want to design modules of your own.

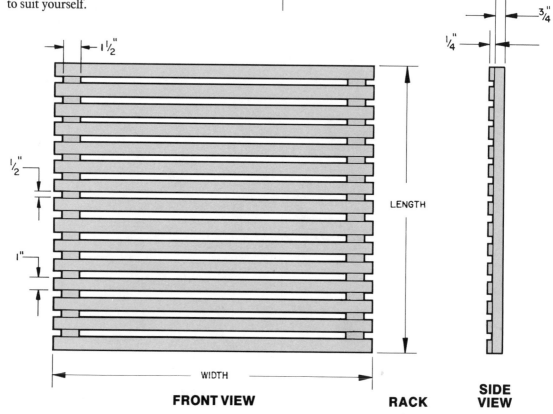

FRONT VIEW **RACK** **SIDE VIEW**

5. Build the modules you need. These are all simple units that are nailed or screwed together. They each have two ¼"-diameter holes drilled in the upper corners, which you'll use later to hang them from the rack. Here is a brief discussion of each one:

Hanging pocket—This is just a deep box, glued and nailed together. The sides are shaped with a sabre saw.

Shelf—This is a 'bracket' shelf, braced at both ends.

Belt or tie rack—Make the rack by setting ⅜"-diameter dowels in a board. If you wish, you can use commercially-made pegs instead of dowels.

Divided tray—This is a shallow box with partitions. Like the pocket, the sides and the partitions are shaped with a sabre saw.

Bat/racket holder—The bat/racket holder is made like the shelf, except it has notches cut in it with a sabre saw. Space and size the notches as you need them—for holding baseball bats, tennis rackets, and the like.

Boot hanger—Make this precisely as you made the bat/racket holder, but cut two deep notches in the shelf. Use these notches to hang boots or anything else that fits in them. You can adjust the width and depth of the notches to fit the item you want to hang.

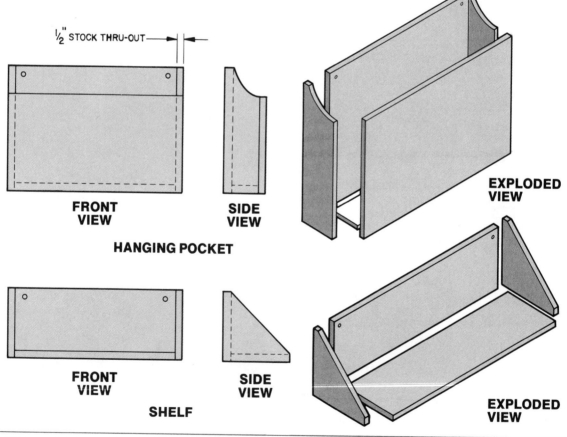

½" STOCK THRU-OUT

FRONT VIEW **SIDE VIEW**

HANGING POCKET

EXPLODED VIEW

FRONT VIEW **SIDE VIEW**

SHELF

EXPLODED VIEW

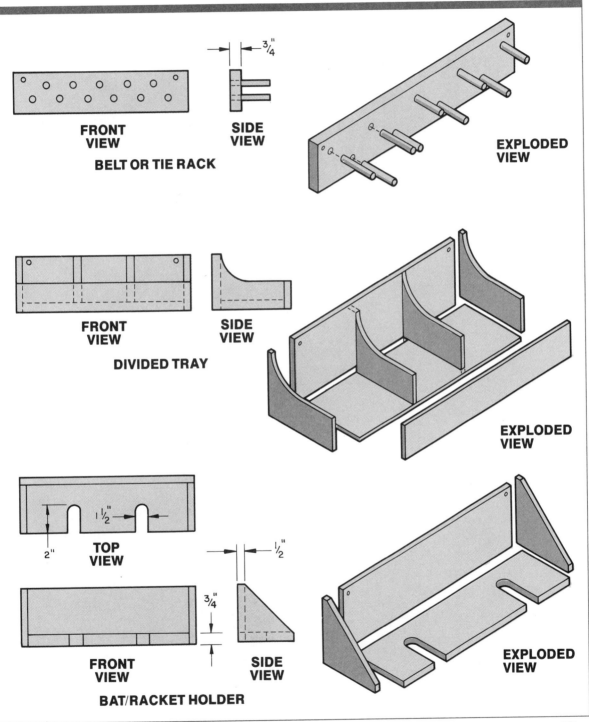

FRONT VIEW

SIDE VIEW

BELT OR TIE RACK

$3/4"$

EXPLODED VIEW

FRONT VIEW

SIDE VIEW

DIVIDED TRAY

EXPLODED VIEW

$1 1/2"$

$2"$

TOP VIEW

$1/2"$

$3/4"$

FRONT VIEW

SIDE VIEW

EXPLODED VIEW

BAT/RACKET HOLDER

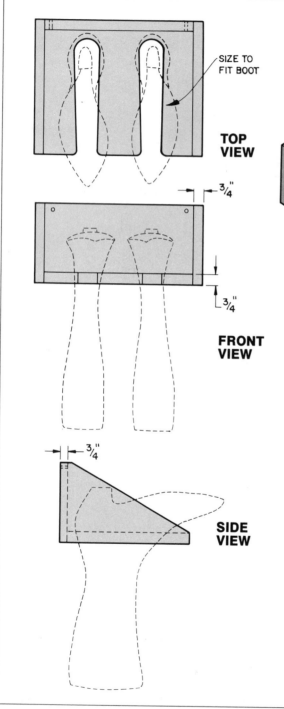

SIZE TO
FIT BOOT

**TOP
VIEW**

$3/4''$

$3/4''$

**FRONT
VIEW**

$3/4''$

**SIDE
VIEW**

BOOT HANGER

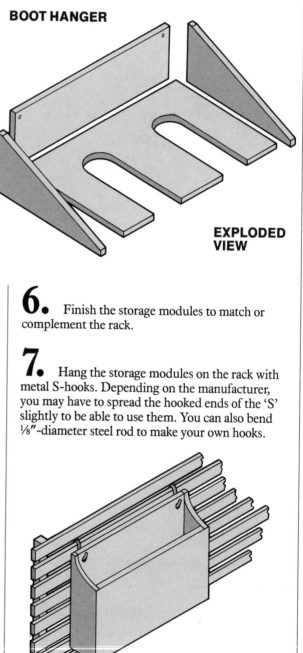

**EXPLODED
VIEW**

6. Finish the storage modules to match or complement the rack.

7. Hang the storage modules on the rack with metal S-hooks. Depending on the manufacturer, you may have to spread the hooked ends of the 'S' slightly to be able to use them. You can also bend $1/8''$-diameter steel rod to make your own hooks.

7

Increased Organization in the Bathroom

The major purpose of the bathroom in the home is cleanliness, so it only follows that it should be orderly. Whether large or small, your bath will be stocked with certain items: towels and washcloths, soaps, shampoos and bath oils, medicines, paper products, articles for grooming hair and skin—all the familiar necessities. If there's room, you may also have some cleaning products, a first-aid kit, the shoe-shine kit, the kids' rubber ducky and on and on ad infinitum.

Considering the fact that baths are statistically unsafe rooms, it is especially important that we keep them neat and accessible. In this chapter, several ideas and projects will be presented to aid you in your quest of better organizing your bathroom. First and foremost is the traditional

vanity base cabinet, the most common storage unit in a bathroom. The "Vanity Bins and Shelves" offer suggestions for better organizing the space in one of these vanities.

Next, there's a custom-built wall-hung vanity or 'medicine cabinet', as it's more commonly called. If you don't have one, the "Recessed Bathroom Shelves" project shows you how you might install one. If you already have one, the space inside it might be better organized with a "Medicine Caddy".

If you can spare the space in your bathroom, build some of the other projects, such as the shelving units and towel racks. All these were designed to take up as little space as possible, while creating useful storage space where none was before.

Finding Room in the Bathroom

It's really a change in lifestyle that has increased our need for more bathroom storage space; people now bathe and groom more frequently, read books and even talk on the telephone in their bathrooms.

Unless you have a custom-built home, your bath is liable to be a small space loaded with plumbing fixtures and a few shelves. Consequently, it seems like there's never enough space in this room for all we want to do. Modern appliances for grooming hair and teeth and products for pampering and soothing our bodies take up more space than is available in most baths.

At times, the plumbing installations will provide space. Examples of this include the typical bathroom lavatory which is usually enclosed by a vanity cabinet. Although the primary purpose is to hide the pipes, the cabinet can be fitted with shelves for additional bathroom storage. When making adaptations to such fixtures, be sure to use removable shelves or to position them so as not to interfere with the plumber's work.

Another example is the space directly above a standard toilet tank. As long as the tank top can be removed and the tank parts are accessible, the space above the toilet can be fitted with a shelving unit mounted to the wall. Perhaps you are installing a bathtub in a space that measures a little longer than the tub. You can use the leftover space to create a tub-side storage space, lined with redwood shelves if you need them. In short, look everywhere for dead space in your bathroom and put it to use.

Many older homes had built-in medicine cabinets fitted between the studs, a wise use of limited storage space. Take inventory of all your bathroom supplies and if you find that you can use more of this narrow space, knock out an interior wall between two studs and install a built-in shelving unit or cabinet, as shown in this chapter. Be careful, though, not to break into a wall where plumbing, heating ducts, or electrical equipment are installed and not to cut into a structurally vital wall.

Also be sure to utilize any structural quirks in your bathroom. Two facing walls located very close to each other are a natural place to put a shelving unit. For such a project, you should always check the wall materials first, in the planning stages, and use the proper fasteners.

Choosing Suitable Materials.   Perhaps more than any other room in your home, your bath is subject to wetness and dampness. That's why it's important to use moisture-resistant materials. Purchase plywood made with waterproof glue, and subject to wetness and dampness. That's why it's important to use moisture-resistant materials. Purchase plywood made with waterproof glue, and moisture-resistant woods such as redwood, cedar, cypress, teak, and mahogany. Ensure the beauty of these materials by applying long-lasting finishes, such as spar varnish or enamels. Countertops and other horizontal surfaces should be covered with plastic laminates to make them resistant to spills and splashes.

Other materials that are excellent for bathroom storage projects are acrylic plastic, metal, and glass. Acrylic in clear, opaque, or solid colors can be incorporated into projects that are primarily wood, or it may be used as the primary material. Aluminum, chrome-plated, or brass-plated hardware will stay free from rust for longer periods than other metals. They give your bath a shiny and gleaming appearance. Glass and mirrors should be used freely, since they give us plenty of 'self-image space' and help to psychologically enlarge small rooms.

As always, don't neglect to check home improvement stores, catalogs, and magazines for other ideas and materials. There are so many ready-made units that require merely a screwdriver for easy assembling and mounting. Plastic stackable bins afford you inexpensive, easy-to-move, and easy-to-clean storage. These might come in colors to coordinate with your bath's decor. Don't forget to use wall and door space for towel bars, rings, hooks, racks and pockets.

WARNING :

Use these safety tips for planning and using storage units:

1.   The bathroom is often a tiny space where people are prone to slip and tumble; so, in your designs, avoid sharp corners on any projecting piece. Try to plan your projects so that items will be easily within reach.

2.   Avoid storing important items up high, where reaching for them could cause a fall.

3.   Keep dangerous substances like cleaning supplies and medications, and sharp objects like scissors and razors well beyond the reach of small children.

4.   Most importantly, if you have children in the home, keep electrical appliances stored far away from outlets and standing water. (For extra protection from electrocution, install a Ground Fault Circuit Interrupter, a special receptacle that serves as a safety device.)

5.   Once all your storage projects are built or installed, work at keeping this room neat and free of clutter, a good way to prevent accidents.

PROJECT/Spare Towel Rack

There's always a need for a spare towel or two in a bathroom, and rarely a place to hang one. To solve this problem, consider building this simple rack. It will mount to almost any unused wall space, or even the back of a door.

1. Decide where you want to mount the rack, and measure the available space. This will determine the dimensions of the finished rack.

2. Cut the parts of the rack to size. Drill holes in the sides to mount the dowels, and round the corners, as shown in the *Side View.*

3. Finish sand all the parts of the rack, and assemble them with finishing nails and glue. When the glue dries, apply a finish to the rack.

4. Mount the rack where you want it. If you're mounting it to a wall, secure the rack with flathead wood screws (to frame studs) or molly anchors (to the hollow spaces between the studs). If you want to attach it to a door, secure it with wood screws (to a solid door) or panel adhesive and wood screws (to a core door).

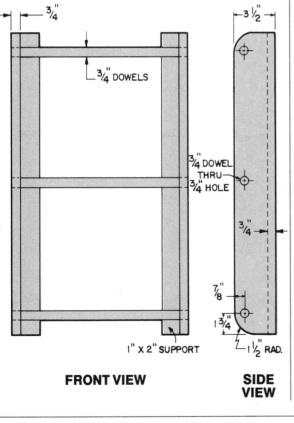

FRONT VIEW

SIDE VIEW

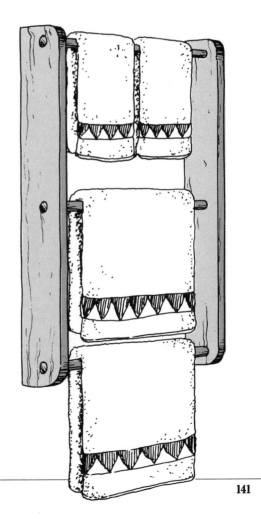

PROJECT/Bathroom Display Shelves

Some bathroom items deserve to be displayed rather than hidden away in vanities and closets: colorful, aesthetic bottles of perfume and cologne; well-crafted shaving and hair-care accessories, colorful towels and washcloths. For those things that you want to be seen rather than hidden, make a simple set of display shelves.

1. Measure the wall space where you plan to mount the shelves. If necessary, adjust the dimensions on the plans, so that the completed project will fit the space.

2. Cut all the parts to size, with the exception of the bead molding. (This molding is available at most lumberyards and building supply centers.) The molding must be fit to the shelving unit *after* it's assembled.

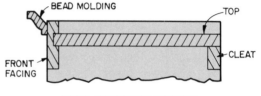

TOP JOINERY DETAIL

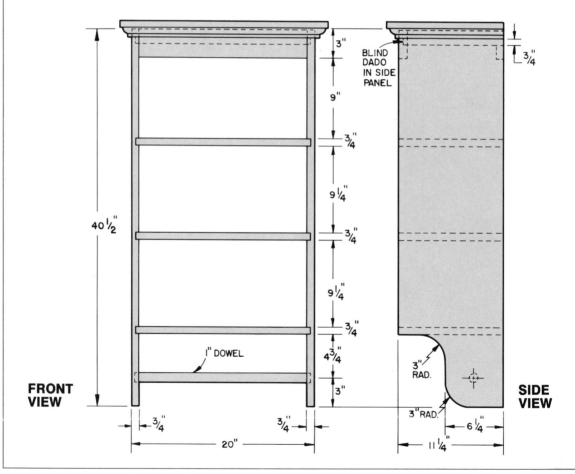

FRONT VIEW

SIDE VIEW

INCREASED ORGANIZATION IN THE BATHROOM

EXPLODED VIEW

6. Cut the molding to fit around the top of the shelving unit. Miter the ends where the front molding meets the side moldings. Attach the moldings to the shelves with glue and finishing nails.

7. Finish sand any parts of the shelving unit that still need it, and apply a finish.

8. When the finish dries, mount the completed project to the wall, using screws and molly anchors. Where you can attach it directly to a frame stud, drive flathead wood screws through the cleat and into the stud. Where you must mount the unit between the studs, use molly anchors.

3. Cut or rout the dadoes in the sides, then drill the holes for the towel bar. After you have made the joinery, use a band saw or sabre saw to cut the shapes of the sides.

4. Test-fit the parts to make sure they fit properly. *Don't* glue them up just yet.

5. When you're satisfied that the parts fit as they should, finish sand all surfaces. Assemble the shelves with glue and finishing nails.

PROJECT/Diagonal Shelving

While towels and linens are traditionally stored in vertical stacks on horizontal shelves, this may not be the best way. Stacks of towels tend to fall over, and a few toppled stacks will make a mess out of your bathroom linen closet. To solve this problem, consider making a *diagonal* shelving insert for the closet. (If you don't have a linen closet, the insert can hang on the wall or rest on a counter.) The stacks can't topple over—they've already toppled, in a sense. Paradoxically, that's what keeps the stacks of towels neat in this non-traditional shelving unit.

1. Measure the space where you want to put the diagonal shelving. Will it be an insert in a closet? Or will it be mounted somewhere else in your bathroom? If necessary, adjust the dimensions on the plans so that the completed unit will fit the space available.

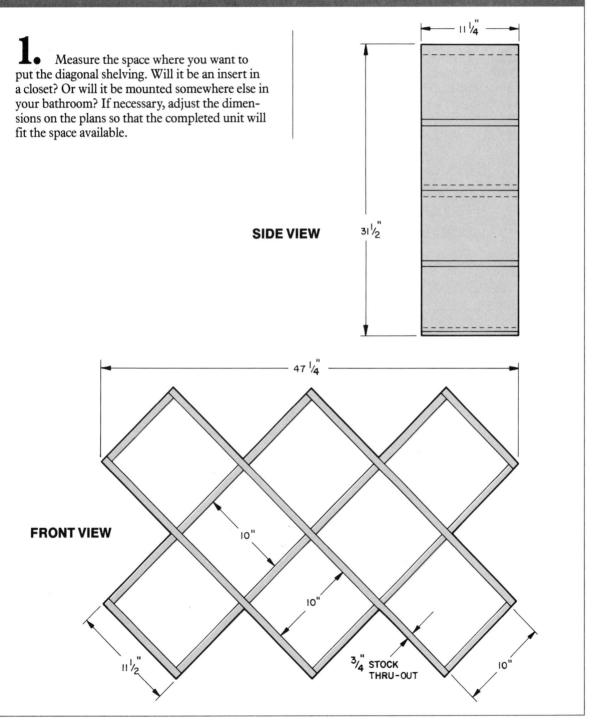

SIDE VIEW

FRONT VIEW

$11\frac{1}{4}$"

$31\frac{1}{2}$"

$47\frac{1}{4}$"

10"

10"

10"

$11\frac{1}{2}$"

$\frac{3}{4}$" STOCK THRU-OUT

PROJECT/Diagonal Shelving/Cont'd.

2. Cut all the parts to size, as shown in the drawings. Note that several of the longer boards must be 'trimmed', so that the pieces will fit together properly.

3. The diagonal shelves fit together with lap joints, like the dividers in an egg carton. Cut the long edges of the lap joint slots with a handsaw, then remove the waste with a chisel.

4. Test-fit the parts of the shelving unit, but don't glue them together at this time. The lap joints should be snug, but not too snug. If a joint is too tight, enlarge the slot slightly. If it's too loose, remake the piece.

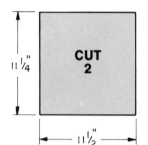

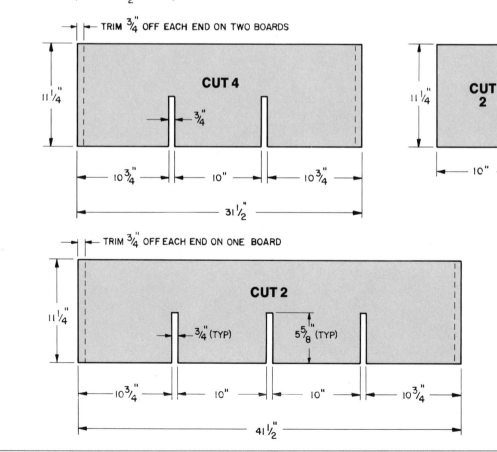

5. When you're satisfied with the fit of the parts, disassemble them. Finish sand all surfaces, then reassemble the unit with glue and finishing nails.

7. Apply a finish to the completed project. When the finish dries, set the unit in place.

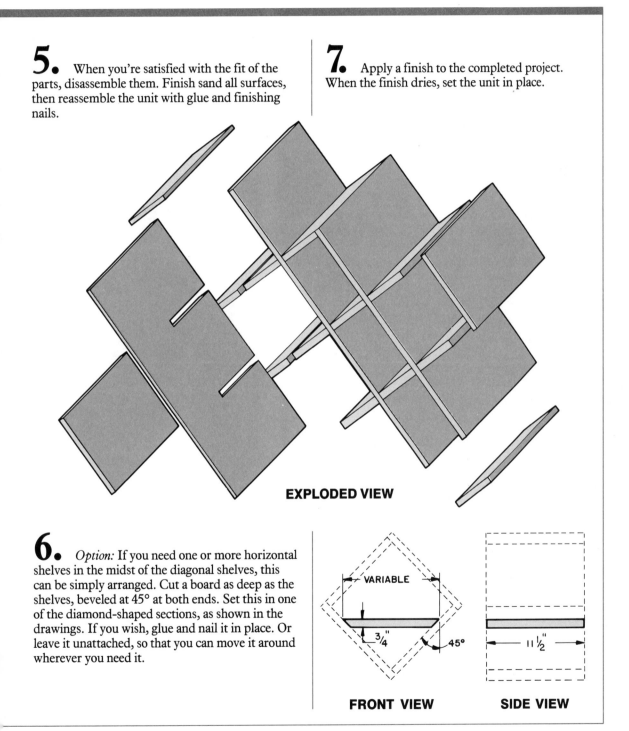

EXPLODED VIEW

6. *Option:* If you need one or more horizontal shelves in the midst of the diagonal shelves, this can be simply arranged. Cut a board as deep as the shelves, beveled at 45° at both ends. Set this in one of the diamond-shaped sections, as shown in the drawings. If you wish, glue and nail it in place. Or leave it unattached, so that you can move it around wherever you need it.

VARIABLE

3/4"

45°

11 1/2"

FRONT VIEW

SIDE VIEW

PROJECT/Medicine Caddy

Among the smallest items you store in your bathroom are medicines. These come in small, short containers that are rarely tall enough to occupy all the space on a shelf inside a wall vanity. As a result, there's a lot of wasted space in the vanity above these short containers. To remedy this, build a 'medicine caddy' to store and organize all those tiny bottles on just one shelf.

1. Consider the medicine that you regularly store in your bathroom. How large are the bottles? How many different sizes? If you built this caddy, how many shelves should it have? What is the spacing between the shelves? How will it fit in your wall vanity? How will you keep the medicines safe from children? The answers to all the questions will determine the dimensions of the caddy and where you put it.

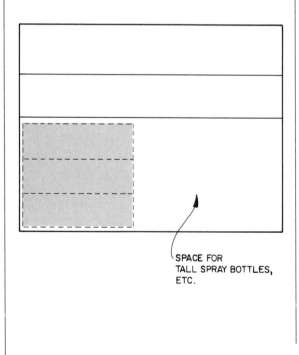

SPACE FOR
TALL SPRAY BOTTLES,
ETC.

2. Cut the parts of the caddy to size. Cut or rout dadoes in the sides for the shelves, then drill stopped holes to hold the dowels.

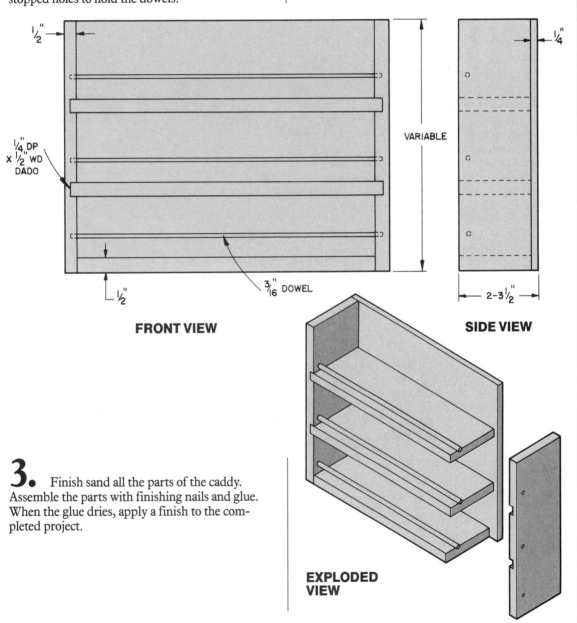

$\frac{1}{2}''$

$\frac{1}{4}''$ DP x $\frac{1}{2}''$ WD DADO

VARIABLE

$\frac{1}{2}''$

$\frac{3}{16}''$ DOWEL

FRONT VIEW

$\frac{1}{4}''$

2-3$\frac{1}{2}''$

SIDE VIEW

3. Finish sand all the parts of the caddy. Assemble the parts with finishing nails and glue. When the glue dries, apply a finish to the completed project.

EXPLODED VIEW

PROJECT/Recessed Bathroom Shelves

Sometimes the only space you have available for extra storage is *in* the wall, between two studs. Wall vanities or 'medicine cabinets' are commonly mounted in a bathroom wall, for example. The space between the studs also makes a good place to build small shelving units. Here's how:

1. Locate the studs in the wall. Drill a ½"-diameter hole in the wall and probe into it with a wire. By angling the wire one way or the other, you'll eventually feel it hit a stud. By marking how much wire you had to feed into the wall to hit the stud, you can calculate how far the stud is from the hole. The other stud, on the opposite side of the hole, will probably be either 14½" or 22½" away from the first stud, since studs are normally spaced 16" or 24" on center.

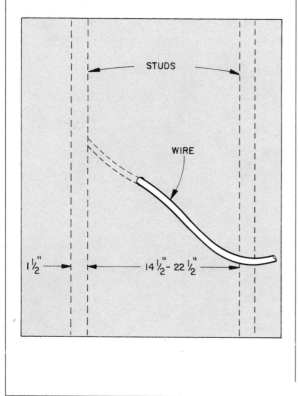

2. Having located the studs, outline the opening you want to make in the wall. Use a level to get the top and bottom lines horizontal, and the side lines vertical. Trace the wiring and the plumbing in this section of the wall to determine if there is a possibility you will run into any wires or pipes. (Remember to check the opposite side of the wall for electrical outlets and faucets. If you find any, use another part of the wall to build your shelves.) For safety's sake, turn off the water and the electrical breakers before you cut.

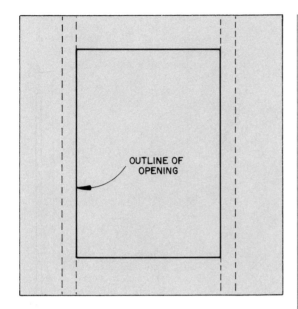

OUTLINE OF
OPENING

3. Drill a series of holes along one of the lines that you've marked on the wall. Insert a saw in these holes, and cut along the lines to remove the section of wall where you want to put the shelves.

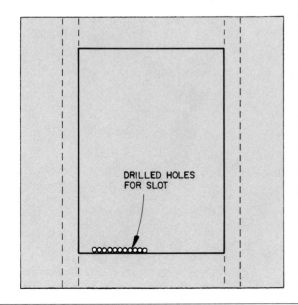

DRILLED HOLES
FOR SLOT

4. Using a carpenter's square, draw lines on the studs inside the wall, level with the bottom of the opening. Repeat this procedure at the top of the opening.

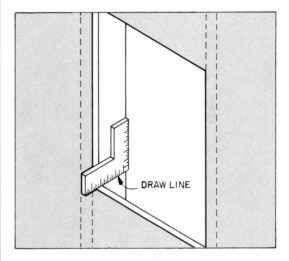

DRAW LINE

5. Cut 1 x 2 cleats 3½″ long, or as long as the studs are wide. Fasten them to the studs so the edge of the cleat is flush with the opening.

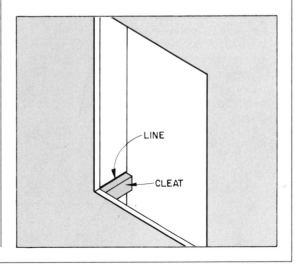

LINE

CLEAT

6. Cut a panel of ¼″ plywood to fit snugly at the back of the opening. Apply panel adhesive to the back of this piece, rest it on the cleats, and press it into place against the back of the opening.

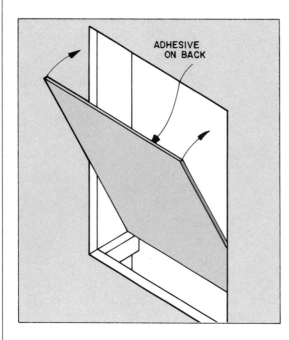

ADHESIVE ON BACK

7. Cut a top and a bottom from ¾″-thick stock to the same width and depth as the opening. Include the thickness of the wall material so that the edges of these pieces will be flush with the surface of the wall when you install them. Put the *bottom* in place and nail it to the cleats. Don't install the top yet.

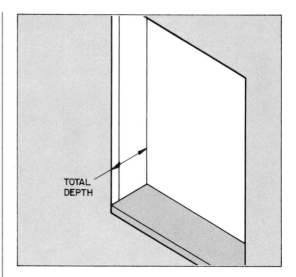

TOTAL DEPTH

8. Determine the length of the side panels. Measure from the top of the opening to the bottom piece that you have just installed, and subtract ¾″. The width of these panels should be the same dimension as the depth of the top and bottom panels. Cut the side panels accordingly.

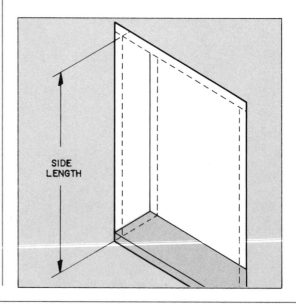

SIDE LENGTH

9. Clamp the two sides together and drill ¼″-diameter holes for the shelf support pins. (You can also use other types of hardware or joinery to support the shelves.)

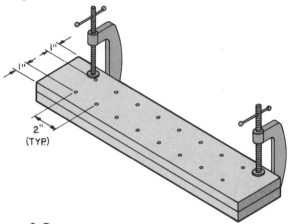

2″
(TYP.)

10. Glue and nail the top to the two sides. Insert this assembly in the opening, and nail the sides to the studs.

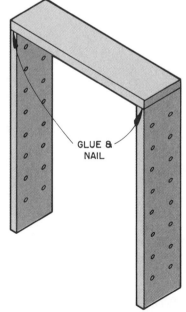

GLUE &
NAIL

11. Attach 2″-wide flat molding around the edges of the recessed shelving unit, to hide the ragged edge where you cut the opening in the wall. Cut the shelves and put them in place, supporting them with pins at the heights you want.

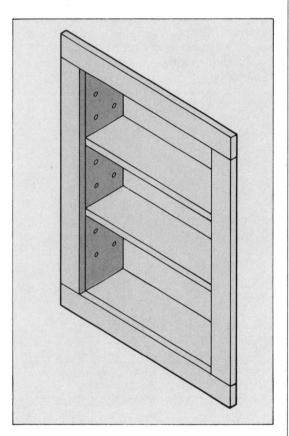

12. *Option:* If you wish, make doors for the shelves. You can use commercially-available shutters for these doors, or make your own.

PROJECT/Vanity Bins and Shelves

The purpose of most bathroom vanities is to enclose the sink and its pipes. This effectively disguises the plumbing and makes it easier to keep the bathroom clean. It also creates storage space under the sink, although most of that space is wasted. Vanities are usually 28″ to 30″ tall, and the things you keep in them—spare towels, soap and shampoo, hair dryers, and so on—are never that large. This space can be more efficiently used if you divide it up with sliding trays and shelves, as shown here.

1. Measure the available space inside your vanity, taking into consideration the plumbing. With this in mind, decide what items you want to store under your vanity, and how you want to store them. There are two storage units shown here— bins and shelves. *Important:* Remember, because the pipes sweat, this space may be somewhat damp. Don't plan to store anything under a vanity that could be damaged by the moisture.

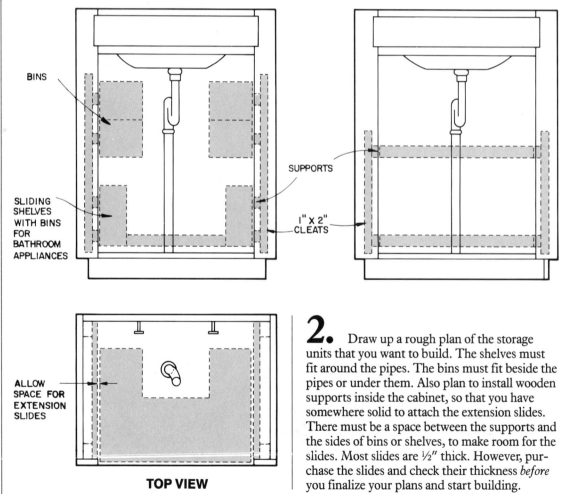

BINS

SLIDING SHELVES WITH BINS FOR BATHROOM APPLIANCES

SUPPORTS

I″ x 2″ CLEATS

ALLOW SPACE FOR EXTENSION SLIDES

TOP VIEW

2. Draw up a rough plan of the storage units that you want to build. The shelves must fit around the pipes. The bins must fit beside the pipes or under them. Also plan to install wooden supports inside the cabinet, so that you have somewhere solid to attach the extension slides. There must be a space between the supports and the sides of bins or shelves, to make room for the slides. Most slides are ½″ thick. However, purchase the slides and check their thickness *before* you finalize your plans and start building.

3.
Build the bins and shelves you need. The bins have an open side, enclosed only by dowels, so that you can see what is stored in them. The shelves are bordered by a 1 x 1 lip, so that items won't fall off when you pull the shelves out of the cabinet.

½" STOCK THRU OUT

¼ DOWELS

SIDE VIEW

FRONT VIEW

SLIDES

EXPLODED VIEW

BIN

PROJECT/Vanity Bins and Shelves/Cont'd.

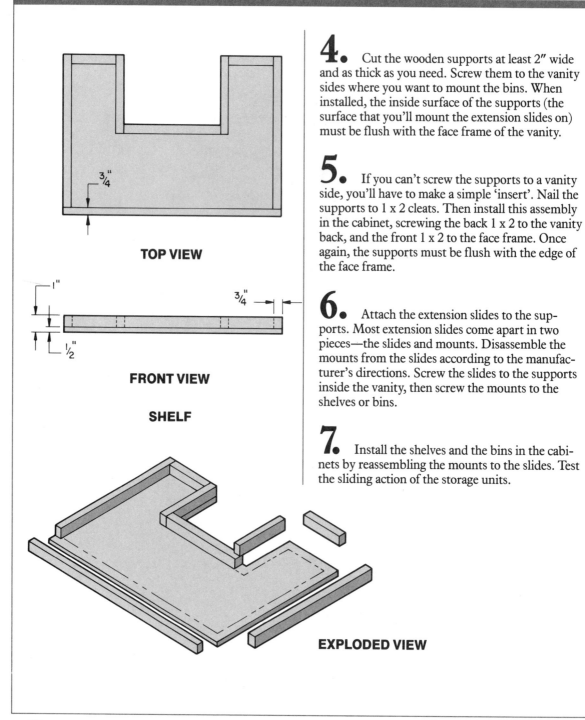

TOP VIEW

FRONT VIEW

SHELF

EXPLODED VIEW

4. Cut the wooden supports at least 2″ wide and as thick as you need. Screw them to the vanity sides where you want to mount the bins. When installed, the inside surface of the supports (the surface that you'll mount the extension slides on) must be flush with the face frame of the vanity.

5. If you can't screw the supports to a vanity side, you'll have to make a simple 'insert'. Nail the supports to 1 x 2 cleats. Then install this assembly in the cabinet, screwing the back 1 x 2 to the vanity back, and the front 1 x 2 to the face frame. Once again, the supports must be flush with the edge of the face frame.

6. Attach the extension slides to the supports. Most extension slides come apart in two pieces—the slides and mounts. Disassemble the mounts from the slides according to the manufacturer's directions. Screw the slides to the supports inside the vanity, then screw the mounts to the shelves or bins.

7. Install the shelves and the bins in the cabinets by reassembling the mounts to the slides. Test the sliding action of the storage units.

8

Uncluttering Family Work and Play Areas

Living rooms, great rooms, recreational rooms, dens and playrooms...whatever they're called, these are the spaces where there is plenty of activity going on. Often, too, there are many people sharing the space. Books, magazines, toys, games, paperwork, albums, cassettes, prized collections, sporting equipment—all the above and more pile up almost overnight as we struggle to 'get a handle on it'.

For the people who can weed through such items regularly and keep their shelves and cabinets lean and clean, this isn't a problem. But for the savers and hoarders, it seems like the only solution is to buy a new, larger home. When your family work and play areas begin to fill up, you'll find a screaming need for new storage systems. Here,

you'll find several ideas for new storage solutions. But don't forget there are many kinds of specialty hardware available from which you can make your own projects and there are also many ready-made and easy-to-assemble kits on the market.

The projects in this chapter solve a variety of different problems. Perhaps the most recent storage crisis to hit the home is what to do with the home computer and all the peripherals? We've designed a simple-to-build computer desk that can be easily adapted to your system. The portable 'game file' will end your woes about where to put, and how to easily get to, board games. For those of you with a large picture window, there's a window seat that doubles as a chest for storing toys, blankets, almost anything.

The Need for Neatness

Both work and play activities involve the use of many materials, and often there is a need to store them when they're not in use. Living areas are the places where everything from firewood to home

movie equipment might be stored. (Note: In this chapter, we will *not* discuss specific work areas, such as laundry rooms, woodworking shops, and the like. You'll learn about those in later chapters. Here the primary focus will be on desk work.

Traditional pieces of furniture come to mind.

Toy chests, desks, file cabinets, and bookshelves all provide obvious storage spaces for the items intended to be housed there. There are also specialty items—magazine racks, hall trees, little organizers for keeping keys sorted, pencil holders and the like.

Ready-made storage units are widely available in department and furniture stores. Often called 'entertainment centers' or 'wall systems', these are shelf-cabinet combinations with special features such as concealed holes in their backs for the routing of electrical wires. Often these are large, attractive pieces of furniture that require a long wall for placement. For more versatility, you can purchase modular systems. Available at furniture, home improvement, and unfinished wood stores, these can be mixed and matched to conform to your storage needs. Modules can also be rearranged to suit your decorating whims, and they will prove to be very adaptable as you move them from room to room and house to house.

Solving a storage problem might be a matter of filling a space that a standard store-bought unit will not fill properly. Or it might involve making a custom-built unit for a lower price than you would have to pay for a comparable ready-made piece. For example, if you have extremely limited living space, you can make a bench seat with a lid that opens up to serve as a storage chest. Whatever the reason—making your own projects assures you an unlimited choice of materials and sizes.

Here are just a few quickie solutions that you might consider:

■ Border sofas and loveseats, either on the ends or at the backs, with interesting shelving units.

■ In a recreational room, mount brackets for the support of flat cardboard storage boxes. In these you can store sporting goods, clothing, play materials, or hobby equipment. The boxes can be painted in attractive colors and labeled. Not quite shelves and not quite drawers, this project is exceptionally easy to complete.

■ Divide a large family room up into several work areas with stand-alone shelving. Not only does this add storage space, it gives your family members a feeling of privacy in a communal space.

■ Mount shelves high on the walls, 12″ to 15″ from the ceiling, all the way around a den. This makes use of otherwise unusable space to store and display keepsakes, trophies, collectables, and similar items.

To solve your particular storage problem, take an inventory, as we discussed earlier in this book. Refer to Chapter 4 on bookshelves and cabinets, as well as other projects in other chapters. Then begin brainstorming on your own, taking a good look around your living areas and imagining how wonderful it would be to have a designated storage spot for everything.

Hardware for Special Needs.   Hardware can be purchased to transform plain cabinets and shelves into special ones. For example, counterbalanced lid supports keep a lid raised until it is hand-lowered. Excellent for toy chests, these supports open and close without a bang or a pinch. Supports are available too, for the attachment of trays, such as those that 'pop out' of cedar chests or jewelry boxes.

You can purchase locks to keep desks and cabinets secure or hardware for the use of swinging-up shelves and worktables. Heavy-duty units are available for the support of typewriters or sewing machines. Even metal partitions for separating record albums are available; wire-like, these are simply inserted into drilled holes to create dividers. Although you might have to shop by catalog or at a store that caters to woodworkers, you'll find that just about any kind of hardware that you've seen on manufactured pieces is available.

Making Play Areas Handier.   If you're looking for ways to organize a purely recreational room, you might not wish to spend a lot of money on storage projects, or you might not be overly concerned about its attractiveness. If the area will be used specifically by children, incorporate their ideas in your plan and, of course, make the finished products safe and convenient for them. For example, for toddlers, you can make open bins with bottoms that slant to the rear. This aids them in keeping little toys, such as blocks, inside the bin.

Consider projects that involve recycling: use old orange and soda pop crates or old typesetting drawers for mini-shelves. Clean them and apply new finishes in stimulating colors, if you wish. Gather heavy, round ice-cream cartons and cover them with adhesive-backed paper. If you use anything metal, be sure to check the corners and edges for sharpness. Lightweight baskets are excellent organizers for children, as are plastic stackable bins; the latter are usually available in colors that catch little ones' eyes.

Don't forget about ready-made or home-built storage boxes; as long as the boxes aren't stacked too high or with heavy toys, these make excellent units that can grow up with the children. If a play area is large, then toys tend to become strewn further and further from their storage haven. Help youngsters out by providing them with movable storage units. Put casters on the bottoms of bins so they can roll the place to the toys rather than the toys to the place.

Making Work Spaces More Serviceable. Desks and worktables are the centerpiece of many work areas. These can be located in novel places in the home, such as under stairways, in former closets, and between bookshelves. Use special hinges and supports for pull-up or pull-down desks. This way, a part-time writing table can serve another purpose—covering up storage space. Little box-like pigeonholes create storage space, aid organization, and they are super-simple to build. Create these as simple modules and keep them portable, if you like, or fasten them to existing desk- and table-tops.

Build special shelves and adapt cabinet space for reference books, your telephone book, or a large atlas. Consider a lectern for a large dictionary. Convert a deep drawer to a two-tiered drawer with a sliding tray. This way you'll have two shallow storage spaces rather than one deep drawer. Purchase plastic drawer dividers or choose from a whole array of plastic desktop organizers—if you're satisfied with their appearance. These inexpensive office aids can help you and your family to better manage paperwork chores and studying.

Of course, there are many ready-made products available at home improvement, department, and furniture stores. Also shop at office supply stores which, these days, have styles to suit a wide range of tastes. Depending on your budget, you might also check used furniture stores for desks and cabinets that need touching up or minor repair work.

Tips for Storing Audio and Video Equipment. Televisions and some stereo components should have adequate ventilation so it's best to keep them out of cramped quarters or to use perforated panels on the backs of cabinets built for them. Receivers generate more heat than any other component; unvented, they can create enough warmth to blister a cabinet's finish. Stereo speakers, on the other hand, require no ventilation. Record albums and tapes should be stored nearby, but they are also susceptible to heat and, therefore, should be kept away from receivers, as well as heaters and windows.

If you wish to put the TV in closed storage when it's not being watched, consider placing it on a heavy-duty slide-out tray. To make it even more accommodating, mount a ball-bearing lazy susan on the tray so the TV can be swiveled in many directions.

This easy-to-build shelving unit serves many purposes. It's an entertainment center and a reference center, plus it's ideal for the display of decorative items.

PROJECT/Computer Desk

Personal computers can be an asset to home organization, since they store valuable information. Often, however, the 'friends of the user-friendly' invest in the equipment without realizing that the computer needs a special storage space. Of course, there are many kinds of computer desks and stands available at office supply stores and furniture stores. But if you want a specific look or a specific size, the best solution is to build a stand yourself.

1. Consider the configuration of your computer. Also consider the space where you want to set up the computer. Will the desk we show here work for you? Or do you need to change the measurements somewhat?

2. Cut the parts for the desk only. (You don't need to build the shelving unit at this time—it's optional.) Lightly sand the parts you've just cut.

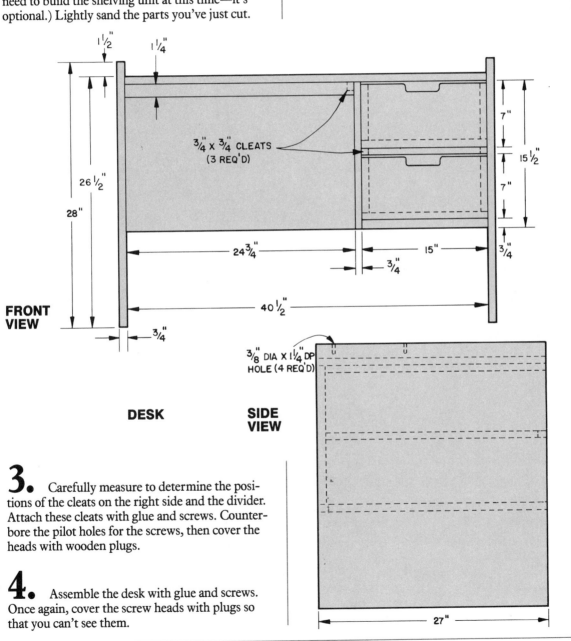

$1\frac{1}{2}$" $1\frac{1}{4}$"

$\frac{3}{4}$" x $\frac{3}{4}$" CLEATS
(3 REQ'D)

7"

$15\frac{1}{2}$

7"

$26\frac{1}{2}$"

28"

$24\frac{3}{4}$"   15" $\frac{3}{4}$

$\frac{3}{4}$"

$40\frac{1}{2}$"

**FRONT
VIEW**

$\frac{3}{4}$"

$\frac{3}{8}$" DIA X $1\frac{1}{4}$" DP
HOLE (4 REQ'D)

DESK   **SIDE
VIEW**

27"

3. Carefully measure to determine the positions of the cleats on the right side and the divider. Attach these cleats with glue and screws. Counterbore the pilot holes for the screws, then cover the heads with wooden plugs.

4. Assemble the desk with glue and screws. Once again, cover the screw heads with plugs so that you can't see them.

5. Cut the rabbets and the notches in the drawer fronts, then dry-assemble (assemble without glue) the drawer parts. Hold the parts together with masking tape. Test fit the drawers in the desk. If you're satisfied with the fit, remove the tape and reassemble the drawers with glue and finishing nails.

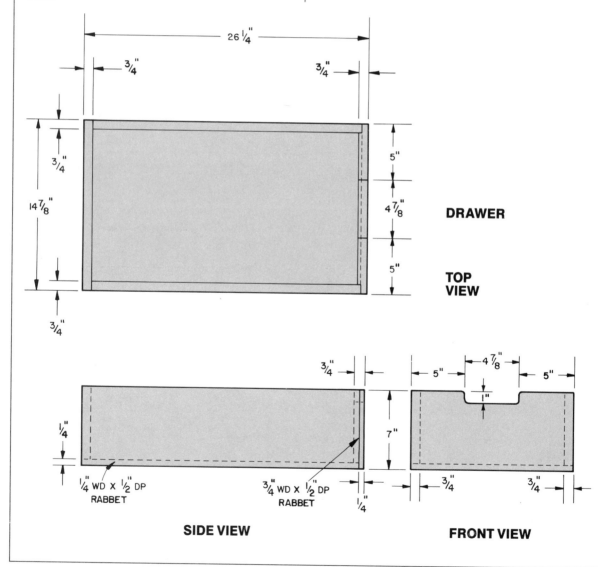

DRAWER

TOP VIEW

¼" WD X ½" DP RABBET

¾" WD X ½" DP RABBET

SIDE VIEW

FRONT VIEW

6. If you've made this desk from plywood, cover all the visible edges with veneer tape. This tape is available at most lumberyards and building supply centers. Trim the tape, and finish sand all the surfaces of the desk and drawers. Apply a finish to the completed desk.

**DESK AND DRAWER
EXPLODED VIEW**

PROJECT/Computer Desk/Cont'd.

7. *Option:* If you wish to make the shelving unit, first measure your computer components and consider how you want to stack them. This will determine the width and the height of the shelves.

8. *Option:* The wood you choose for the shelving unit should match the desk. You can use solid wood, but it should match the surface veneer of the desk plywood. Cut the parts for the shelves, and lightly sand them.

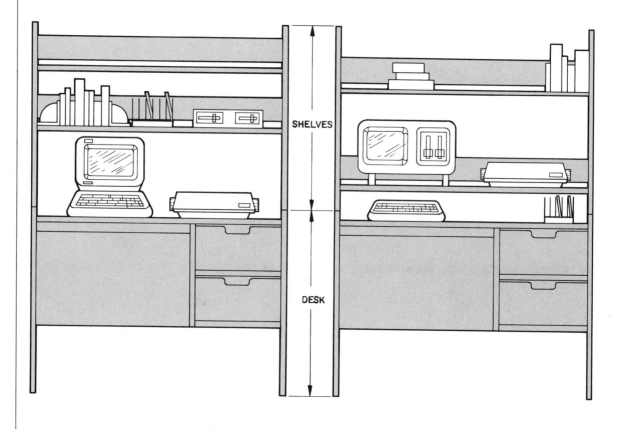

9. *Option:* Assemble the parts with glue and screws. Cover the screw heads with wooden plugs.

10. *Option:* Cover all the visible edges of the plywood with veneer tape, if necessary. Finish sand all surfaces, and apply a finish to the shelves.

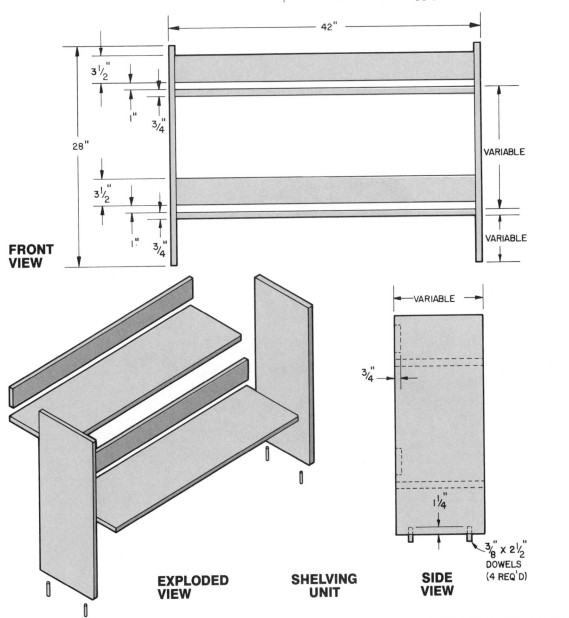

FRONT VIEW

42"

3½"

1"

¾"

28"

3½"

1"

¾"

VARIABLE

VARIABLE

VARIABLE

¾"

1¼"

⅜" x 2½" DOWELS (4 REQ'D)

EXPLODED VIEW

SHELVING UNIT

SIDE VIEW

PROJECT/Video Cart

A s your collection of videotapes grows, you'll want a handy place for storing them, close to the TV and VCR. This stand accomplishes that and more. It holds your portable television at the ideal viewing height on a stand that can roll about to suit your needs. It offers drawers of the exact dimensions for holding VCR tapes. Moreover, it's a fine-looking piece of furniture.

1. Be certain that your television and VCR will fit on the cart, as we have designed it. If not, adjust the dimensions so that they will.

2. If you're building this project from solid wood, glue up boards to make the wide stock you need for this project. Cut all the parts to size. If you're using plywood, cut additional trim parts from solid wood to hide the edges of the sides and shelves, and glue these to the plywood parts.

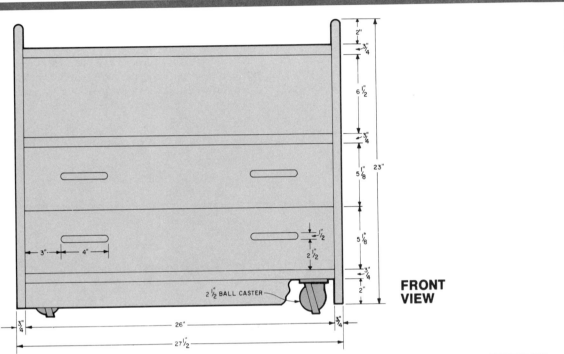

FRONT VIEW

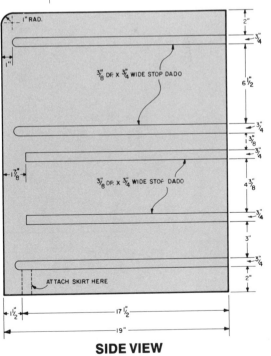

3. Cut or rout the dadoes in the sides. Note that the blind end of the dadoes for the shelves must be round. If you use a router with a ¾″ straight bit, the bit will leave the dadoes rounded. If you use a dado cutter, you'll have to round the dadoes with a chisel. After you make the dadoes, round the top front corners with a sabre saw.

4. Using a router, round over the front edges of the shelves, and the front and top edges of the sides. Finish sand all parts.

5. Test-fit the shelves to the sides. If you're satisfied with the fit, assemble the sides and the shelves with glue and screws. Counterbore the screws, then cover the heads with wooden plugs.

SIDE VIEW

UNCLUTTERING FAMILY WORK AND PLAY AREAS

PROJECT/Video Cart/Cont'd.

6. Cut the joinery in the parts of the drawer. As drawn, the front, back, and sides are joined with half-blind dovetails. You can make these joints with a router and a dovetail template. If you don't have these tools, you can instead use 'lock' joints. Lock joints can be made on your table saw. Cut grooves in the front, back, and sides for the drawer bottom. After you assemble the drawer, cut more grooves in the sides for the drawer guides.

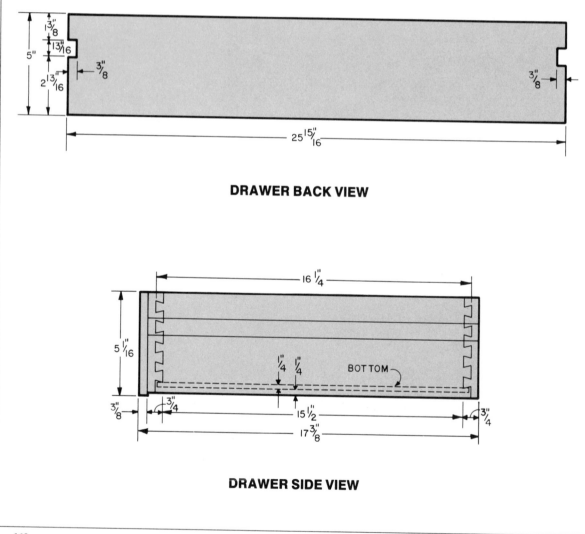

DRAWER BACK VIEW

DRAWER SIDE VIEW

7. Test-fit the drawer guides in their dadoes, and dry-assemble (assemble without glue) the drawer parts. Then test fit the drawer in the cart assembly. If you're satisfied with the fit of the parts, glue the drawer guides in place, and assemble the drawer with glue.

8. Finish sand any parts of the cart that still need it, then apply a finish. When the finish dries, wax the grooves on the sides of the drawers so that the drawers slide easily.

EXPLODED VIEW

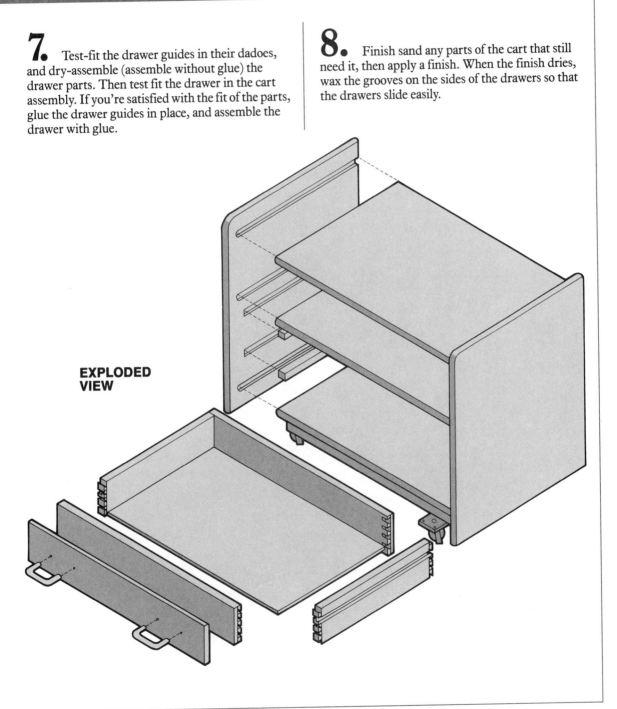

PROJECT/Cassette Racks

If you're a stereo or movie buff, you might find that your living quarters become filled with cassettes faster than you can find a place to put them. For audio and for videocassette recorder tapes, there are certainly many ready-made racks available—in molded plastic, simulated wood-grain or wood. If you want the cost of the inexpensive type but the looks of the more expensive models, make your own racks.

1. Decide whether you want to make these racks for audio cassettes or videocassettes. We show the measurements for both types.

2. Cut the parts to the sizes shown in the drawings. When you cut the shelves, bevel the front and back edges at 45°.

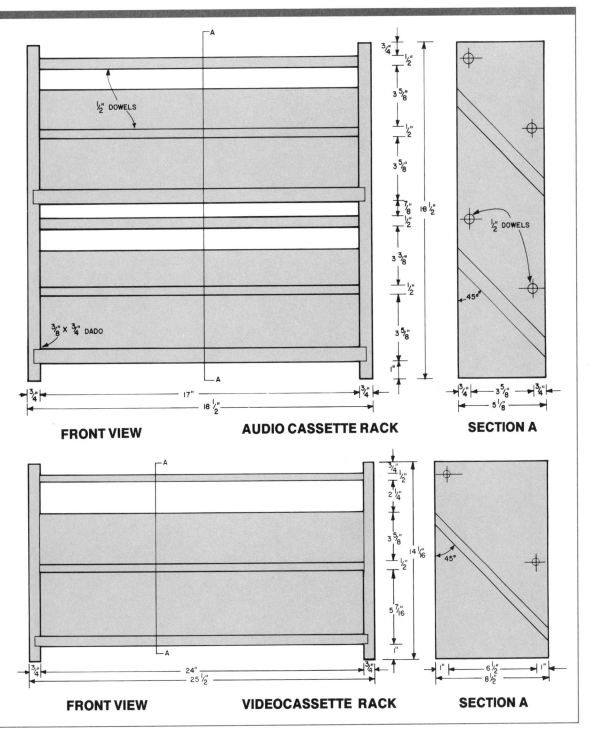

FRONT VIEW **AUDIO CASSETTE RACK** **SECTION A**

FRONT VIEW **VIDEOCASSETTE RACK** **SECTION A**

PROJECT/Cassette Racks/Cont'd.

3. Rout or cut dadoes in the sides for the shelves. Since these shelves are canted, the dadoes must be cut at a 45° angle. After making the dadoes, drill stopped holes in the sides for the dowels.

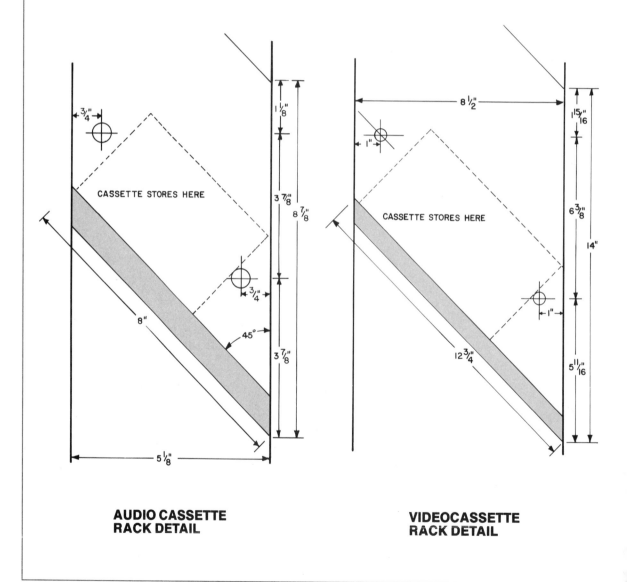

AUDIO CASSETTE RACK DETAIL

VIDEOCASSETTE RACK DETAIL

4. Test fit the parts of the cassette rack together. If you're satisfied with the fit, finish sand all parts and reassemble them with glue.

5. Finish sand any parts that may still need it and apply a finish to the completed project.

6. *Option:* If you need more than one of these racks, they will *stack,* one on top of the other. To keep them from shifting, pin the sides of the top rack to the bottom one with dowels.

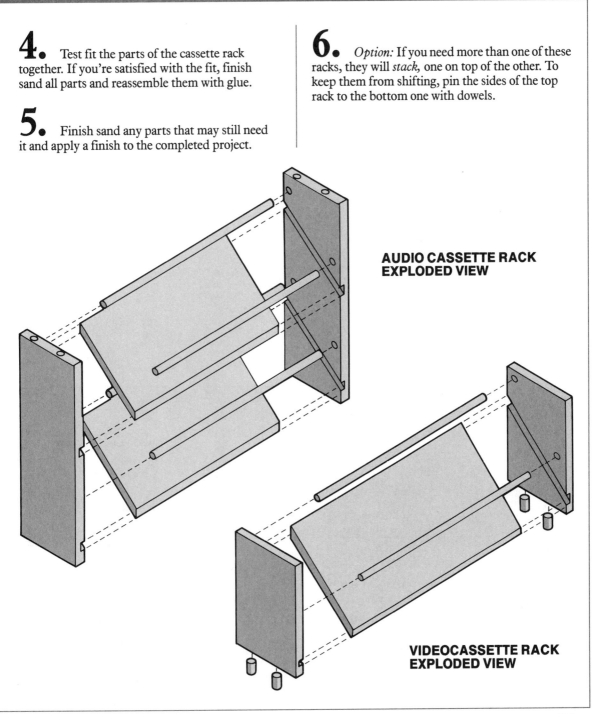

**AUDIO CASSETTE RACK
EXPLODED VIEW**

**VIDEOCASSETTE RACK
EXPLODED VIEW**

PROJECT/Window Seat

If you have a picture window, you probably also have a place where you can sit and enjoy it. This window seat, however, can be made to do double duty as a storage unit. This seat is actually a long chest that can be used to store linens, toys, and dozens of other items, both large and small.

1. Measure the length of your window. This will determine the length of the window seat.

2. Cut the parts of the chest to size (except for the moldings). If you use plywood, then you should also cut extra trim parts to cover the edges that would otherwise show. Glue these trim parts in place, and lightly sand all surfaces.

3. Assemble the front, back, ends, and bottom of the chest with glue and finishing nails. Set the nails, and cover the heads with wood putty. *Option:* Use square 'cut' nails, and don't cover the heads. This will give the chest an old-time 'country' look.

4. Cut the recesses in the base parts that form the feet. Then glue and screw the base parts together. Counterbore the pilot holes for the screws, then cover the screw heads with wooden plugs so that you won't see them.

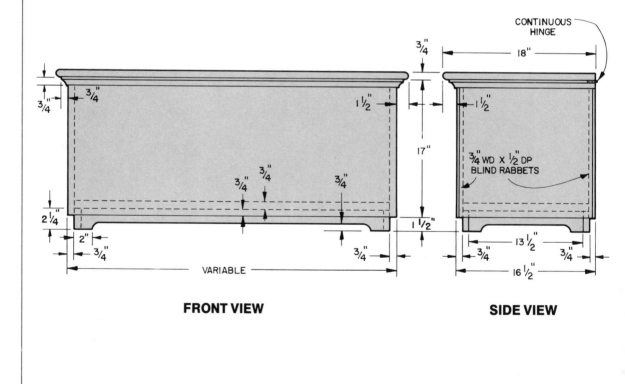

FRONT VIEW

SIDE VIEW

5. Attach the base to the chest with glue and screws. Drive these screws from the inside surfaces of the base into the chest. That way, they won't be visible on the completed project.

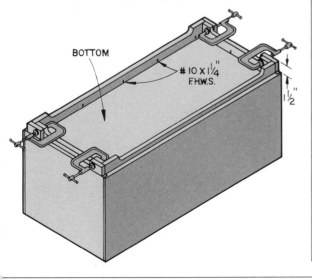

BOTTOM

10 X 1¼"
F.H.W.S.

1½"

6. Cut cove molding to length, and miter the ends where the molding meets. Attach the molding to the front and the sides of the chest by driving screws from the inside of the chest into the molding. The top edge of the molding must be flush with the top edge of the chest.

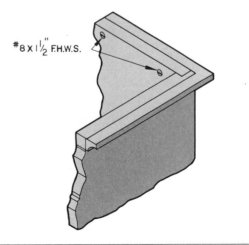

#8 X 1½" F.H.W.S.

7. Attach half-round molding or 'beading' to the front and side edges of the lid. Glue the molding in place, and reinforce it with finishing nails.

8. Hinge the lid to the chest with a continuous or 'piano' hinge.

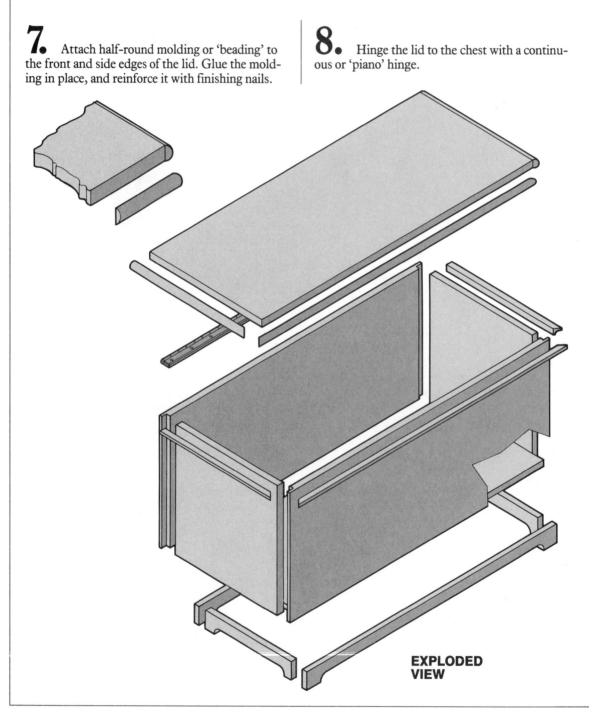

EXPLODED VIEW

9. *Option:* If you wish, you can make this window seat so that it opens at the front. To do this, make the front part ¾″ shorter than shown on the *Front View.* Also make a 1 x 1 strip the same length at the front part. Cut the front in half and don't cut the rabbet in the front edges of the ends. Instead, attach the front 'doors' to the chest with continuous hinges, and nail the 1 x 1 strip in place above the doors.

10. *Option:* Attach cleats to the underside of the lid. Note that the side and back cleats are 1 x 1's, but the front cleat is ¼″ taller than the rest. This will create a 'stop' for the doors. Attach the lid to the chest, driving screws through the cleats and into the ends, back, and front strip from the inside. Attach cove molding to the sides and front of the chest, just under the lid, with glue and finishing nails.

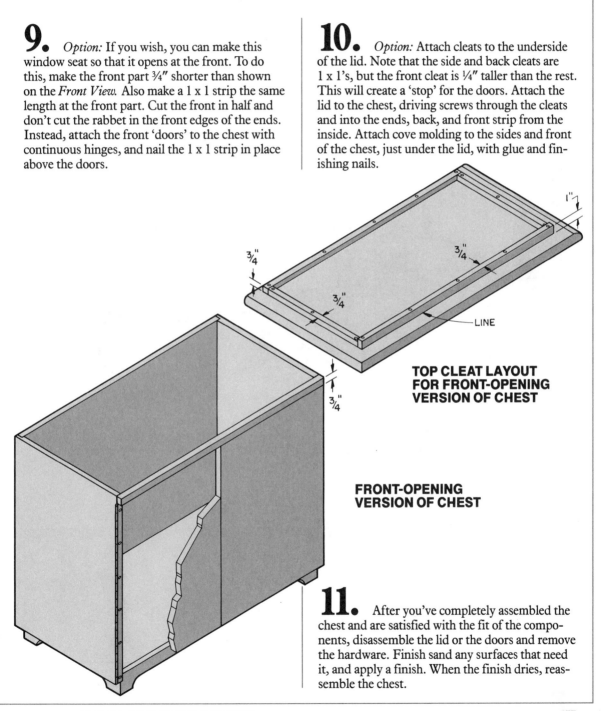

**TOP CLEAT LAYOUT
FOR FRONT-OPENING
VERSION OF CHEST**

**FRONT-OPENING
VERSION OF CHEST**

11. After you've completely assembled the chest and are satisfied with the fit of the components, disassemble the lid or the doors and remove the hardware. Finish sand any surfaces that need it, and apply a finish. When the finish dries, reassemble the chest.

PROJECT/Desktop Boxes

Small boxes offer wonderfully versatile storage. They can be stacked sideways like small shelves, or turned up like miniature bins. They can be used to sort office supplies, hold coins and coupons, display miniatures, or store thousands of other small items that would otherwise clutter your life. Best of all, they're easy and inexpensive to build.

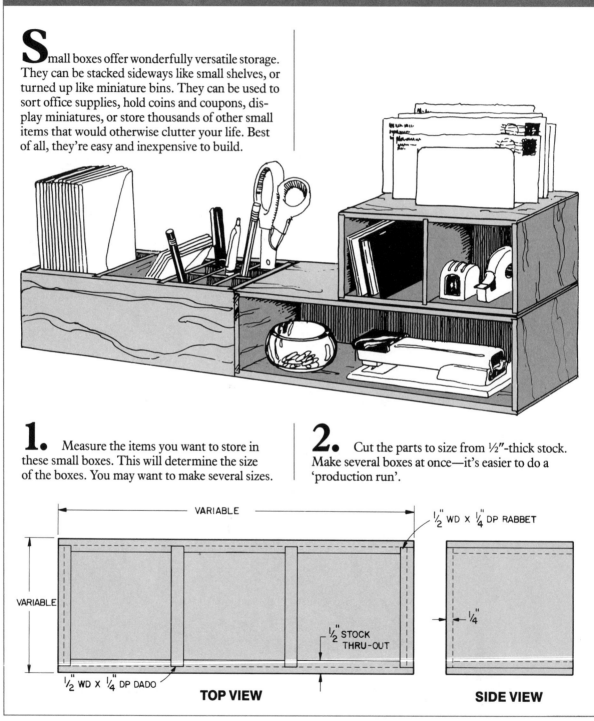

1. Measure the items you want to store in these small boxes. This will determine the size of the boxes. You may want to make several sizes.

2. Cut the parts to size from ½″-thick stock. Make several boxes at once—it's easier to do a 'production run'.

VARIABLE

½″ WD X ¼″ DP RABBET

VARIABLE

½″ STOCK THRU-OUT

¼″

½″ WD X ¼″ DP DADO

TOP VIEW

SIDE VIEW

3. Cut or rout the rabbets and dadoes in the sides and ends, then test fit the parts. If you're satisfied with the fit, finish sand the parts.

4. Assemble the parts with glue and brads. When the glue dries, apply a finish.

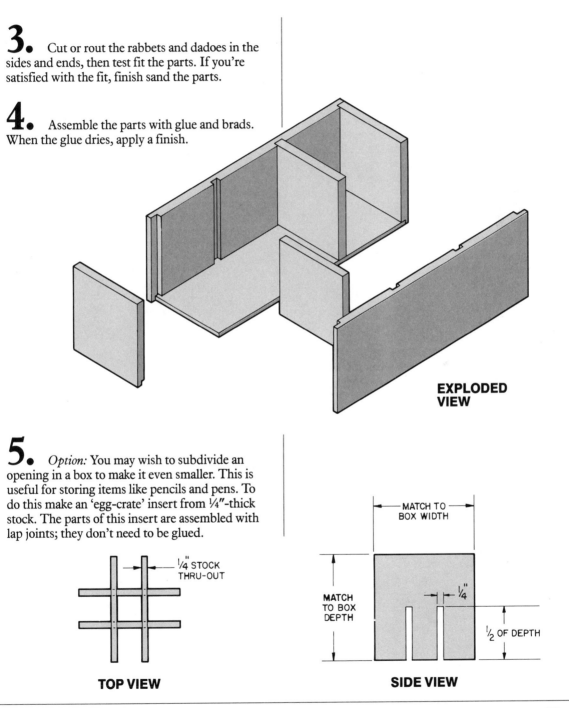

EXPLODED VIEW

5. *Option:* You may wish to subdivide an opening in a box to make it even smaller. This is useful for storing items like pencils and pens. To do this make an 'egg-crate' insert from ¼"-thick stock. The parts of this insert are assembled with lap joints; they don't need to be glued.

¼" STOCK THRU-OUT

TOP VIEW

MATCH TO BOX WIDTH

MATCH TO BOX DEPTH

¼"

½ OF DEPTH

SIDE VIEW

PROJECT/Game File

Board games are, traditionally, an excellent form of family entertainment. But what happens when family game time arrives? Sometimes it's more trouble to find the game and all its pieces than it is to calculate a good chess move. A search in the tops of closets and bottoms of toy chests sends a barrage of other stuff tumbling. When children decide to go on this treasure hunt, it can be exasperating if not downright dangerous. What's needed to solve this storage problem is a simple 'game file' for board games.

1. Decide how many games you want to store, then add a few more for future purchases. As shown here, our game file will hold twelve standard-sized board games—two per shelf. If you need it to hold more, simply make the case taller and add more shelves.

2. Cut the shelves from ¼" plywood, and the case parts from ¾" plywood. Make the lips at the front and the back of each shelf from quarter-round molding.

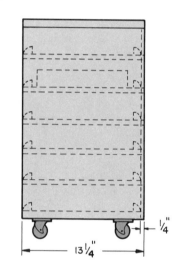

SIDE VIEW

13¼"

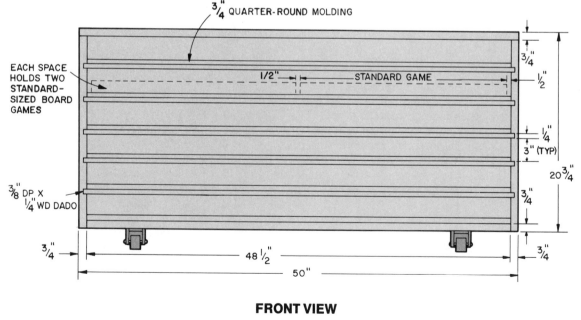

¾" QUARTER-ROUND MOLDING

EACH SPACE HOLDS TWO STANDARD-SIZED BOARD GAMES

½" — STANDARD GAME

¾"

½"

¼"

3" (TYP)

20¾"

¾"

⅜" DP X ¼" WD DADO

¾"

48½"

50"

¾"

FRONT VIEW

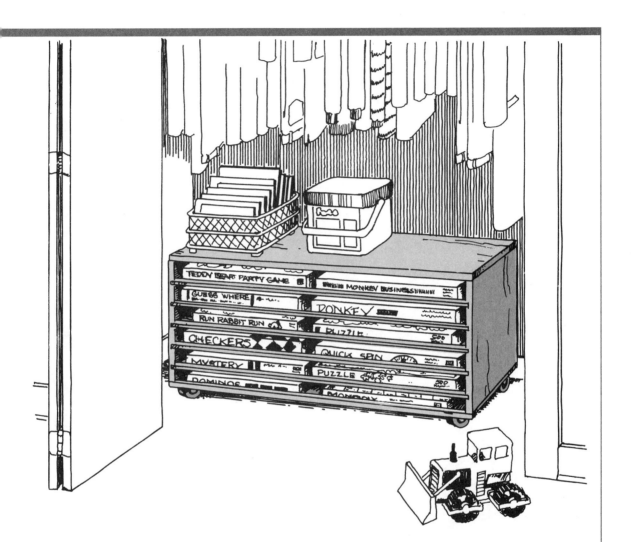

3. Rout or cut ¼″ dadoes in the sides. These sides will hold the shelves, so that they can slide in and out of the case.

4. Finish sand all the parts, and assemble the case with glue and screws. Use 'veneer tape' to hide the edges of the plywood on the front and sides of the case. (This tape is available at most lumberyards and building supply centers.) Notch the tape where you have applied it over the dadoes.

5. Glue the moldings to the shelves, and slide the shelves into the case. If the shelves seem tight, sand a little extra stock off the edges. You might also wax the edges of the shelves to ensure that they slide smoothly.

6. Finish sand any parts of the case that still need it, and apply a finish. If desired, attach casters to the bottom of the completed project to make it mobile.

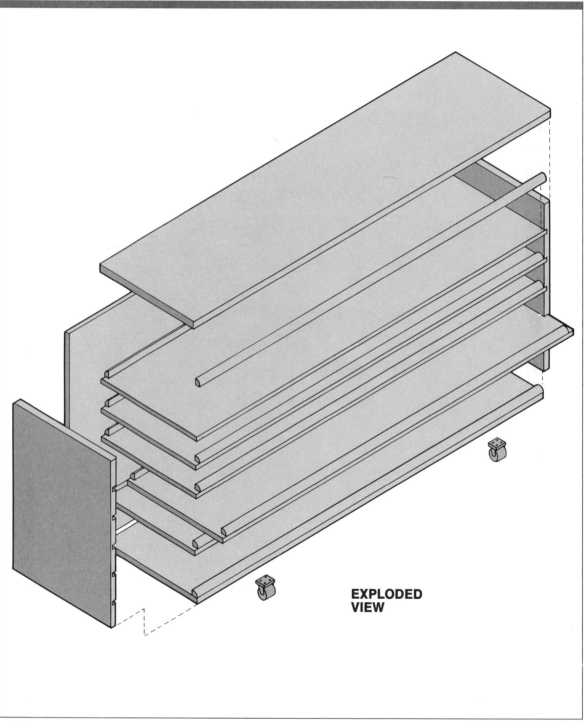

**EXPLODED
VIEW**

9

Utilitarian Storage — Attic, Garage, and Basement

These three spaces, though they might be located far from each other, have some common properties. For many families, they are used primarily for storage, since we don't, as a rule, live in these areas. They are usually 'unfinished', as are the storage units that you build for these areas. They do, however, need to be organized. Attic, garage, and basement units require as much careful planning as any other storage units.

Keeping things stored neatly in these areas will give you a sense of pride about your home being 'in order' and will eliminate the feeling that the space is off limits to visitors. Most importantly, when you want something, you'll be able to find it, without wading through stacked-up stuff and rooting through unmarked boxes.

Though each area presents unique problems, read the entire chapter to search for ideas; some can be used in two or more places. The "Stacking Storage Boxes" can be used in all three areas; so can the "Between-Joists Pocket Storage". If you need to solve a particular problem, borrow elements from this chapter—or elsewhere in the book —and combine several to create a unique solution.

Attics—Up and Away Storage Areas

Typically, items to be stored in an attic include seldom-used or even never-used things—luggage, clothes that have been outgrown or out-dated, holiday decorations, furniture that is no longer needed. What is stored in the attic depends on the amount of space available, not only in the attic, but in the other utilitarian areas. For example, if the house has no basement, then the attic and the garage will probably be used to a greater extent than otherwise. It may also depend on the *access* to the attic. You're more likely to store things in a walk-up attic than you are in an attic whose only entrance is a tiny hatchway in the ceiling of some closet. In any case, to give you an idea of what size storage units you may want to build, use the chart below to find the typical sizes of items that are commonly stored in the attic.

When you're considering using your attic as a storage space, the first thing that you should determine is whether or not the attic is finished. There are great fluctuations of temperature and humidity in unfinished attics, and you might first want to install insulation between the rafters and/or a ventilating fan. This will help protect the items you store there from extreme heat or coldness. (These installations also make your home more energy-efficient, so you should consider them no matter what your storage needs are.)

Once you have made such installations, however, you should still beware of storing certain materials in the attic—things that are liable to melt, crack or chip over an extended length of time. Especially vulnerable are items made of wax and older articles held together by glue.

Ideally, there will be a floor in the upstairs attic so that you can walk around on it, set things down on it, and mount storage shelves and bins to it. That's *ideally*. Often, especially in ranch-style homes, there will be a relatively tall space in the center of the attic, then the roof will slant downward to short walls (called *kneewalls*) or no walls, leaving some unusable space. Generally, too, these attics will not have floors.

Making usable floor space in an attic is a common problem. This, coupled with the need to insulate between the joists for energy conservation,

creates a double problem. How can a homeowner have an energy-efficient house (insulated between the attic joists) and still have an attic floor that can be walked upon? Here is a way to have both—and you don't have to be a finish carpenter to accomplish it:

1. Your ceiling joists will probably measure 6 to 8 inches high. The recommended amount of insulation in most areas of the country is 18 inches. Create 'pockets' for the insulation by attaching 2 x 4 vertical braces to the existing joists. These should measure exactly 18 inches high.

2. Install the insulation; once it is in place, run 2 x 4 'stringers' between the braces and parallel to the floor joists to create new joists. Attach these stringers flush to the tops of the vertical braces.

3. Over your newly-created joists, lay ½-inch plywood flooring. Make the flooring airtight and also, if you've raised the floor above your attic hatchway, line this opening with plywood to make sure that it too is airtight.

CAUTION:

Insulating materials irritate the skin, nose, eyes, and lungs. Therefore, take precautions by wearing gloves, goggles and a painter's mask when installing them. Also, do not cover with insulation anything that produces heat, such as recessed light fixtures and electric fans. If your insulating material includes a vapor barrier, peel this flammable sheet back 3 inches from chimneys, stovepipes, and flues.

If you decide not to put insulation between the attic floor joists, then you can simply lay plywood flooring over the existing bare joists. Depending on how the space is to be used, you may not even need to anchor the plywood down. Remember, however, that whoever uses the attic should be well aware that they might fall through a downstairs ceiling if they happen to tip over or step off the edge of one of these plywood sheets.

Attic Storage Tips. As mentioned earlier, attics often have tiny doors or hatches. Whatever you plan to do in your attic, think it through carefully. Will a sheet of plywood fit through the attic opening? If not, then what size must it be cut to? Answer these and similar questions before you're

---

Standard Sizes of Attic Items
(in inches)

Large Piece of Luggage	26 W x 20 H x 6¾ D
Shoe Box	7 to 14 W x 4 to 6 H x 13 D
Footlocker	30 W x 13 H x 17 D
Cardboard Storage Box	24 W x 11 H x 13 D

UTILITARIAN STORAGE—ATTIC, GARAGE, AND BASEMENT

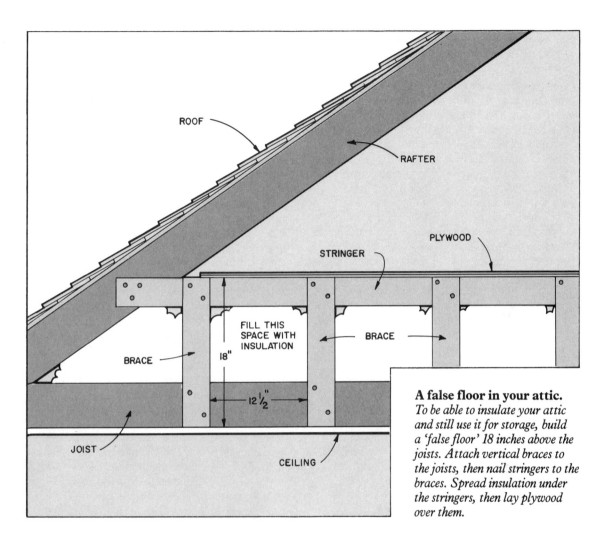

Labels within image:
ROOF
RAFTER
STRINGER
PLYWOOD
FILL THIS SPACE WITH INSULATION
18"
BRACE
12½"
BRACE
JOIST
CEILING

A false floor in your attic.
To be able to insulate your attic and still use it for storage, build a 'false floor' 18 inches above the joists. Attach vertical braces to the joists, then nail stringers to the braces. Spread insulation under the stringers, then lay plywood over them.

standing on the ladder trying to shove something through the hatchway, or before you've purchased a large storage trunk.

If the roofline is low, build triangular racks or specially shaped chests tucked under the sloping ceiling. If, instead, you have a walk-up attic with plenty of headspace, then you can revert to more conventional storage units. Buy inexpensive or used racks, bins, chests, and footlockers—and label everything. Leave plenty of space between items so you'll be able to easily see where things are located and retrieve them. Recycle and use all kinds of containers—shoe boxes, tins, cardboard boxes and shopping bags. If you want to keep items dust-free, save plastic sheeting and old

sheets for this purpose. To help you keep track of what's in the attic, group related objects together even if they're different shapes and sizes. Always label concealed items and, for a fool-proof system, prepare an inventory list. In a roomy attic, you can create your own monument to organization.

If the attic is tall enough, you can suspend rods across the rafters for hanging garment bags. Or mount shelves on the gable end wall. Another way to take advantage of a high roofline is to drive nails or hooks into the rafters and use them for hanging sporting equipment, clothes, and so forth. Home-improvement stores are filled with useful 'ready-mades' and hardware.

Surrounding the Hatch with Usable Units

Low-clearance attics often present a special problem—only the space within reach around the open hatchway is available for storing things. Objects at the back of this pile tend to get pushed back under the eaves. The solution? To keep your possessions from straying out of reach, put them in a series of boxes or shelves (like the stacking boxes or the rafter storage shelves shown later in this chapter) that surround the hatchway opening.

These projects will provide simplified and very accessible storage places for attics that have a hatchway opening. They eliminate the need for you to crawl into the attic. Even if you do have a walk-up attic, though, these boxes or shelves may be positioned on three sides of the hatchway. This gives you an easily accessible storage area for items that you need more often, but still lets you use the rest of the attic to store seldom-used articles. In this way, the attic isn't restricted, only enhanced.

The boxes or shelves can have shelves and partitions to separate what you plan to store in them. One or more of the boxes can have openings in a side or back through which long objects can protrude. If dust-proofing is a factor, the shelves can be enclosed or the faces of the boxes can be covered with flaps of clear vinyl held in place with Velcro® tape.

Gathering Things in the Garage

Generally, the garage is a hodge-podge space for storing sports and outdoor equipment, garden and workshop tools and various seasonal goods. Stuff to be stored in the garage can range from small to bulky, from lightweight to heavy. As always, the things to be stored will vary according to the life-style of your family and, also, how your home is built.

If a garage is detached, it will be less convenient than a garage connected to the house, and it will be more susceptible to weather. You might store outdoor clothing such as boots and rain gear in an attached garage, or goods that are sometimes used in the home, like cleaning supplies or insecti-

cides. You might even place an old but working refrigerator in this space.

Because they're usually at ground level and have wide doorways, garages have a wider assortment of things stored in them than other utilitarian areas. It's not easy hauling spare tires, step ladders, and lawn furniture up and down stairs or in and out of hatchways. And because this area is *so* accessible, sometimes household accumulations simply take over and cars must be parked in the driveway.

Garage organizers, shelves, and cabinets—although they should be well made—do not have to win awards for attractiveness. Here is an area where you can use inexpensive materials, as long as they're strong enough to do the job. Commonly used materials include plywood, particleboard, pegboard, simple hinges, and sturdy brackets for attaching racks of all kinds. And though many of the organizers that we show in this chapter are built into or attached to the structure of the garage, don't forget that you can also build free-standing units—things that you can rearrange if the need arises or take with you if you move. Consider making large units on casters to make them portable.

As always, begin planning the storage areas in your garage by taking inventory. Special items may require special treatment: Any potentially dangerous substances should be stored in a locked cabinet, especially if there are small children in the household. Avoid placing heavy items up high—in hard-to-reach places. Keep safety in mind as you make a plan for better garage storage.

Great Ideas for Garages.   As you look over your inventory, here are a few tips and ideas to consider: Store loose garden materials like potting soils and fertilizers in their bags in enclosed cabinets. Charcoal briquettes, bird seed, and dog food require extra protection from mice and moisture; place these in metal or plastic containers with tight-fitting lids. Bicycles that are stored for long periods are best kept hung on racks since leaving them on the floor gradually flattens and cracks the tires.

Exposed beams and joists are naturals for suspending racks of all kinds for hanging things. Suspended storage doesn't have to be fixed; consider using pulleys. You can build a platform that will be raised overhead by pulleys. This, however, should be used only for relatively light objects.

Long-handled implements like rakes and brooms can be hung on strategically-placed pegs or even long nails driven into wood strips. Our 'implement shelf', shown in this chapter, provides a shelf for small tools and a hanging storage for large ones in the same space.

If you plan on mounting a lot of pegboard and using metal hooks for the storage of rather large items, you might consider doing a brief study of relative costs. Pegboard and metal can add up, used in great quantities. A cost-saving option is to mount 1 x 3s to the frame studs. Drill these 1 x 3s so that you can insert wood dowels in them every 1 or 2 inches. Securely mounted and glued, these should adequately serve the same purpose as pegboard at a fraction of the cost.

Storage Down Below...
In Basements

Basements offer plenty of space but, because they are often humid, you may not be able to use this space to store certain items. If you can get rid of the dampness, then the space will be much more usable. The remedy may be simple—just install a dehumidifier. Or it may be more drastic—uncover the foundation walls and apply waterproofing materials. What you do (or what you can afford to do) to control humidity in your basement will partly determine what you can store in it.

If you store fabrics in the basement, take special precautions to combat mildew. Leave plenty of room for air to circulate around the cloth items. Ideally, units for storing clothing should be raised about 4 inches off the floor and furred out from the foundation wall at least 1 inch. Spread heavy plastic sheeting between the base of a storage unit and the concrete basement floor for extra protection against dampness. To get the clothes off the ground completely, suspend a rod between exposed pipes and hang garment bags from it.

When purchasing ready-made units, choose metal storage units over wood—metal won't swell in the high humidity. If you do use wood products for building storage units, make sure that you incorporate legs or supports in the designs. Concrete acts like a 'wick' for ground water. Any wood that contacts the concrete may become damp.

Utilizing Basement Space. Your basement may or may not be finished, and this will not only influence what you store in the basement, it will also determine how those projects look when you complete them. Storage units for a finished basement typically require more care than those for unfinished spaces. To get started, take an inventory of what is to be stored, and think about how you want the completed projects to look. Then consider some of the following ideas:

Many people use their basements for doing laundry or ironing. If this is the case at your house, consider storage for items relating to these chores, such as bins to sort soiled laundry, folding tables, and pull-down ironing boards. Create shelving units for all your laundry-care products and paint them in bright colors to perk up these 'dull-duty' spaces.

Built-ins can be attached to joists in the basement. Attach vertical stiles to the joists so that they run from the ceiling to the floor. Use these as supports for simple shelving. Shelves built in this manner can hold small to medium loads.

In order to attach shelves or cabinets to basement walls, explore these methods: Drill a hole in concrete with a carbide-tipped masonry bit and tap in a lead or fiber anchor; then drive a bolt or screw in. Another way is to use a hammer-activated stud driver to drive special nails or threaded metal studs into concrete. When working with concrete block walls, drill into the hollow space inside the blocks and use toggle bolts.

If you're storing food or drink, you'll find that some areas of your basement might be more ideal than others. Older homes with dirt-floor root cellars are wonderful for this purpose. Books on preserving foods will give you tips on how to transform spaces and build special storage units for certain types of foods. Install wine racks on outside walls; this will keep a vintage collection at the ideal temperature.

Look over the projects in this chapter, as well as those in other parts of the book, and put together the basement storage solutions that work best for you.

PROJECT/Rafter Storage

Whenever you can, use the structure of the house to help solve your storage problems. By attaching shelving and other storage units directly to the exposed frame, you can cut down on the time and the expense it takes to build a storage project.

These attic shelves hang from the attic rafters. Because the roof frame provides all the support, they are simple and cheap to make—just a few boards, some chain, and some hardware.

1. Measure the space available, and cut the shelves to the width and length you need. Light loads can be stored on ¾" plywood shelves. These shelves should be supported by chain every 32"- 36". Heavier loads must be supported every 16"- 24", or make the shelves from thicker stock. If you want, use inexpensive core doors for shelves that will support heavy loads.

2. Measure and cut the lengths of chain you'll need to support the shelves. Attach the upper end of each chain to the rafters with an eye screw and S-hook.

3. If you're hanging ¾″ plywood shelves, drill 1″ holes where you want the chain to go through the shelves. Insert the chain through the holes, then hold each shelf at the proper height with nuts and bolts. Pass each bolt through a link of the chain just below the shelf, and hold it in place with a nut.

4. If you've made the shelves from thicker stock or core doors, hang the shelves with lag bolts. Drive the bolts through links of the chain and into the ends of the shelves.

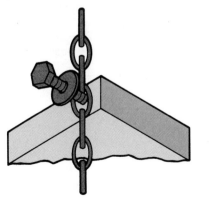

5. If you need to prevent these hanging shelves from swinging, secure the lower ends of the chain to the attic floor with eye screws and S-hooks.

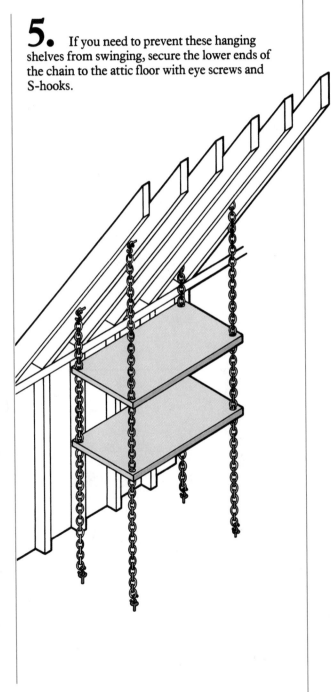

PROJECT/Over-the-Car Storage

If you have a one-car garage, you probably have room for a car and not much else. If you want to use the garage for storage, then the car is banished to the driveway.

There is, however, a way to have this particular piece of cake and eat it too. There's plenty of wasted storage space over the *hood* of your car. By building a set of wide, hanging shelves, you can make use of this space.

1. Pull your car in the garage, hood first. Measure the available area over the hood where you can build hanging shelves. If you need to walk around your car when it's in the garage, plan to hang the shelves 2'-3' away from the wall of the garage. This will leave a walkway in front of your car.

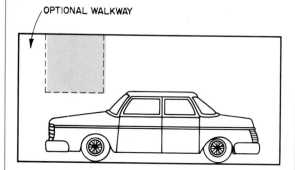

OPTIONAL WALKWAY

2. This shelving unit must be hung from the ceiling joists or roof rafters of the garage. In most garages, these will run side to side and you can simply bolt the shelving supports to them. However, if the joists or rafters run lengthwise, either nail 2 x 4 'purlins' between them or lay long 2 x 4's across them. Attach the shelving supports to these purlins or long 2 x 4's.

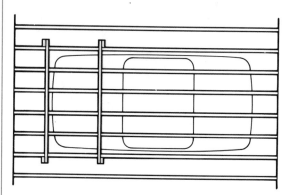

3. Cut shelving supports from 2 x 4 stock. Cut 1½"-wide, ¾"-deep dadoes in the supports where you will later mount the shelves. The spacing between the shelves is up to you; it should depend on what you plan to store on the shelves. Above each dado, drill one or two ¾"-diameter holes. These holes can hold dowel 'rails' to keep your stuff from sliding off the shelves. Secure the shelving supports to the garage frame with carriage bolts.

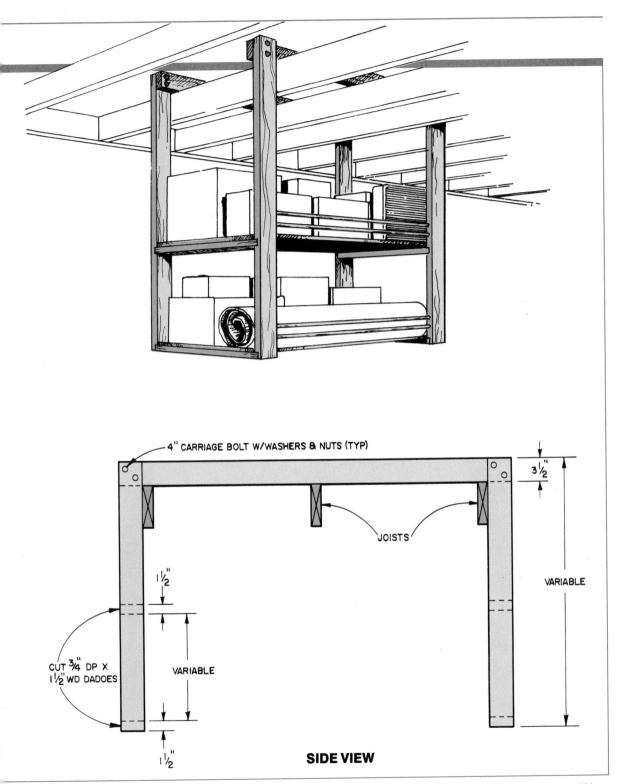

4" CARRIAGE BOLT W/WASHERS & NUTS (TYP)

$3\frac{1}{2}''$

JOISTS

VARIABLE

$1\frac{1}{2}''$

CUT $\frac{3}{4}''$ DP X $1\frac{1}{2}''$ WD DADOES

VARIABLE

$1\frac{1}{2}''$

SIDE VIEW

UTILITARIAN STORAGE—ATTIC, GARAGE, AND BASEMENT

4. Cut stringers from 2 x 4 stock. Fit these stringers in the dadoes between the shelving supports, and secure them in place with screws.

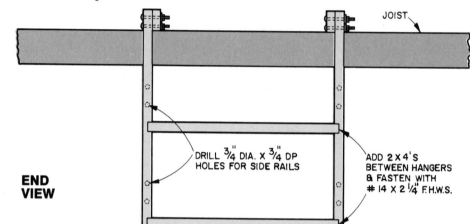

JOIST

DRILL ¾" DIA. X ¾" DP HOLES FOR SIDE RAILS

ADD 2 X 4'S BETWEEN HANGERS & FASTEN WITH # 14 X 2 ¼" F.H.W.S.

END VIEW

5. Cut ¾"-diameter dowels to length to make the rails. Insert them in the holes in the shelving supports—you may have to loosen or remove several of the carriage bolts that hold the shelving supports to do this. Cut sheets of ¾" plywood to size and lay them in place across the stringers to make the shelves. Secure these shelves to the stringers with 4d nails.

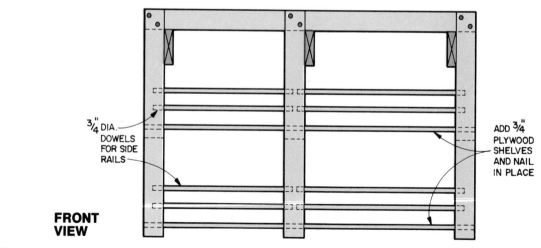

¾" DIA. DOWELS FOR SIDE RAILS

ADD ¾" PLYWOOD SHELVES AND NAIL IN PLACE

FRONT VIEW

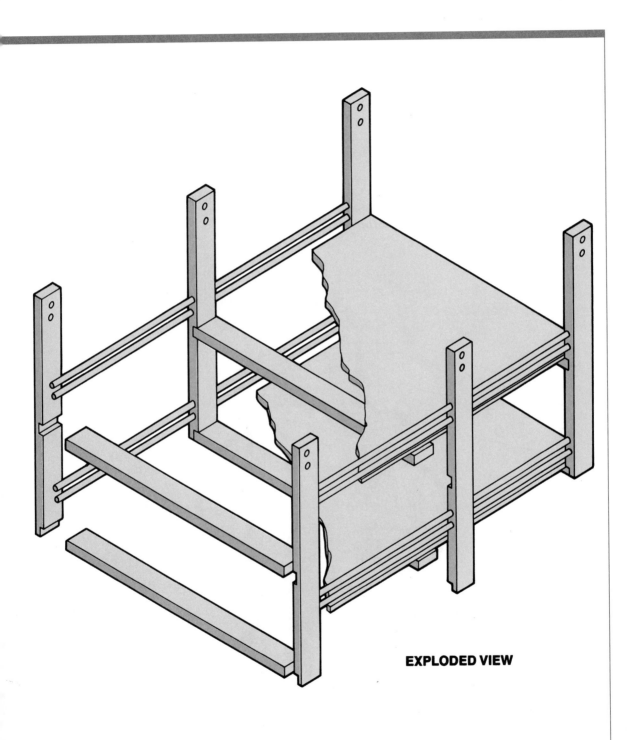

EXPLODED VIEW

PROJECT/Bicycle Rack

How to store the bicycles is one of the most common storage problems. Line them up in the garage, and there's no room for the car. Leave them outside in the driveway and they get rusty or stolen.

The best solution is often a bicycle rack. A rack makes it possible to store a lot of bicycles in just a little space. The rack you see here is *adjustable,* so that you can change the position of the pegs as the members of your family trade their old bikes and acquire new ones.

1. Decide where you want to put the bike rack. We show two different versions for various areas of your garage. If you can mount the rack in the center of your garage (between two cars, perhaps), then you can store bikes on either side of the rack—use the 'hanging' version. If you must attach it to a wall, you can only store bikes on one side—use the 'wall-mounted' version.

2. Decide how far apart to mount the uprights. These should be spaced to fit the *largest* bike you have to store.

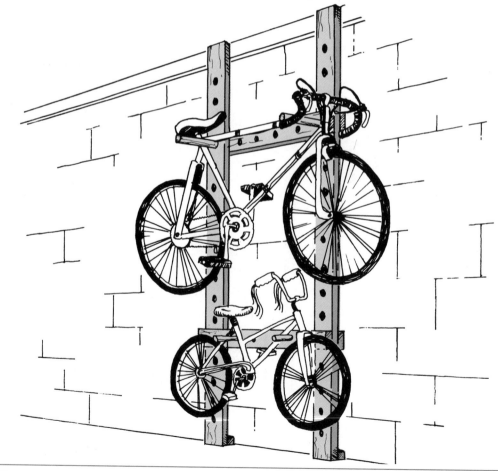

3. Cut all the frame parts from 2 x 2 and 2 x 4 stock. Make the pegs from 1¼″-diameter 'closet pole'. Drill 1¼″-diameter holes, spaced every 4″, in the supports.

4. If you're making the 'wall-mounted version', nail the long and the short parts of the stringers together. Drill 1¼″-diameter holes, as needed in the stringer assemblies. If you're making the 'hanging version', you won't need to nail any parts together; just drill the holes.

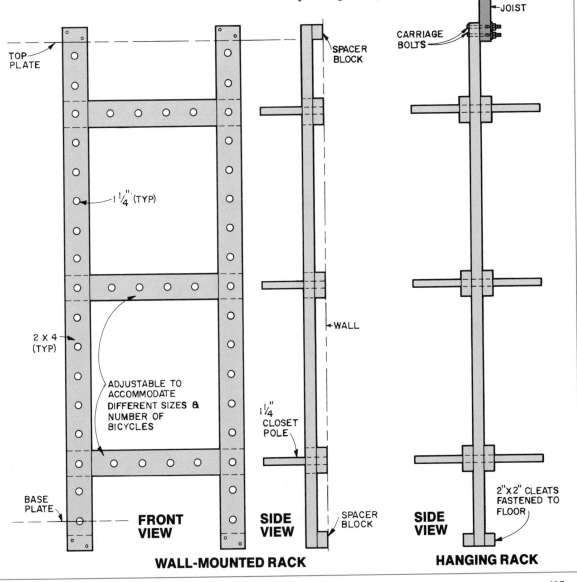

TOP PLATE

1¼″ (TYP)

2 X 4 (TYP)

ADJUSTABLE TO ACCOMMODATE DIFFERENT SIZES & NUMBER OF BICYCLES

BASE PLATE

FRONT VIEW

SPACER BLOCK

WALL

1¼″ CLOSET POLE

SPACER BLOCK

SIDE VIEW

WALL-MOUNTED RACK

JOIST

CARRIAGE BOLTS

2″X2″ CLEATS FASTENED TO FLOOR

SIDE VIEW

HANGING RACK

5. Attach the vertical supports to the frame of the garage with lag screws or carriage bolts. If you build the 'hanging version', you'll have to drill holes in the garage floor. Use lag screws and expandable lead shields to attach the lower end of the rack to the floor.

6. Put the pegs and the horizontal stringers in place. Insert the pegs through the holes in the supports and into the holes in the stringers. Leave enough of the peg 'hanging out' to support a bicycle. If you need to use any of the holes in the stringers *between* the supports to hang a small bike, secure the stringers to the supports with short pegs, then insert the long pegs where you want them.

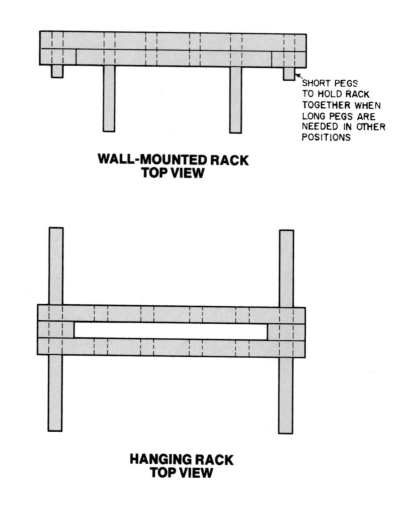

SHORT PEGS
TO HOLD RACK
TOGETHER WHEN
LONG PEGS ARE
NEEDED IN OTHER
POSITIONS

**WALL-MOUNTED RACK
TOP VIEW**

**HANGING RACK
TOP VIEW**

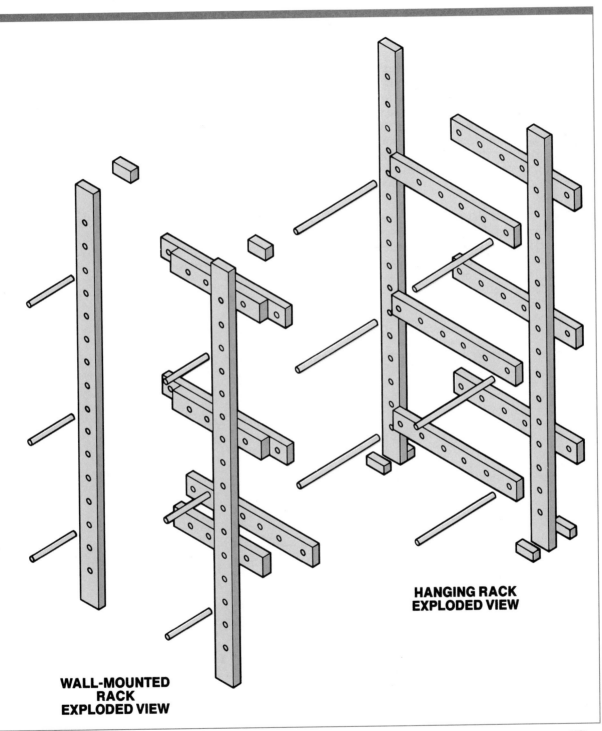

**WALL-MOUNTED
RACK
EXPLODED VIEW**

**HANGING RACK
EXPLODED VIEW**

PROJECT/Implement Shelf

Many gardeners hang their larger gardening implements—rakes, hoes, shovels, etc.—on a rack, and store the small tools and supplies on shelves. However, if you have limited space, you can make a simple 'implement shelf' that will do both jobs. The implements hang from notches in the front edge of the shelf, and the smaller items sit in the space behind the notches.

1. Plan how long you need to make your implement shelf. Line up your large garden tools on the floor of the garage and measure how much space they take up. Also measure the spacing between the handles of the tools. This will tell you where to make the notches.

2. Cut the shelf, ledger, and braces from ¾" stock. Note that the braces are large right triangles—you can make two braces from a single piece of stock, 10½" x 10½". The shelf should be braced at least every 36" along its length. If the implements, small tools, and gardening supplies are heavy, you may have to brace it more often.

3. Measure and mark the notches along the shelf. To cut a notch, first drill a 2½"-diameter hole with a hole saw. Then 'open up' the notch to the outside edge of the shelf by removing the waste with a sabre saw or handsaw.

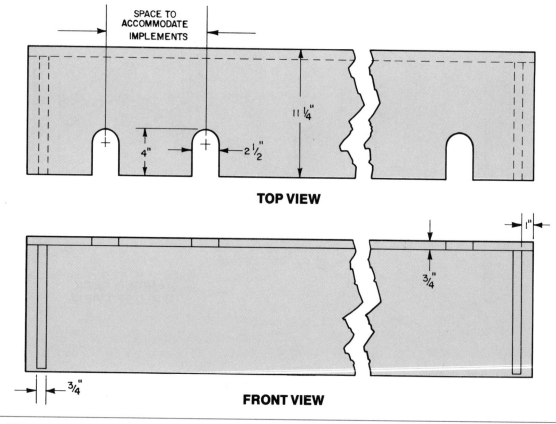

SPACE TO ACCOMMODATE IMPLEMENTS

11 ¼"

4"

2 ½"

TOP VIEW

1"

¾"

¾"

FRONT VIEW

UTILITARIAN STORAGE—ATTIC, GARAGE, AND BASEMENT

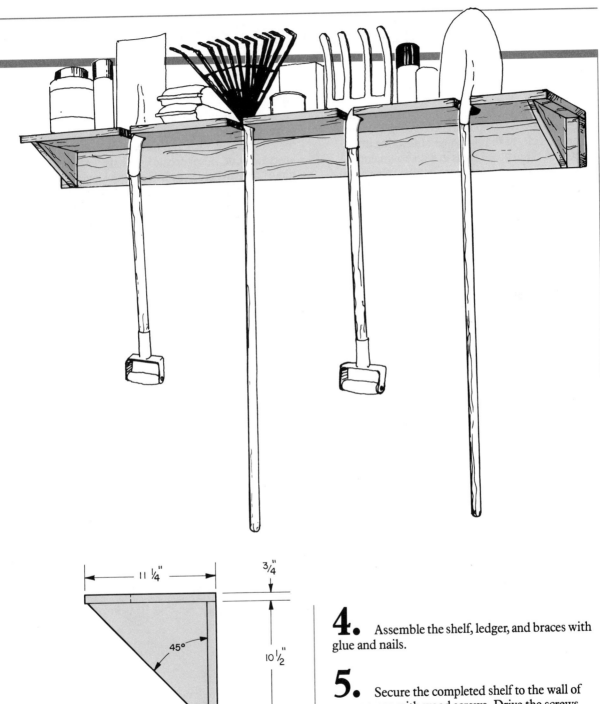

SIDE VIEW

11 1/4"

3/4"

45°

10 1/2"

3/4"

4. Assemble the shelf, ledger, and braces with glue and nails.

5. Secure the completed shelf to the wall of your garage with wood screws. Drive the screws through the ledger and into the frame studs. If you want to attach this project to a masonry wall, use lag bolts and expandable lead shields.

PROJECT/Between-Joists Pocket Storage

If you look hard enough, you can find room for storage where you thought there was no room at all. For example, have you thought of storing items between the exposed joists in your basement or garage? There's a lot of room between those joists! Make a few simple boxes, mount them on hinges so they swing down, and you can create an enormous amount of extra storage space.

1. Measure the space between the joists. Plan to build boxes 1″ narrower than that space, so that they'll fit easily. They should be no deeper than the joists are wide. Also, decide how long you want these boxes to be. If you make them longer than 18″, plan on putting partitions in the boxes so that things won't all slide to one end when the box swings down out of the joists. And don't plan on making them longer than 36″—they will be too heavy when they're filled.

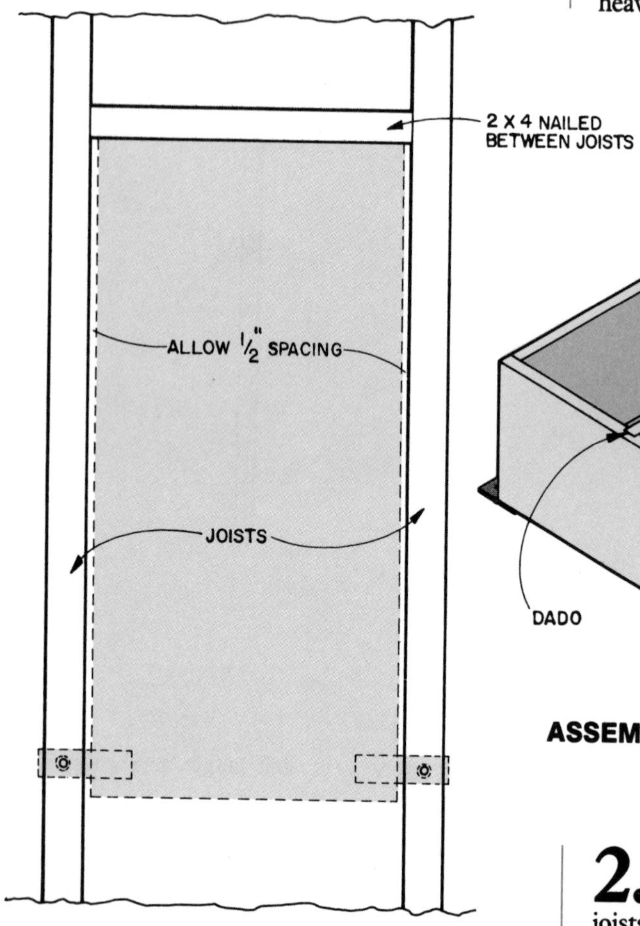

2 X 4 NAILED
BETWEEN JOISTS

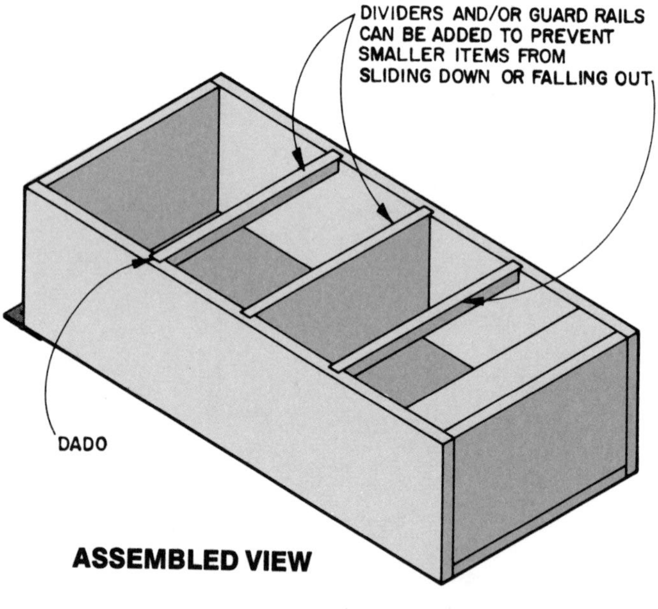

DIVIDERS AND/OR GUARD RAILS
CAN BE ADDED TO PREVENT
SMALLER ITEMS FROM
SLIDING DOWN OR FALLING OUT

ALLOW ½″ SPACING

JOISTS

DADO

ASSEMBLED VIEW

**BOTTOM VIEW
OF FLOOR JOINTS**

2. Cut a length of 2 x 4 to fit between the joists. Secure this in place with 12d nails where you want to hang the box. The 2 x 4 must be square to the joists. If it isn't, the box will rub on the joists when it swings up and down.

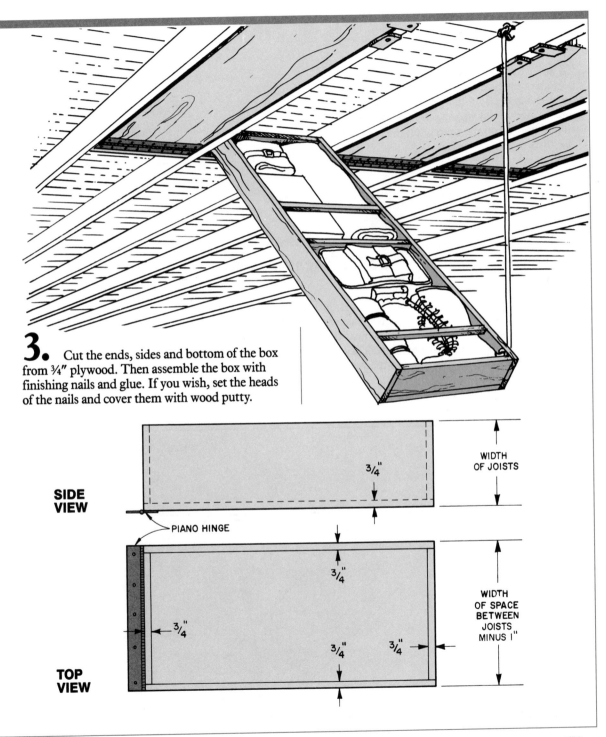

3. Cut the ends, sides and bottom of the box from ¾″ plywood. Then assemble the box with finishing nails and glue. If you wish, set the heads of the nails and cover them with wood putty.

SIDE VIEW

¾″

WIDTH OF JOISTS

PIANO HINGE

TOP VIEW

¾″

¾″

¾″

¾″

WIDTH OF SPACE BETWEEN JOISTS MINUS 1″

4. Attach one leaf of a piano hinge to the bottom of the box at one end. Then attach the other leaf to the 2 x 4 that you nailed between the joists. Check the swinging action of the box. It should not rub on the joists or on the floor above the joists.

BOX

JOIST

BOX IN PLACE/SIDE VIEW

5. Using roundhead screws and flat washers, mount short strips of 1 x 2's to the joists, near the end of the box opposite the piano hinge. These strips will serve as 'turndogs' to keep the box in the 'up' position.

6. To prevent the box from swinging down too far and spilling its contents, attach a length of chain or rope between the floor above the joists and the end of the box opposite the hinge. The length of this rope may vary, depending on the size of the box and how far you want it to swing down.

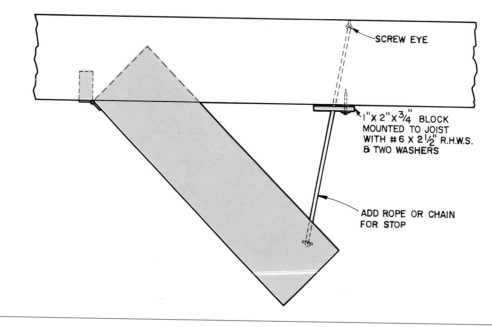

SCREW EYE

1" X 2" X ¾" BLOCK MOUNTED TO JOIST WITH #6 X 2½" R.H.W.S. & TWO WASHERS

ADD ROPE OR CHAIN FOR STOP

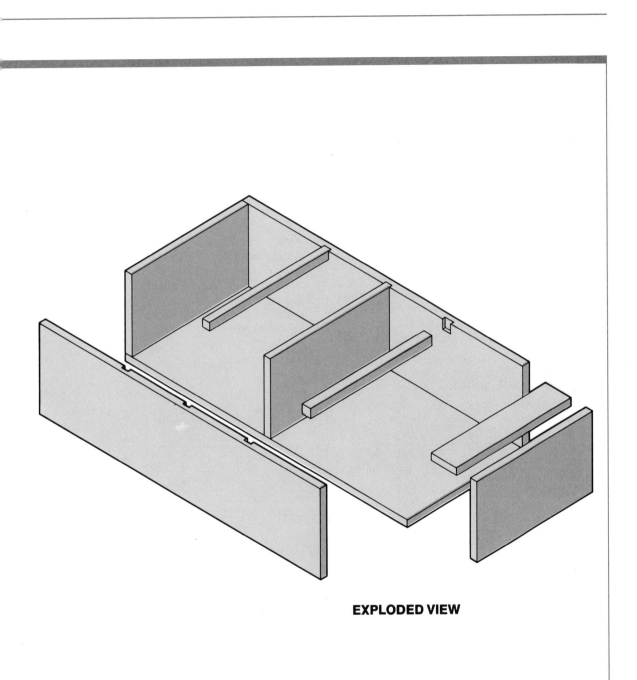

EXPLODED VIEW

PROJECT/Tool Caddy

Tool storage presents a special problem: Tools are often used in locations other than where you store them. For example, you use your pipe wrench and drain auger in the kitchen or the bathroom, but you probably store them in the garage or the basement. If you just need one or two tools for a job, this isn't much of a problem. But when the job requires several tools, it's a nuisance. What you need at times like these is a tool caddy.

Caddies come in many forms and can be made to do many jobs. The caddy shown here does three jobs. First of all, it hangs on the wall like a cabinet so that you can store tools and materials in it. Open it up while it's hanging, and a drop-down shelf provides a small workspace. Take it off the wall, and you can carry all the tools and materials inside it to the job.

1. Consider the tools you're going to store in this caddy. You may have to adjust the dimensions so that your tools will fit properly. We suggest, however, that you don't make this caddy much larger than what we show. If the caddy gets too big, it will be difficult to carry.

2. Cut the parts to the sizes you need. Most of these parts are made from ½" stock—this cuts down on weight without sacrificing too much strength. Using a dado cutter or a router, make the dadoes to hold the shelves in the sides of the back assembly. Just above the dadoes, drill holes for the ¼" dowel rails.

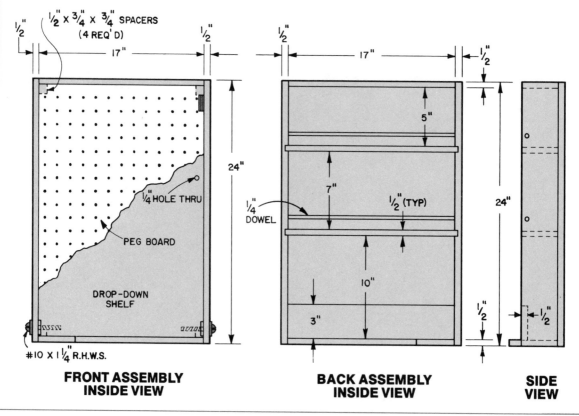

FRONT ASSEMBLY INSIDE VIEW

BACK ASSEMBLY INSIDE VIEW

SIDE VIEW

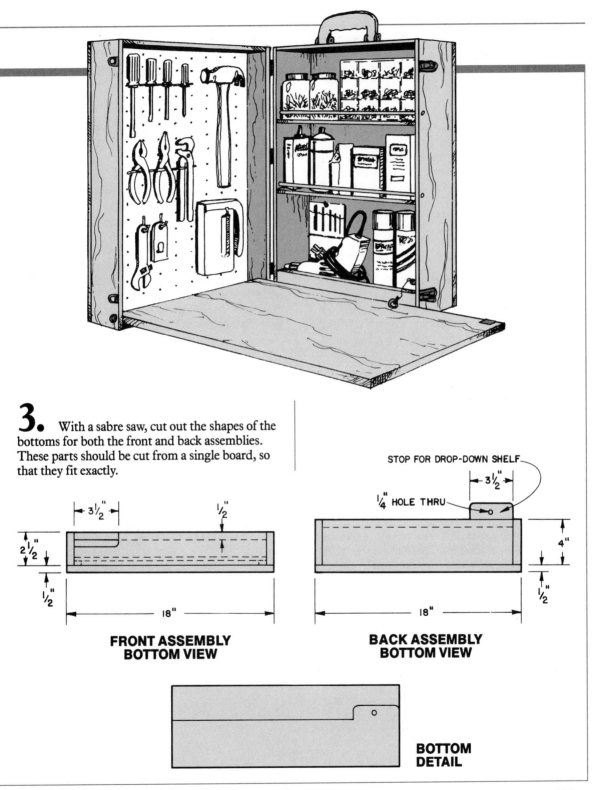

3. With a sabre saw, cut out the shapes of the bottoms for both the front and back assemblies. These parts should be cut from a single board, so that they fit exactly.

**FRONT ASSEMBLY
BOTTOM VIEW**

STOP FOR DROP-DOWN SHELF

1/4" HOLE THRU

**BACK ASSEMBLY
BOTTOM VIEW**

**BOTTOM
DETAIL**

4. Assemble both the front and back of the tool caddy with glue and screws. Secure the rails, shelves, and bin front in the back assembly as you put it together. Build the basic box—sides, top, bottom, and front of the front assembly. Then glue spacers to the inside, at each of the four corners. Attach pegboard to these spacers with glue and screws.

5. Attach the two assemblies with a piano hinge. Check the hinge action—when the caddy is closed, the ledge or 'stop' for the drop-down shelf must fit in the notch in the front assembly. Install surface catches to hold the caddy closed.

6. Mount the drop-down shelf in the front of the tool caddy. Use roundhead wood screws and flat washers as pivots for the shelf. Screw these pivots through the sides and into the shelf, near the bottom edge.

7. Open the caddy so that the front and back assemblies are at 90° to each other. Drop the shelf down so that it rests on the stop. Drill a ¼"-diameter hole through the shelf and the stop, and insert a small eyebolt in this hole. This will stop the caddy from opening too far, and keep the shelf in place. So that you don't lose the eyebolt, attach it to the back assemblies with a string and an eyescrew.

8. Install a handle at the top of the caddy so that you can carry it easily.

9. Make four L-shaped brackets from ¾"-thick *hardwood.* Using glue and screws, attach two brackets to the back of the back assembly, near the top and bottom edges. Attach the other two brackets to the wall where you want to hang the caddy. Make sure these wall brackets are secured to the frame of the house at one or more points. To hang the caddy on the wall, simply slip the two sets of brackets over one another so that the L's interlock. To take the caddy down, just lift up slightly.

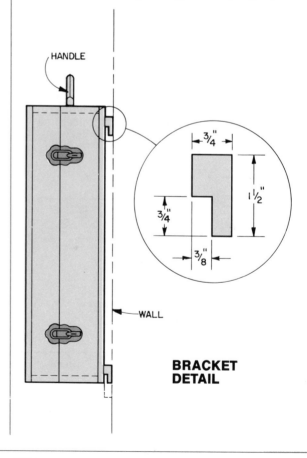

HANDLE

WALL

BRACKET DETAIL

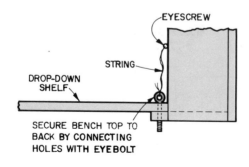

EYESCREW

STRING

DROP-DOWN SHELF

SECURE BENCH TOP TO
BACK BY CONNECTING
HOLES WITH EYEBOLT

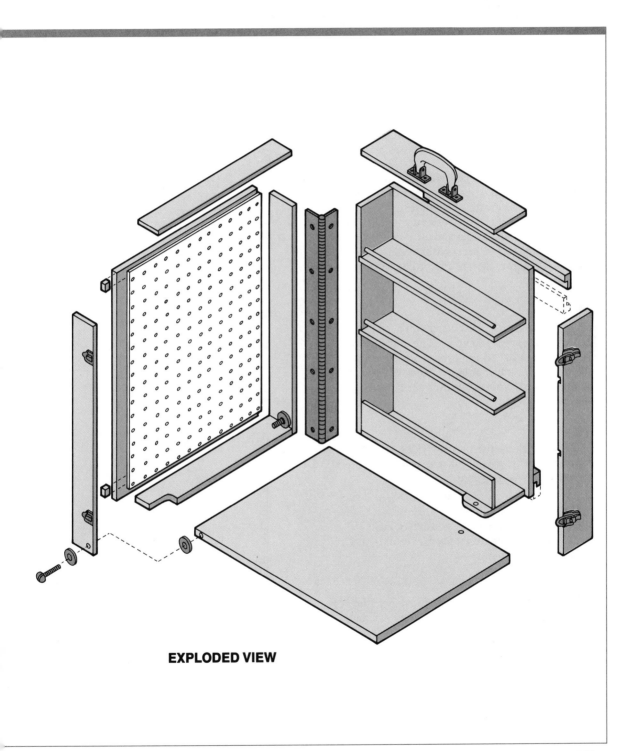

EXPLODED VIEW

PROJECT/Stacking Storage Boxes

Boxes are, perhaps, the most universal storage system. You can make them any size, and they can be made to hold almost anything. Consequently, a simple box can solve many of your utilitarian storage problems. An entire *set* of boxes may solve most of them.

The boxes you see here are meant to be *stacked*. When placed one on top of another, these boxes will store a great deal more stuff in a limited amount of space. Stack the boxes upright like bins, or turn them on their sides and use them as shelves. Or mix them up: Use some boxes as bins, others as shelves. Configure the stack according to your storage needs.

1. Decide how many boxes you need to make, and what sizes they should be. The drawings show boxes that are 20″ on a side, but you can make them slightly smaller or larger. However, you should make all your boxes the same size so that they will stack easily.

2. Cut all the parts—ends, sides, and bottoms from ¾″ plywood. Fill any 'voids' between the plies with wood putty.

3. With a router or a dado cutter, make ¾″-wide, ⅜″-deep rabbets in the edges of the ends, as shown in the drawings.

4. Cut the handholds near the upper edges of the sides. To make a handhold, drill two 1″-diameter holes approximately 5″ apart. Remove the waste between the holes with a sabre saw.

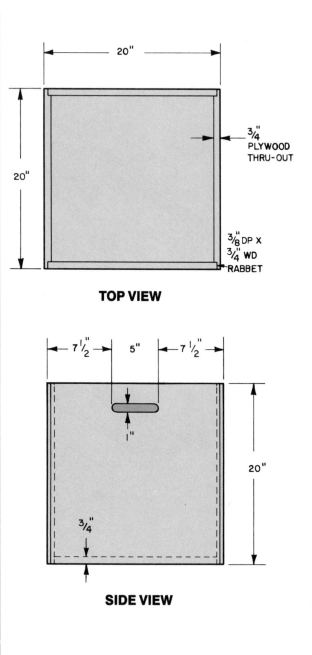

TOP VIEW

SIDE VIEW

5. Assemble the boxes with finishing nails and glue. 'Cross' the nails on each corner—that is, nail from both directions so that the nails cross each other at 90°. This will help hold the boxes together. Set the heads of the nails below the surface of the wood, and cover them with wood putty.

6. When the glue dries, sand the boxes smooth. Be especially careful to sand the inside edges of the handholds so that you won't get splinters when you move the boxes. If you wish, paint or finish the completed boxes.

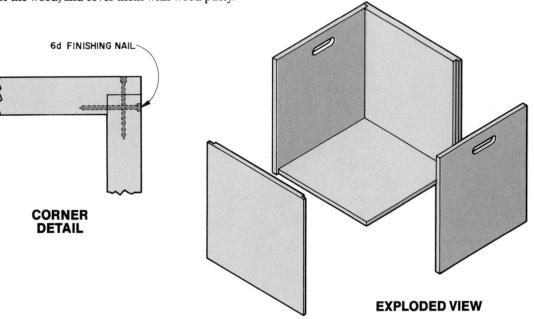

6d FINISHING NAIL

CORNER DETAIL

EXPLODED VIEW

PROJECT/Under-Stairs Bins and Shelves

The space under the basement stairs is rarely used as well as it should be. A few builders install closets in this space, but usually it's left open. An odd assortment of boxes and other stuff begin to accumulate under the stairs, with no real plan or order.

A set of roll-out storage units will make better use of this space. These bins and shelves are simple to make. The only tricky part is cutting the top edges—these edges must be angled so that they fit under the staircase.

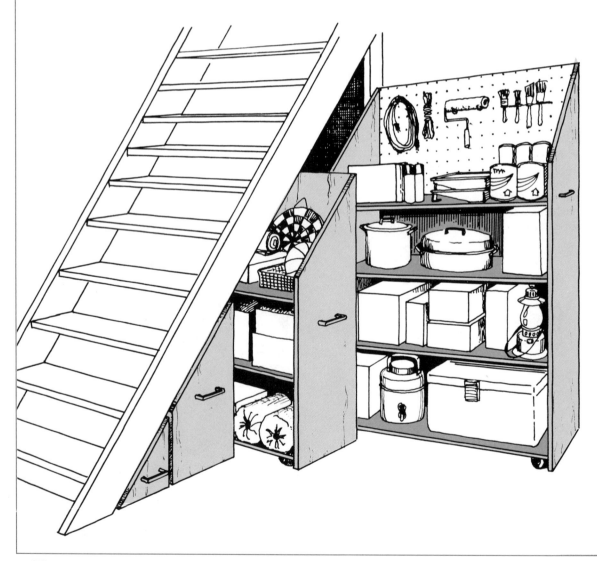

1. Using a tape rule and a plumb bob, measure the exact amount of space you have under the stairs. Carefully draw a plan and determine just how many bins/shelves you have room for, how wide and tall they should be, and at what angle you should cut the top edges. In your plan, leave at least ½″ of space between each unit.

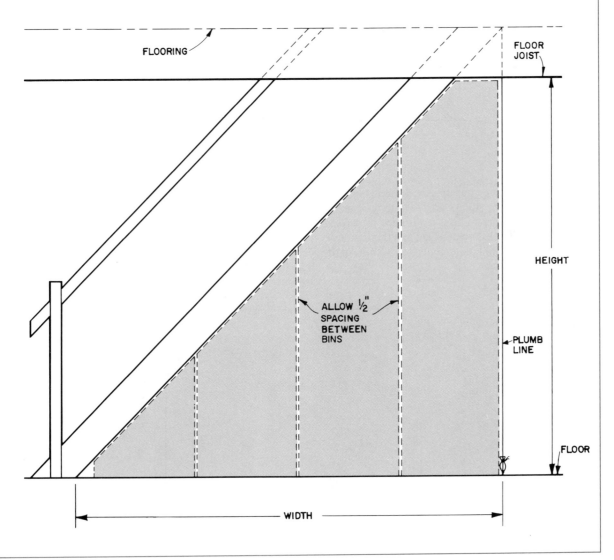

2. If you have open stairs in your basement, cover the back of the staircase with ¼″ plywood. This will keep dirt from falling onto the storage units.

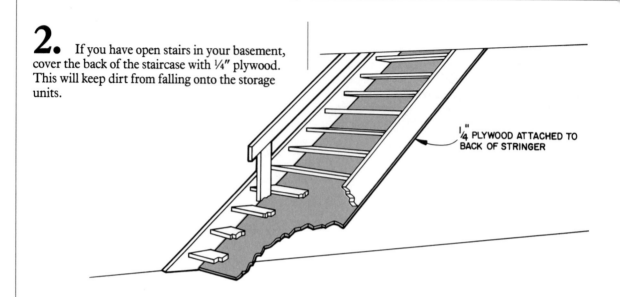

¼″ PLYWOOD ATTACHED TO BACK OF STRINGER

3. If necessary, put up a 2 x 4 frame to close in the 'back' of the storage area—directly beneath the top of the stairs. (This is not needed if there is already a wall at this point.) Nail together a simple frame, then put it in place. Attach this frame to the floor joists with nails, and to the basement floor with lag screws and expandable lead shields. Cover the frame with plywood or drywall, depending on how 'finished' you want this project to look.

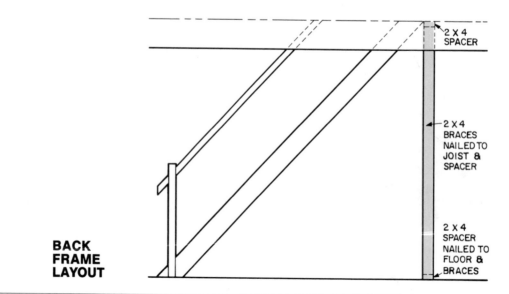

2 X 4 SPACER

2 X 4 BRACES NAILED TO JOIST & SPACER

2 X 4 SPACER NAILED TO FLOOR & BRACES

BACK FRAME LAYOUT

Cont'd.

4. Cut the parts you'll need for the roll-around storage units. Make the sides, ends, shelves, and bin bottoms from ¾″ plywood, and the cleats and other reinforcing parts from 1 x 2 stock. Cut the top edges of the ends and sides at the proper angle.

5. The joints required to make this project are a ¾″-wide, ⅜″-deep dado and a rabbet of the same size near the bottom edges of the front ends. These hold the bottom in place. Make the dadoes with a router or a dado cutter. If you use a router, clamp a straightedge to the workpiece to guide the cut.

6. Build the smallest unit first. This is just a single shelf with triangular ends. Two cleats reinforce the butt joint between the ends and the side. Assemble the unit with glue and screws.

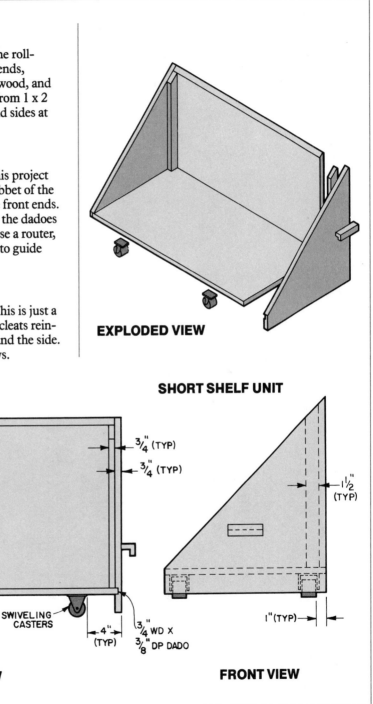

EXPLODED VIEW

SHORT SHELF UNIT

¾″ (TYP)

¾″ (TYP)

¾″ (TYP)

1½″ (TYP)

NON-SWIVELING CASTERS

SWIVELING CASTERS

4″ (TYP)

¾″ WD X ⅜″ DP DADO

¾″ WD X ⅜″ DP RABBET

1″ (TYP)

SIDE VIEW

FRONT VIEW

7. Consider making the second-to-the-smallest unit a bin. This is made almost exactly the same as the smallest unit, except there are four cleats and two sides.

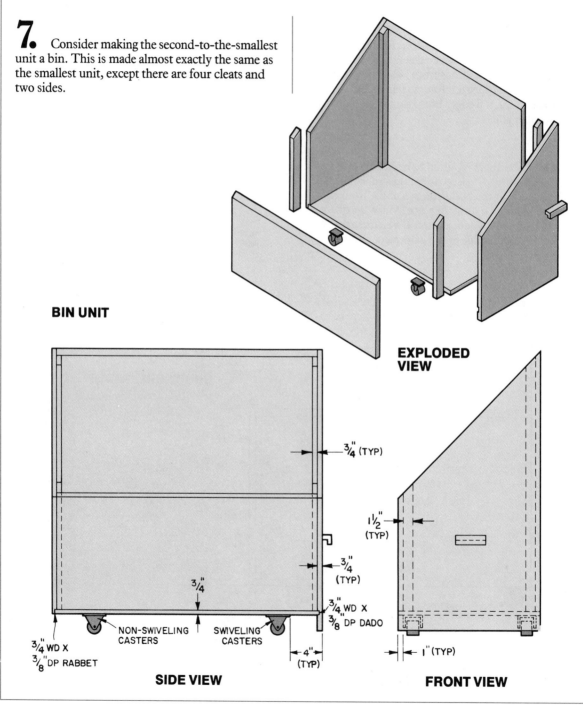

BIN UNIT

EXPLODED VIEW

$\frac{3}{4}$" (TYP)

$1\frac{1}{2}$" (TYP)

$\frac{3}{4}$" (TYP)

$\frac{3}{4}$"

$\frac{3}{4}$" WD X $\frac{3}{8}$" DP DADO

NON-SWIVELING CASTERS

SWIVELING CASTERS

$\frac{3}{4}$" WD X $\frac{3}{8}$" DP RABBET

4" (TYP)

1" (TYP)

SIDE VIEW

FRONT VIEW

Cont'd.

8. The larger units should be shelving units (unless you need some *very* deep bins.) The spacing of the shelves is up to you; it will depend on what you want to store on the shelves. Use cleats to attach these shelves to the sides and ends.

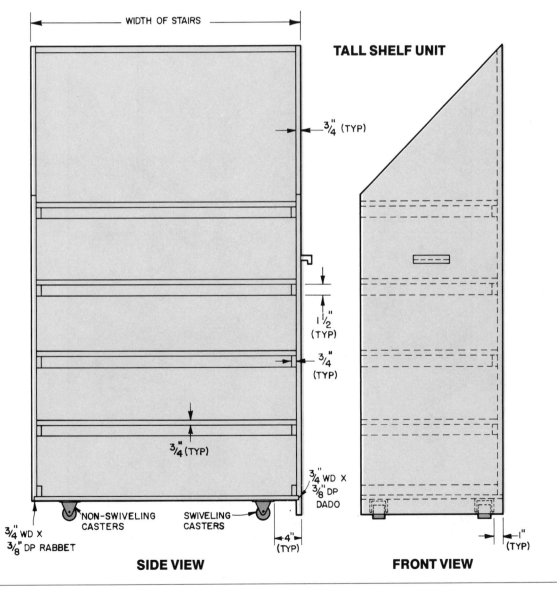

WIDTH OF STAIRS

TALL SHELF UNIT

$\frac{3}{4}$" (TYP)

$1\frac{1}{2}$" (TYP)

$\frac{3}{4}$" (TYP)

$\frac{3}{4}$" (TYP)

$\frac{3}{4}$" WD X $\frac{3}{8}$" DP DADO

NON-SWIVELING CASTERS

SWIVELING CASTERS

$\frac{3}{4}$" WD X $\frac{3}{8}$" DP RABBET

4" (TYP)

1" (TYP)

SIDE VIEW

FRONT VIEW

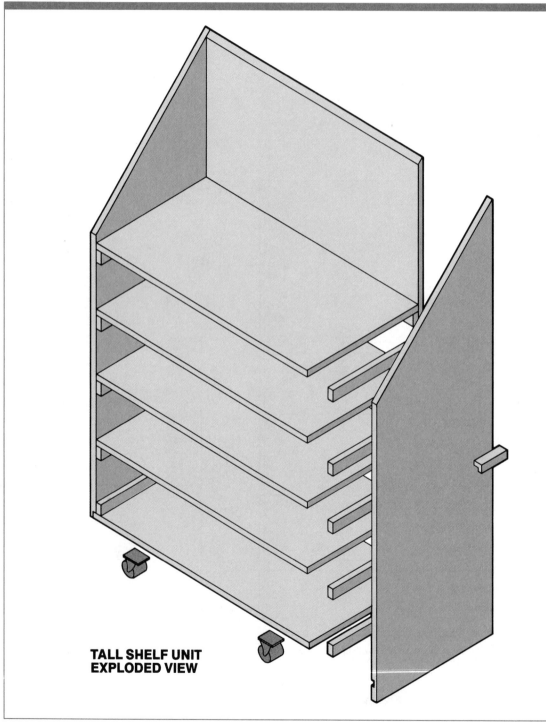

**TALL SHELF UNIT
EXPLODED VIEW**

Cont'd.

9. Attach pulls to the front ends of the units and casters to the bottoms. Put regular swiveling casters on the front of each unit and 'fixed' or non-swiveling casters on the back. With concrete nails or similar fasteners, attach guide strips to the basement floor. These help to keep the storage units properly aligned.

10. If you want, paint or finish the storage units. Then put them in place under the stairs.

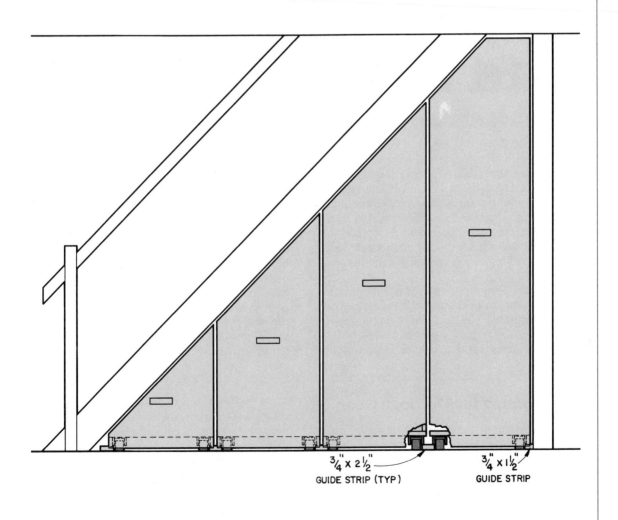

3/4" x 2 1/2"
GUIDE STRIP (TYP.)

3/4" x 1 1/2"
GUIDE STRIP

10

Adding Storage Outdoors — Backyard Storage

Summer's over and it's time to drag in the garden hose and all the patio furniture and find a place to store it. If you have children, you need to find places for more outdoor stuff—sandbox toys, bicycles, the croquet set, and so on. Add your lawnmower and other lawn-care equipment. And if you have a fireplace, where will you put the firewood?

All these things can be stored in your garage. But if you don't have a garage, or if your garage is simply overloaded, you can build storage spaces in your backyard. The great outdoors, however, sometimes presents great problems. Cold weather can ruin certain materials. Dogs and other critters will tear into stored goods if they are not properly protected. This chapter offers tips on how to solve such problems.

Some projects are very specific. For example, there is an outdoor rack for stacking firewood. A hose rack holds the garden hose and related tools. Other projects have several uses. The "Trash Can Bins" can be used to store dog food, bird seed, or potting soil. The "Outdoor Work Center" can be used as a potting bench or a barbecue table. And the "Houseside Shed" holds a variety of outdoor implements and objects.

Safekeeping for Outdoor Gear

No matter where you live, you're likely to have a need for outdoor storage. Even if you leave goods outdoors year-round, you can better protect them by putting a roof over them. You'll keep items more secure by placing a structure around them, complete with door and lock. Best of all, your yard or patio will look much neater if outdoor things are orderly arranged.

One simple way to create storage units is to attach them to already-standing structures, as we have done with the houseside shed. Use these sheds as outdoor 'closets'; install shelves or partitions in them to help organize the things you have to store.

If you would rather locate your storage area at some location away from your house or garage, then build a free-standing shed or storage barn. There are many, many kits on the market for storage barns, or you can custom-build your own to meet your needs. Most people find the kits fairly easy to work with—even beginning carpenters and do-it-yourselfers.

Checking Local Codes. Before you build or assemble any shed, barn, or any type of 'permanent' structure or addition to your existing buildings, you should check your local building code for any restrictions. In some areas, detached storage sheds or even attached ones are prohibited. In other communities, there are regulations regarding their proximity to fences or property lines.

Often, codes will allow you to put a shed anywhere you want as long as it isn't on a concrete slab or in some other way anchored to the ground. The only way to know for sure what is permitted is to contact your local building inspector. Checking the code first could save you the agony of tearing down a structure which has taken much time and effort to build.

Ideas for Storing Specific Items. Here are some ideas for purchasing and building storage units for various outdoor items. These can be self-sufficient structures or they can be incorporated on the inside of other structures:

Purchase a reel for your garden hose so that it simply rolls up into its designated storage space. Or build the hose rack we show here. Remember the between-the-studs shelves from a previous chapter? You can do the same thing on the *outside* of your house. Line the space with metal and attach a door. Use this to store a hose, garden tools, anything that's not too wide. You can make yet another place for the garden hose by constructing a narrow bench against a building, lining it with metal, and hinging a lid to it.

Using metal for lining is a good idea for many outdoor projects. The structures will be better protected from the weather and destructive insects.

Certain rules of thumb pertain to firewood storage. If you're seasoning your wood, then you should allow for as much air circulation as possible but still keep the wood sheltered from the rain. Wood should be elevated from the ground and should not be piled flush against a house wall. For safety's sake, too, you should avoid excessively tall and unseparated stacks. Dividers will prevent wood from tumbling down on you.

Outdoor furniture such as lightweight lawn chairs can be placed in divided bins; so removing one will not upset an entire stack, or they can be hung on long brackets mounted in a storage shed. Cushions for outdoor furniture can be stored in racks made especially for this purpose. These, of course, should be protected from weather and dust.

If you have a small workspace for potting plants or a potting shed, make specific bins for holding various types of soil and fertilizer. These can be stored in plastic or metal cans with lids and be placed at an angle for easy access. The trash can bin storage system, in this chapter, shows you how.

Important Principles for Outdoor Storage. As always, the first thing to do when considering new outdoor storage structures is to take inventory. Think about the equipment you now own and about what you might own in the future.

Size it all up and then make a list of priorities. The most important factor is accessibility. Design and build structures with doors and openings that are large enough to permit you to easily remove and replace the stored item. If you want to make a shed for the storage of a ladder or a roto-tiller, make sure that it is long enough or wide enough to hold these items. Also be certain that family members will have easy access to their outdoor stuff. Will a small child be able to reach his wagon or tricycle?

Use these guidelines when storing outdoor goods:

■ Keep all potentially unsafe articles far from the reach of small children.

■ If sharp implements are stored in the open, make sure that they are securely mounted on pegs or hooks.

■ Flammables and toxic substances should not only be stored in remote places but they should additionally be locked in a cabinet. This extra precaution is particularly important if a storage shed is used by the entire family. The reason is that children, both yours and the neighbors', will view the shed as an ideal playroom. Also, by the nature of the structure, it's impossible for parents to see inside the shed. You may just want to keep the entire shed under lock and key.

■ When you purchase the wood for these projects, buy cedar, redwood, or 'pressure-treated' lumber. These materials will withstand the weather much better than ordinary lumber, and they don't require yearly coats of stains or varnish.

■ Also purchase *galvanized* nails and other hardware to assemble the projects. Ordinary nails will rust and stain the wood.

PROJECT/Houseside Storage Shed

If you only need a small storage shed, consider making a lean-to shed attached to a wall of your house or garage. This saves you a great deal of time and expense. Because the existing structure provides the support for the new shed, you don't need to put up a complex structure.

1. Decide on the size of the shed. The shed shown here is small, just 48″ across. You may need something longer. Don't make the shed too much deeper than what is shown here. If you do, you'll have to beef up the structure. You might as well just make a stand-alone storage shed.

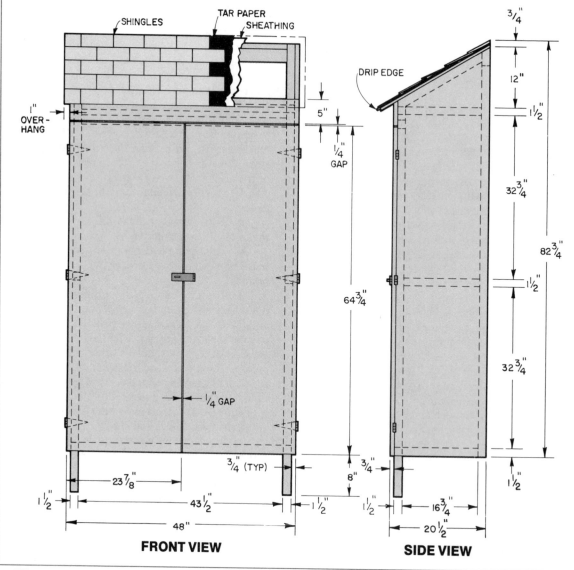

SHINGLES

TAR PAPER

SHEATHING

1″ OVER-HANG

DRIP EDGE

5″

¼″ GAP

64¾″

¼″ GAP

23⅞″

¾″ (TYP)

1½″

43½″

1½″

48″

FRONT VIEW

¾″

¾″

8″

1½″

16¾″

20½″

1½″

SIDE VIEW

12″

1½″

32¾″

82¾″

1½″

32¾″

¾″

ADDING STORAGE OUTDOORS—BACKYARD STORAGE

2. Cut the parts of the frame from 2 x 2 pressure-treated stock, except for the ledger that fits against the house where the roof joins it—this is cut from a 2 x 4. Miter the ends and bevel the edges of the roof frame parts as needed.

3. Assemble the side frames with 12d nails. Since you're working with narrow stock, you may have to drill pilot holes to keep the nails from splitting the boards.

4. Dig 8"-10" deep postholes for the front frame posts, and put flat rocks in the bottoms of these holes to keep the posts from settling. Put the frames in place, tacking them to the house with 16d nails. Don't drive the nails all the way home until you have completed the frame. Check that the frames are level and plumb. If necessary, raise or lower the rocks in the holes by digging out or putting back dirt.

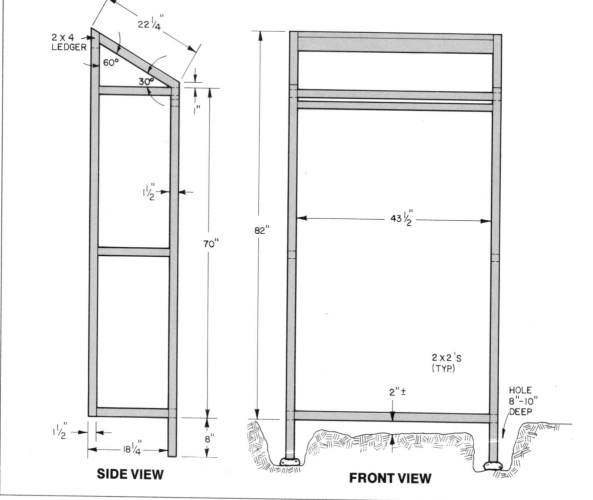

SIDE VIEW

FRONT VIEW

5. Nail the 2 x 4 ledger to the house, between the frames. Then attach the front rails to the frames with 12d nails. The bottom nail must be 2″ above the ground (approximately).

6. Cover the side frames and the top of the front frame with ⅜″ plywood siding, securing the siding with 6d nails. Cover the roof with ½″ exterior plywood sheathing, leaving a 3″ overhang.

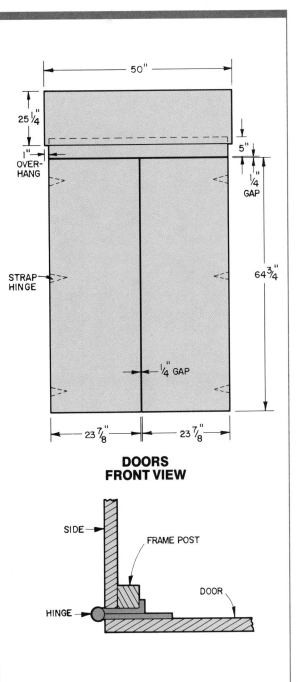

**DOORS
FRONT VIEW**

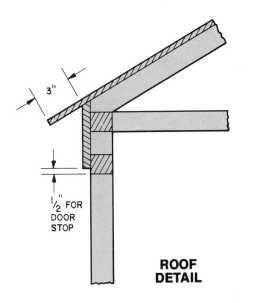

**ROOF
DETAIL**

7. Cut the doors from ⅝″ plywood siding and attach strap hinges to the inside face of the doors. Mount the doors to the shed, securing the other part of the hinges to the frame post. Bend the strap around the post, as shown in the drawing.

8. Install drip edge around the edge of the roof. Caulk the seam where the roof meets the house. Install tarpaper, shingles and flashing to finish the roof.

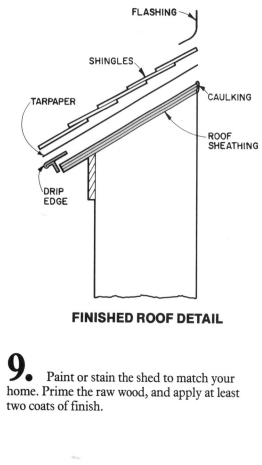

FINISHED ROOF DETAIL

9. Paint or stain the shed to match your home. Prime the raw wood, and apply at least two coats of finish.

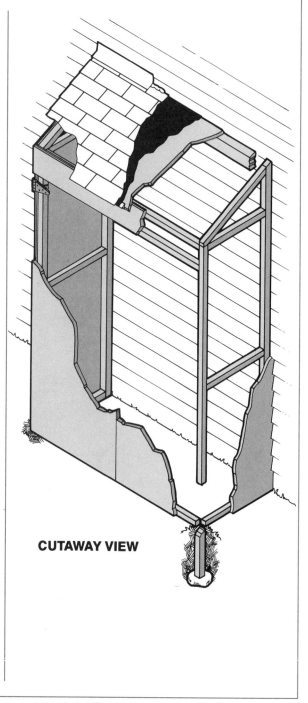

CUTAWAY VIEW

PROJECT/Outdoor Work Center

If you spend much time outdoors, working in the garden or cooking out, then you probably have a need for an outdoor work center. As the name implies, this provides a workspace in your backyard or patio. It also provides a place to store gardening materials or barbecue utensils while you're not using them.

This work center is designed along the same lines as your kitchen cabinets. There is a counter to work on, and storage areas both above and below the counter. If you want, you can even improvise a 'sink' by making a cut-out in the countertop for a plastic tub.

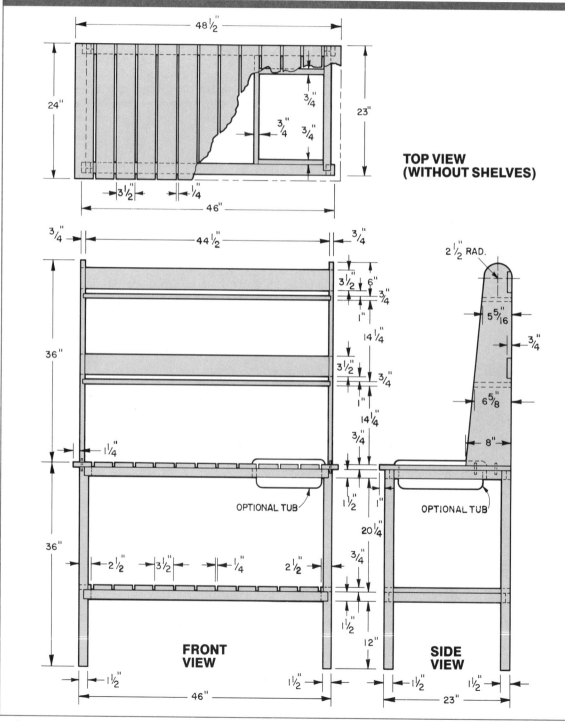

**TOP VIEW
(WITHOUT SHELVES)**

**FRONT
VIEW**

**SIDE
VIEW**

OPTIONAL TUB

1. Cut all the parts of the work center to size. Use an 'outdoor' wood that will hold up in the weather—redwood, cedar, cypress or 'pressure-treated' lumber. If you use the latter, don't place food directly on the countertop.

2. Make dadoes and rabbets in the leg and shelf frames, where shown in the *Front View* and *Top View.* Assemble the frames, then attach the legs to the frames. Use #10 x 2½″ flathead wood screws to join these parts, and countersink the screws so that the heads are flush with the surface of the wood.

3. Cover the shelving frames with 1 x 4's to make the lower shelf and the countertop. Use 4d finishing nails to attach the boards to the frames. Space the 1 x 4's approximately ³⁄₁₆″ apart so that no moisture will collect between the boards. Cut notches in the 1 x 4's on either end of the lower shelf to fit around the legs.

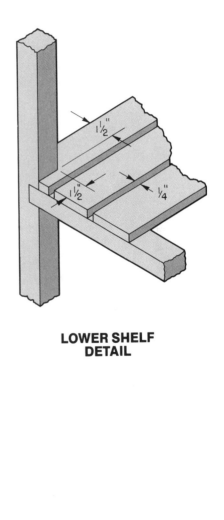

LOWER SHELF DETAIL

FRAME JOINERY DETAIL

SIDE

FRONT OR BACK

LEG

4. If you want to add a 'sink' to your work center, purchase a plastic tub and measure the outside dimensions, just under the lip. Build a 1 x 2 frame under the countertop, near one end, nailing the 1 x 2's to the 1 x 4 countertop. The inside dimensions of this frame must match that of the tub. With a sabre saw, cut an opening in the countertop for the tub.

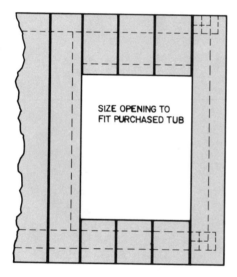

SIZE OPENING TO
FIT PURCHASED TUB

**TUB OPENING
TOP VIEW**

5. With a router or a dado cutter, cut dadoes in the sides of the shelving unit to hold the shelves. Bore the bottom edge of the sides for ⅜″ dowels—later, you'll use the dowels to mount the shelving unit on the work center. Finally, cut the notches for the back braces, the tapers, and the rounded top edges with a sabre saw.

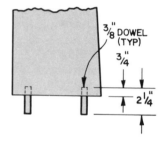

$\frac{3}{8}$″ DOWEL (TYP)

$\frac{3}{4}$″

$2\frac{1}{4}$″

6. Assemble the shelving unit with #10 x 1¼″ flathead wood screws. Once again countersink the heads of the screws.

7. Drill ⅜″-diameter holes in the countertop to attach the completed shelving unit. The position of these holes must match the holes in the bottom edges of the shelves. The easiest way to mark the countertop holes precisely is to use 'dowel centers'. When you have drilled the holes, stick the dowels in the holes in the shelving unit with a waterproof glue such as epoxy or resorcinol. *Do not* glue the other end of the dowels in the countertop holes. Just set the shelving unit in place. That way, you can remove the shelving unit when it's not needed.

8. If you wish, paint or finish the completed work center. If you built this project from pressure-treated lumber, wait several weeks before applying a finish. This will give any chemicals or interior moisture that may have been exposed when you cut up the wood a chance to evaporate.

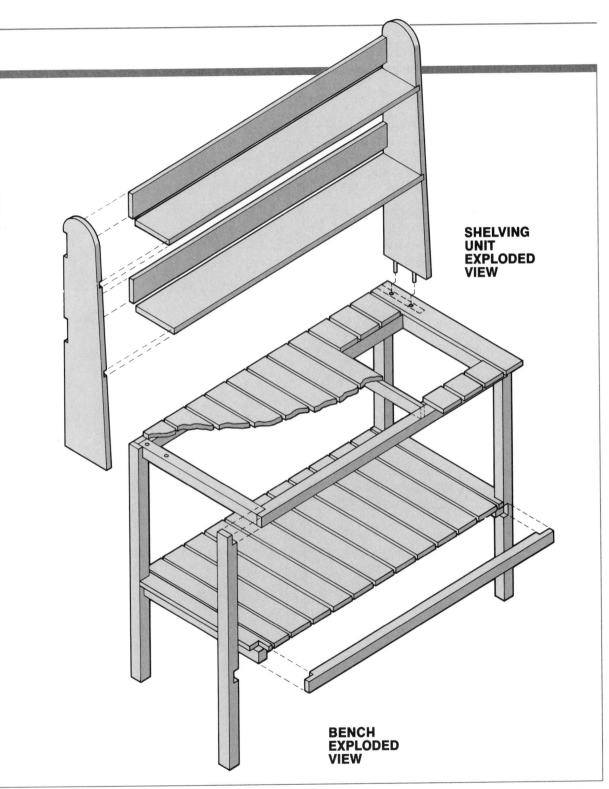

**SHELVING
UNIT
EXPLODED
VIEW**

**BENCH
EXPLODED
VIEW**

PROJECT/Garden Hose Shelves

There are dozens of different types of hose reels and hose hangers on the market to keep your hose neatly coiled beside the outdoor water spigot. None, however, provide any sort of storage for all the accessories that go along with a hose—nozzles, sprinklers, brushes and sponges.

Here's a project to fill that void. This hose rack is actually a small shelving unit that mounts on the side of your house. The hose coils around the rack, while hose accessories are stored on the shelves.

1. Cut the parts needed from ¾″ pressure-treated lumber, redwood, cedar, or cypress. These types of wood resist water damage and rot.

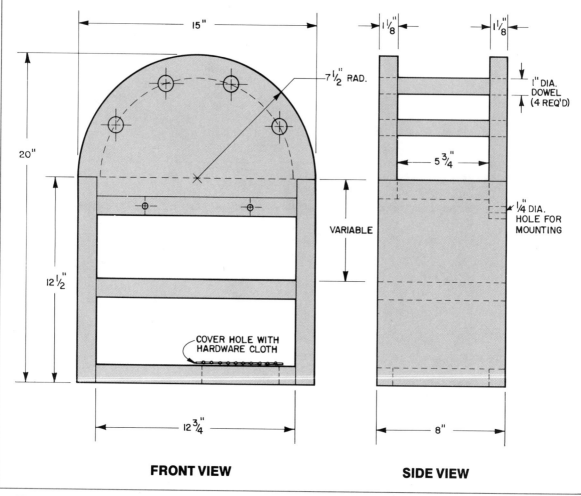

FRONT VIEW

SIDE VIEW

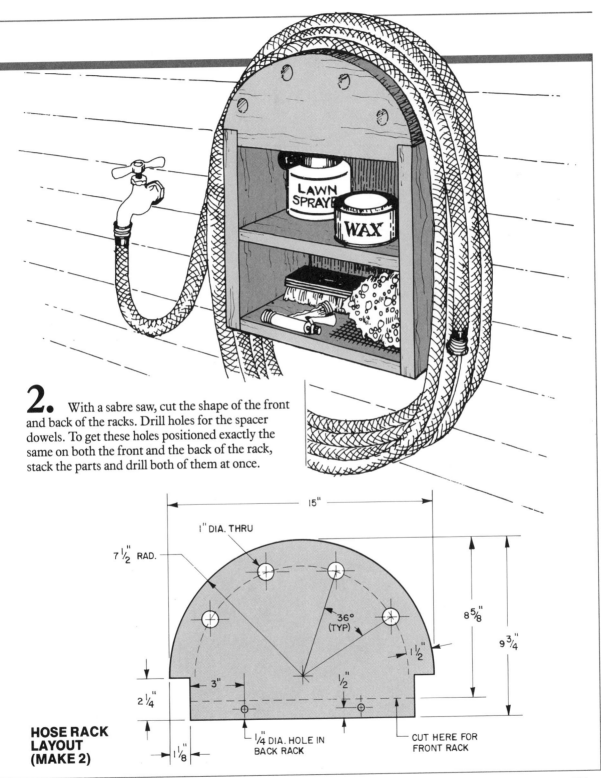

2. With a sabre saw, cut the shape of the front and back of the racks. Drill holes for the spacer dowels. To get these holes positioned exactly the same on both the front and the back of the rack, stack the parts and drill both of them at once.

15"

1" DIA. THRU

7 1/2" RAD.

36° (TYP)

8 5/8"

9 3/4"

1 1/2"

3"

1/2"

2 1/4"

1 1/8"

1/4" DIA. HOLE IN BACK RACK

CUT HERE FOR FRONT RACK

HOSE RACK LAYOUT (MAKE 2)

PROJECT/Garden Hose Shelves/Cont'd.

3. Cut a hole in the bottom shelf. Drill a hole to start the cut, then remove the rest of the waste with a sabre saw. Cover this hole with hardware cloth. This will allow you to store bars of soap on the shelves without having to worry that the soap will dissolve in a puddle of water if it rains.

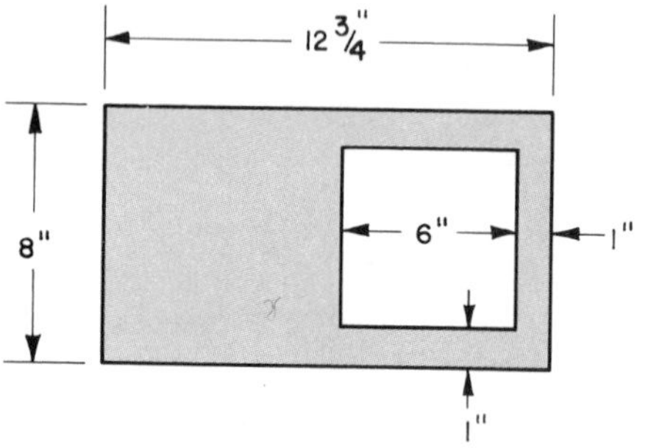

4. Assemble the front, back, spacer dowels, and top shelf with waterproof glue (epoxy or resorcinol) and screws. Also assemble the lower shelves and the sides. Then attach the two assemblies.

5. Paint or stain the completed rack to match your home. Mount the project near the water spigot, driving screws through the back of the rack and into the wall of the house.

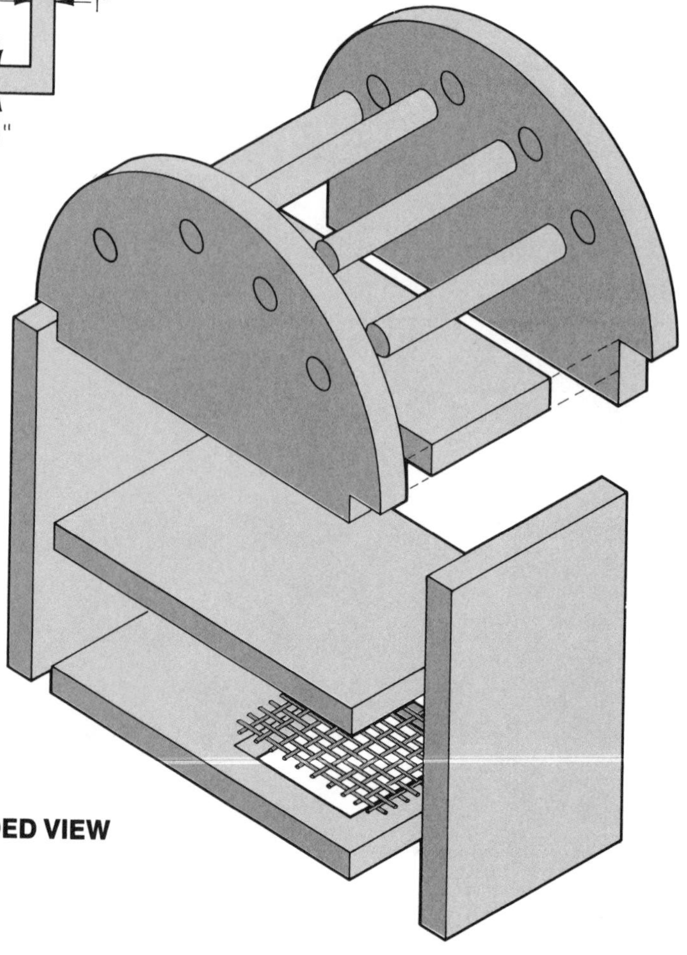

BOTTOM SHELF LAYOUT

EXPLODED VIEW

PROJECT/Trash Can Bins

If you have pets, like to watch birds, or do a lot of potting, you have some special storage problems. You have to keep a supply of pet food, cat litter, bird seed, or potting soil on hand. These things come in a variety of bags, but bags don't always solve all the problems. To store these items *and* keep them accessible, what you need are closed *bins.*

Perhaps the simplest way to make a closed bin is to take a trash can and tip it on its side. Shown here is a frame that will hold three standard-size (30 gallon) metal cans. It also provides a work space on top of the frame. You can easily modify this project to hold one can or twenty, whatever your storage needs are.

1. When you have decided how many cans you want to mount, cut the parts of the frame from pressure-treated lumber. Miter the ends of the pieces, where shown in the drawings.

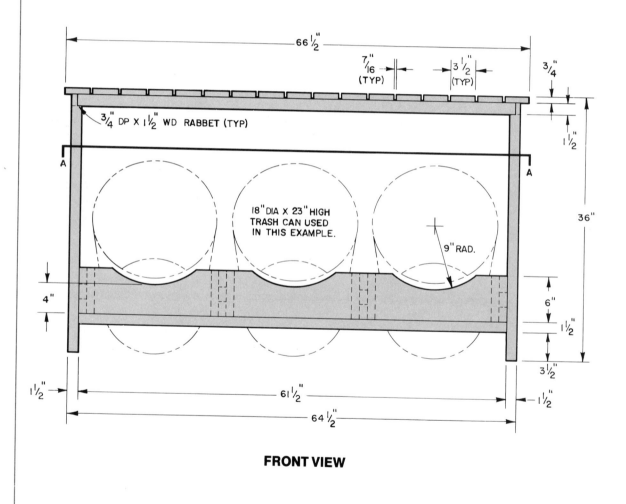

$66\frac{1}{2}''$

$\frac{7}{16}''$ (TYP) $3\frac{1}{2}''$ (TYP) $\frac{3}{4}''$

$\frac{3}{4}''$ DP X $1\frac{1}{2}''$ WD RABBET (TYP)

$1\frac{1}{2}''$

A   A

18" DIA X 23" HIGH TRASH CAN USED IN THIS EXAMPLE.

9" RAD.

36"

4"

6"

$1\frac{1}{2}''$

$3\frac{1}{2}''$

$1\frac{1}{2}''$ $61\frac{1}{2}''$ $1\frac{1}{2}''$

$64\frac{1}{2}''$

FRONT VIEW

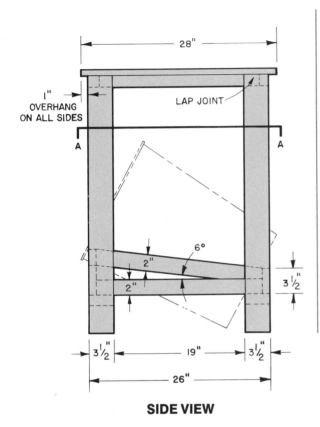

1"
OVERHANG
ON ALL SIDES

28"

LAP JOINT

A   A

6°

2"

2"

$3\frac{1}{2}$

$3\frac{1}{2}$"   19" $3\frac{1}{2}$"

26"

SIDE VIEW

2. With a circular saw and a chisel, cut rabbets in the ends of legs and the ends. Set the depth of cut on the saw and score the end of the 2 x 4 stock several times. This scoring makes it easier to remove the waste with the chisel.

3. Using a sabre saw, cut semi-circular notches in the front bottom rail. These notches will keep the cans from rolling around.

4. Assemble the frame with 12d and 16d nails. Space the top slats ½″ apart to keep water from collecting between them.

5. If you wish, paint or stain the completed wooden frame. Then put the trash cans in place and fill them up.

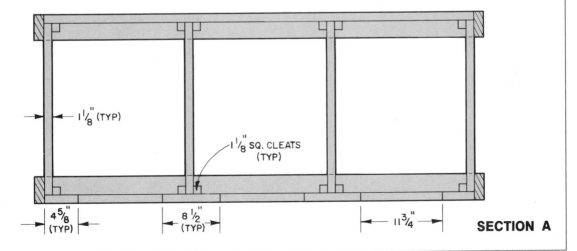

$1\frac{1}{8}$" (TYP)

$1\frac{1}{8}$" SQ. CLEATS
(TYP)

$4\frac{5}{8}$"
(TYP)

$8\frac{1}{2}$"
(TYP)

$11\frac{3}{4}$"

SECTION A

PROJECT/Trash Can Bins

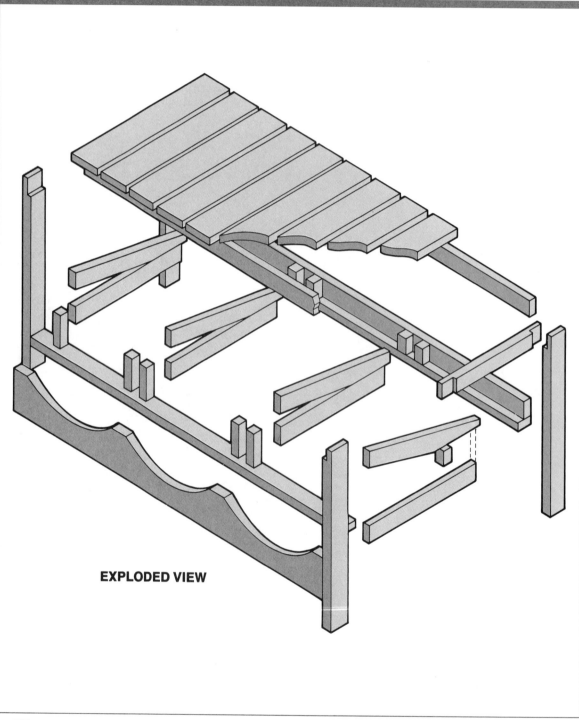

EXPLODED VIEW

PROJECT/Outdoor Storage Chest

If you have small children, you know what a nuisance it is to have their outdoor toys scattered all over the yard. When you make them pick up those toys, where do they put them? Probably on the floor of the garage. This outdoor storage chest makes a great 'toy chest' for those outdoor toys. The chest *and* the toys can stay outside, year round.

Even if you don't have kids, this project comes in handy. It makes a good place to store some types of sports equipment, garden tools and supplies, hoses and sprinklers, car washing supplies—anything that belongs outdoors.

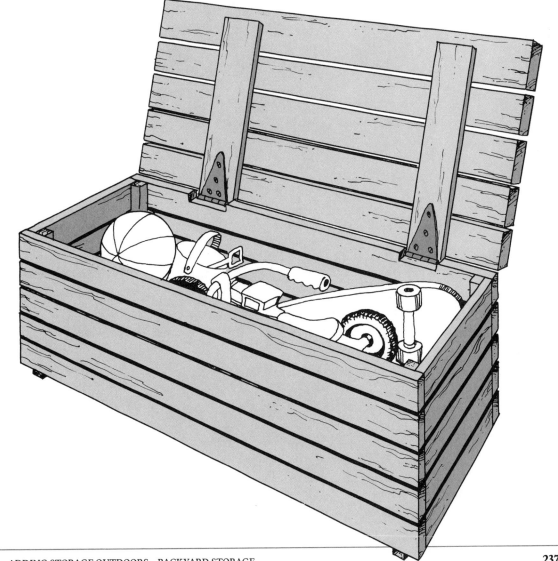

PROJECT/Outdoor Storage Chest/Cont'd.

1. Measure what you want to store in the chest. You may want to adjust the dimensions, making the chest smaller or larger than what we show here.

2. Cut the parts to size from 'outdoor' stock such as redwood, cedar, cypress, or pressure-treated lumber.

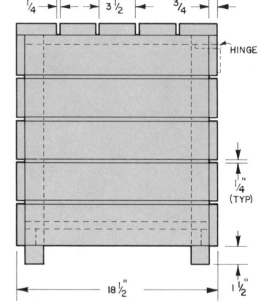

SIDE
VIEW

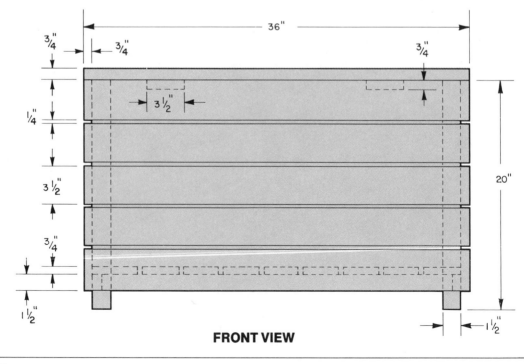

FRONT VIEW

3. Using a router or a dado cutter, make rabbets and dadoes in the legs and bottom frame parts. Join the parts with #10 x 2½″ flathead wood screws. Countersink the screws so that the heads are flush with the surface of the wood.

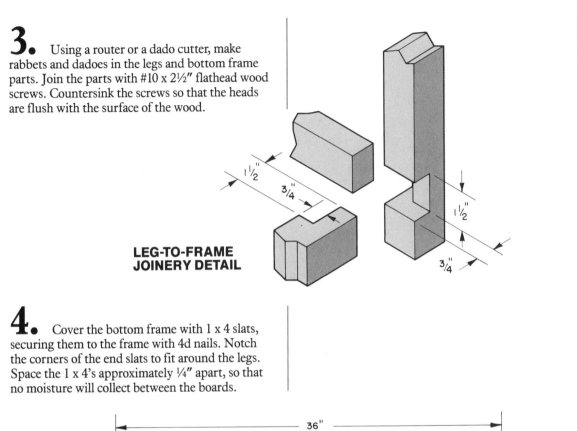

LEG-TO-FRAME JOINERY DETAIL

4. Cover the bottom frame with 1 x 4 slats, securing them to the frame with 4d nails. Notch the corners of the end slats to fit around the legs. Space the 1 x 4's approximately ¼″ apart, so that no moisture will collect between the boards.

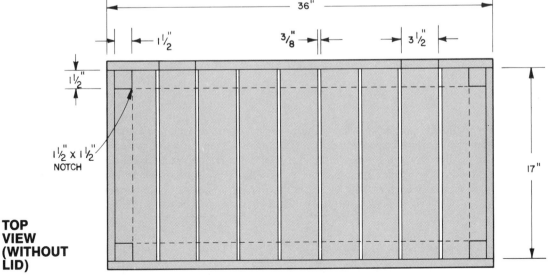

TOP VIEW (WITHOUT LID)

5. Assemble the lid, nailing 1 x 4 slats to two cleats. Space the slats ¼″ apart, and drive the 4d nails at an angle, so that they don't come through the underside of the cleats.

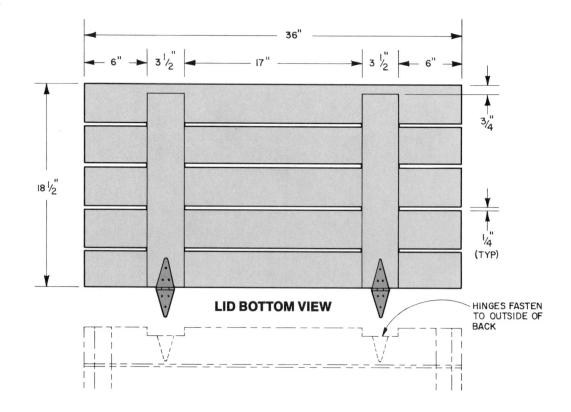

LID BOTTOM VIEW

HINGES FASTEN TO OUTSIDE OF BACK

6. Assemble the side and end slats to the chest frame with 4d nails. Once again, space the slats apart. Work from the bottom up. Before you attach the top back slat, notch the upper edge to accommodate the cleats on the underside of the lid.

7. Attach the lid to the chest with strap hinges. Screw these hinges to the *underside* of the lid cleats, and the *outside* on the back top slat.

8. If you wish, paint or finish the completed chest. If you built this project from pressure-treated lumber, wait several weeks before applying a finish. This will give any chemicals or interior moisture that may have been exposed when you cut up the wood a chance to evaporate.

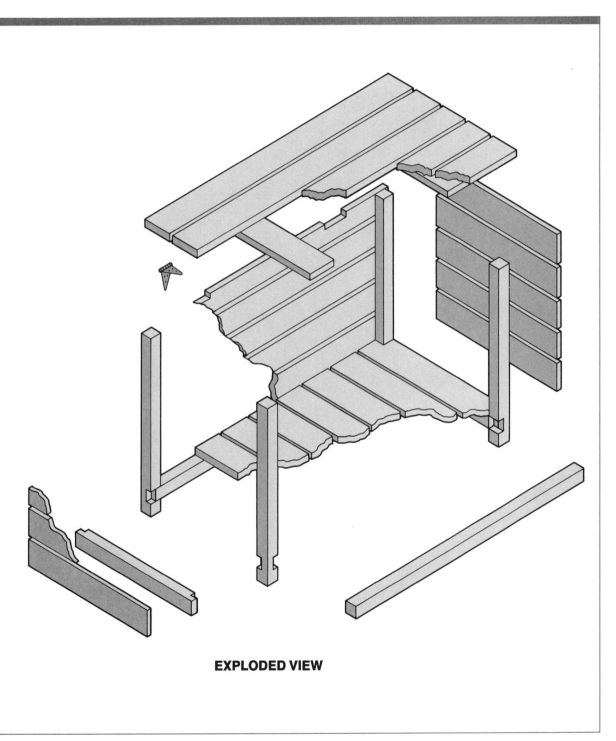

EXPLODED VIEW

PROJECT/Firewood Rack

It's best to keep firewood under cover so that it remains dry. But if you stack it in your garage or under the eaves of the home, termites and other insects that are hiding under the bark may find their way into your home. It's best to store firewood *away* from the house in outbuildings, on a covered rack like the one we show here.

1. Cut the parts to the sizes shown. Make the frame parts from pressure-treated lumber.

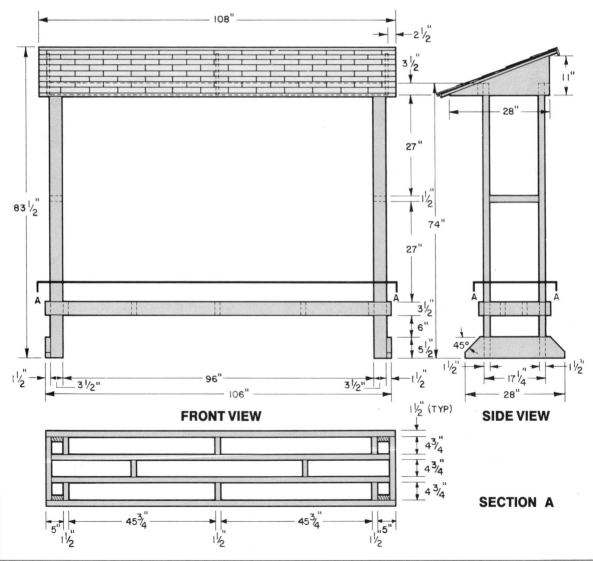

FRONT VIEW

SIDE VIEW

SECTION A

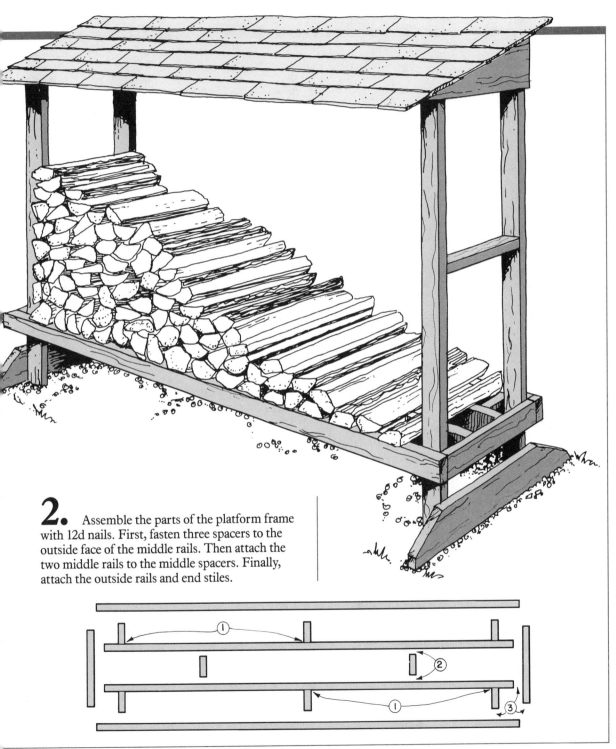

2. Assemble the parts of the platform frame with 12d nails. First, fasten three spacers to the outside face of the middle rails. Then attach the two middle rails to the middle spacers. Finally, attach the outside rails and end stiles.

PROJECT/Firewood Rack/Cont'd.

3. Using carriage bolts, attach the four uprights to the outside rails of the platform frame. The uprights should hold the platform at least 15" off the ground. Cut off the upper corners of the feet, as shown in the drawings, and attach these to the uprights with lag screws.

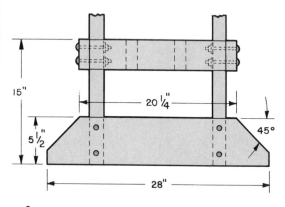

4. Using lag screws, attach braces between the uprights, running side-to-side, 27" above the platform. Attach a second set of braces, running end-to-end, flush with the top end of the uprights. If you're not going to add a roof to this rack, you should also attach side-to-side braces at the top.

5. If you are going to add a roof, decide what sort of roof you want to make. We show two possibilities here—shed and gable. Cut three roof trusses from ¾" *exterior* plywood.

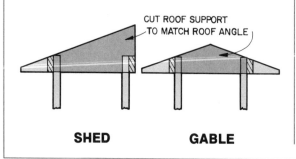

SHED   **GABLE**

6. With 12d nails, attach trusses to either end of the rack assembly, and trim the third truss to fit in between the end-to-end braces. Tack it in place, then cover the trusses with ½" exterior plywood sheathing.

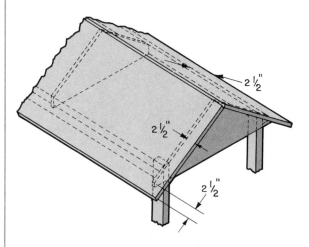

7. Attach drip edge all around the perimeter of the roof. Then cover the roof with tarpaper and shingles.

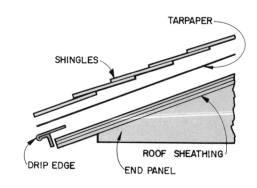

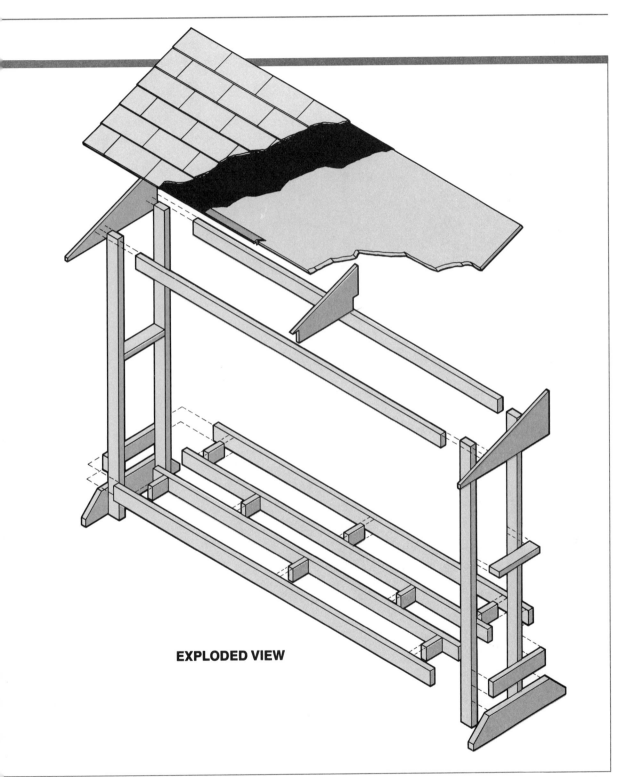

EXPLODED VIEW